Beckett in performance

to Julie

Beckett in performance

JONATHAN KALB

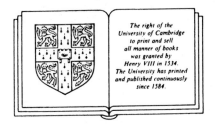

Cambridge University Press

Cambridge
New York   Port Chester
Melbourne   Sydney

Published by the Press Syndicate of the University of Cambridge
The Pitt Building, Trumpington Street, Cambridge, CB2 1RP
40 West 20th Street, New York, NY 10011-4211, U.S.A.
10 Stamford Road, Oakleigh, Melbourne 3166, Australia

First published 1989
First paperback edition 1991

British Library cataloguing in publication data

Kalb, Jonathan
Beckett in performance
1. Drama in English. Beckett, Samuel
Productions
I. Title
792.9'5

Library of Congress cataloguing in publication data

Kalb, Jonathan.
Beckett in performance.
Bibliography.
Includes index.
1. Beckett, Samuel, 1906–1989 —Dramatic production.
I. Title.
PR6003.E282Z7538   1989   792.9'5   88–34017

ISBN 0 521 36549 X hardback
ISBN 0 521 42379 1 paperback

Transferred to digital printing 2000

Contents

Illustrations

vi

Acknowledgments

Beckett in Performance benefited from the generous assistance of a great many people and institutions, and I owe each of them a more singular expression of thanks than these lines can convey.

The book was written partly with the aid of a Fulbright-Hays Grant to West Germany, which gave me access to much European material unavailable in the United States. Among those especially helpful in Germany were Elmar Engels of the Technische Universität Berlin, Georg Hensel, Hans-Thies Lehmann of the Justus-Liebig-Universität Giessen, Robert James Lewis of the SDR, Friedrich Luft, Peter Musolf, Patricia Simpson, Klaus Völker and Susanne Wolfram of S. Fischer Verlag. Ingrid Stanke and Sebastian Zimmermann offered invaluable assistance in transcribing interview tapes

Betty Corwin at Lincoln Center and Tom Bishop at New York University both gave me access to video material without which my study would have been impossible, and I am grateful to Dr. Bishop for meeting with me and providing information where he could. Similar thanks for information and opinions are due to Ruby Cohn, Pierre Chabert, Martha Fehsenfeld, James Knowlson, Dougald McMillan and Barney Rosset. Richard Gilman and Stanley Kauffmann have my warmest appreciation for reading and commenting on the manuscript, as do Gitta Honegger and Daphne Dejanikus for checking my translations.

Permission to reprint was kindly granted by the editors of *American Theatre*, *Modern Drama*, *Theater*, and *Performing Arts Journal*, where sections of the book previously appeared. I am particularly grateful to all the artists who agreed to interviews, the majority of which do not appear in the Conversations section, and to all the photographers who accepted less than standard fees for the use of their work. Others rendered help in ways too various to recount – among them: the Edward Albee Foundation, Bert Cardullo, Glenn A. Clatworthy of PBS, Victoria Cooper and Ruth Sharman of Cambridge University Press, Mireille Delbraccio and Anne-Patricia Chantrefoux, Earle Gister, Beth Greenberg, George C. Hammond, Mona Heinze, Leon Katz, Daniel Labeille, John Lahr, Robert Langdon-Lloyd, Lindsay Law and Stellar Bennett of American Playhouse, Gordon Rogoff,

Laura Ross, Joel Schechter, Laurie Melissa Vogelsang, Glenn Young and Melvyn B. Zerman. My sincere apologies and thanks to anyone I may have omitted.

Last and best, I thank those whose faith and love and sundry other forms of tangible and intangible support helped keep me going from beginning to end: all my parents – Saundra Segan Wheeler, Gerald Kalb, George Wheeler, Mary Sayler, and James and Betty Heffernan; Stanley Kauffmann, whose teaching and friendship have meant much more to me than he may know; and my wife and most trusted editor, Julie Heffernan, who shared the whole project sanguinely, odious parts included.

1 Introduction

Reviewing *Happy Days* in 1961, Richard Gilman wrote:

That question of effectiveness, far more than the meaning of the plays – which are really far less arcane than we have been led to think – has always been to me the interesting one to ask about Beckett's theatre. How does it manage to achieve its high intensity and complete conviction – how, really, does it *reach* us – after its apparent abandonment of most of the traditional means of dramatic communication?[1]

The question is as elusive as it is complex – it changes with each new Beckett text, and in any case there are few enough critical conventions adequate to a discussion of why any theater is effective – but anyone who has seen one of the dozens of exceptional Beckett performances in the past twenty-five years (Jack MacGowran in *Beginning to End*, David Warrilow in *The Lost Ones*, Billie Whitelaw in *Rockaby*, for example) will understand the impulse to continue asking it. It is the kind of question that is never answered with finality, but as data accumulate we can rephrase it in more specific ways.

Actors such as MacGowran, Warrilow and Whitelaw are habitually called "consummate," "ultimate," "quintessential" Beckett actors, but what exactly do those terms mean? How do these actors produce the effects for which they are praised, and precisely what are those effects? How do their techniques differ from those used in other theater? Do they differ? And is the audience's role different? Alan Schneider, who at his death in 1984 was Beckett's foremost director, always insisted he did little critical interpretation of texts. What then does it mean to call someone a "great Beckett director"? Since Beckett has repeatedly made clear that he will not tolerate what he calls "the omnipresent massacre and abuse of directorial function" (letter to Barney Rosset, February 13, 1973), to what extent can one presume to interpret his work, come to some provisional understanding of it, while directing it?

Beckett in Performance is an attempt to address these and other related questions through critical documentation of some of the more significant Beckett performances in Europe and America over the past several decades. It is not a history of Beckett production and makes no claims to exhaustiveness in that regard, but it does involve assessment of some seventy productions I have seen, both live and on video, between 1978 and 1987, and of interviews with actors and directors from those productions. It is a dramaturgical study rather than a literary one in the usual sense, written by someone whose most profound experiences of Beckett have occurred in the theater rather than the reading chair. It is an attempt to be articulate about some of those experiences in the interests of articulating a poetics of Beckett performance and discussing the place of that poetics in theater history. These issues are corollary to text analysis but nevertheless, in my view, equally important.

I was fortunate enough to meet with Beckett in Paris several times while writing this book, and the help he offered me in answering questions is evident throughout. I might mention that I still do not know exactly why he agreed to meet me in the first place. No doubt my case was helped by Warrilow, who did me the honor of sending a letter of introduction, but I would like to think it was also because he approved of my topic of study.

When Beckett and I first sat down together over coffee in the nondescript Hotel PLM in November 1986, my first thought, knowing of his notorious reticence, was to suppress the dozens of specific queries I had formulated in the course of writing *Beckett in Performance*, to say nothing of the hundreds of general questions I had formulated in the course of living my life. To my astonishment, though, he turned out to be more generous, helpful and open than many others of lesser talent and fame whom I have approached during my research. For a while I dodged about for a neutral topic, and then realized I was devising my own obstacles; for the kind of exegesis that always puts him out of patience had little to do with my work, which concerned concrete issues of theatrical production. He was actually interested in hearing about some of the performances I had seen, many done by his friends, and he spoke to me nostalgically about many others.

I remain very grateful to Beckett for his interest and assistance, and for the time he spent with me – which, by any conceivable standard, he need not have spent – and I have tried in the following chapters not to exploit his generosity. Upon leaving him each time, I searched out the nearest quiet place and wrote down everything I could recall about what we said to one another, but I have nevertheless refrained from publishing those notes. Citing a faulty memory, Beckett requested that I keep direct quotation of him to a minimum, and I have therefore quoted our conversations only where memory is not an issue and where I feel that the topic at hand calls for the specificity of his precise words.

Perhaps the best way to describe the point of view of this book – which will doubtless seem unusual to some readers – is simply to explain a few basics of dramaturgical procedure. Since a dramaturg is primarily interested in how plays generate meaning in performance, his analyses naturally focus on performance as related to text and not, as is usual, the other way round. He is, in short, a semiologist, a researcher in the science of significances, except that he has no use for esoteric terminology. Unfortunately, semiology has never overcome the fact that a huge segment of the population stops reading or listening the moment it perceives the words "sign" and "signifier" in the same clause, and a dramaturg, if he is to be useful in production, cannot employ terms that make his collaborators stop listening. I am aware that some of the best recent writing on performance-stage transactions does make use of specialized language (notably the work of Patrice Pavis and Keir Elam), but this study avoids it as much as possible in order to remain useful to practitioners in addition to critics and others interested in Beckett as a literary figure.

The strategy of the book's two critical sections, on acting and directing, is analogy and contrast. Each chapter focuses very closely on three or four productions, either of the same play or with the same practitioner, in order to draw conclusions about the problems of producing that work, or that type of work – type meaning any of the categories I have used to isolate production problems: early works, late works, television plays, works of prose fiction adapted for the stage. A third section contains selected excerpts from some of the interviews used as primary material for the critical study.

All the chapters in parts one and two function both independently as essays and inter-dependently as steps in an argument about Beckett's historical context. That argument is then drawn explicitly in the conclusion, where I relate Beckett to the contemporary (mostly American) avant-garde: e.g. the Wooster Group, Robert Wilson, Richard Foreman, Squat Theater. Most people who bother about such matters at all would agree that, in general, theater has been unambitious and disappointing during the past fifteen years, and in that interval the avant-garde, like a monastery in the Dark Ages, has remained one of few significant focal points for serious contemplation about theatrical art. Any claims about progressiveness or radical originality in Beckett performance, then, must necessarily be held up against those of the avant-garde.

The claims I will make for Beckett have to do with the way in which presentational and representational action is blended in his theater – which is much more relevant to contemporary avant-gardist theories than either the avant-garde artists or most critics have perceived. Beckett's oft-quoted words about Joyce also describe his own work: "You complain that this stuff is not written in English. It is not written at all. It is not to be read – or rather it is not only to be read. It is to be looked at and listened to. His writing is not *about* something; *it is that something itself.*"[2] Beckett's theater does not represent scenes from another time – or rather it does not only do so. It creates scenes whose subject matter is their duration in present time. His

dramas are not *about* experiences; *they are those experiences themselves.*
This heightened authenticity in Beckett, a quality of unnerving straightforwardness, is similar in many ways to the ethic of "immediacy" that
pervades much contemporary performance art and avant-garde theater.

It is also unique, however, because its source is a classic author and not a
director or auteur. As I will explain through numerous illustrations, the
famous resistance to Beckett both in the mainstream and the avant-garde is
attributable partly to his demand, as a writer, for authority in productions,
and partly to this very point about authenticity. The more narcissistic a
theater practitioner is, I have found, the more he or she is threatened by the
honesty in Beckett's work, its tendency to throw duplicity back on itself,
unmasking it. Indeed, part of Beckett's significance is that he shows up the
swollen, desperate egotism at work in the theater, and for that he has paid the
price of unpopularity among a large group of theater professionals.

A few matters of procedure. Although I have written about certain performances as though they were stable entities, I understand that all live productions change from night to night. I am dealing in this book essentially with
ephemera, and those who attended the productions I describe on different
nights (or even the same night) may not have seen what I did. For this
reason, I have tried to use as examples performances recorded on video or
film, and have referred to those recordings in my description even when – as
is true in most cases – I also saw the production live. A surprising number of
films and videos of Beckett productions exist, far more than I thought when I
began researching, so it is actually possible for readers to corroborate the
majority of my observations. There are also important differences between
videos and live performances, however, so even readers who take the time to
go to the archives will occasionally have to take my word for certain points.

Nor have I limited discussion only to productions I have seen, though I
have seen all those I use as main examples, and most of those two or three
times. In order to give the study a broad enough historical base to permit
generalization, I have occasionally relied on reviews, recollections of partici-
pants, and a handful of other excellent secondary sources, including: the
published rehearsal diaries of Walter Asmus, Beckett's Assistant Director in
Germany; the special Beckett issue of *Revue d'Esthétique* edited by Pierre
Chabert in 1986; McMillan/Fehsenfeld's *Beckett in the Theatre*, which
Dougald McMillan kindly allowed me to read in galleys, and the production
sections of Ruby Cohn's *Just Play: Beckett's Theatre.*

On a related topic: as will become obvious, I have not accepted the
unwritten taboo among theater practitioners against comparing different
actors in the same role. Part of this book's significance, I hope, is that it treats
production with a critical seriousness usually reserved for texts, on the

assumption that theatrical performances are, among other things, works of art capable of being read closely. The ephemerality of the theater event has always protected actors and directors from having their work read closely, but video recording must inevitably change that. Some extraordinary precedents exist for the practice of comparing actors, such as Bernard Shaw's delightful "Duse and Bernhardt," and comparison is an invaluable tool for guarding against certain critical fallacies. For example, in most criticism, as Pavis writes, "remarks on . . . *actors' performances* are often preoccupied with the success or failure of illusion or verisimilitude," but Beckett's work, like that of many other twentieth-century theater artists, usually involves a radical critique of common assumptions about dramatic illusionism.[3] Comparing my own perceptions of several different performances decreases the likelihood of my making unjustified assumptions about actor/character distinctions in a given play.

In fact, Beckett's work presents an enormous trap for those prone to a priori assumptions, and I have tried throughout to be vigilant about that, especially when substantiating appraisals of performances. As already mentioned, Beckett helped me with information as much as he could, but at no point in this book do I treat his remarks or opinions as gospel, nor his productions – much as I appreciate them – as unchallengeable models. Where appropriate I explain the textual readings used as bases for judgments and leave the reader to decide their worth. Readers familiar with the field, though, will notice immediately a far greater degree of specificity in observation than that found in the majority of essays and journalistic articles on Beckett acting and directing. I have tried to respect the degree to which the works are composed of minutiae, and to bring to them a level of attention commensurate with what their performers must bring.

PART ONE

_____

Acting

2   *Rockaby* and the art of inadvertent interpretation

Eclipsed among the millions of critical words that have been lavished on Samuel Beckett is an uncomfortable and frequently avoided question: on what level can spectators be expected to understand his theater? Some critics, with limited success, have tried to address this issue by pointing out parallels between the dilemmas of Beckett's characters and those of his audiences, but I want to shift the field of inquiry by discussing affinities between the actor's process of creating characters in rehearsal and the spectator's process of apprehending plays in performance. I focus predominantly on *Rockaby*, because Billie Whitelaw's extraordinary performance is well documented and also because there is an important article by Charles Lyons about the process of perceiving this play.[1] Lyons' essay, which has application to Beckett's other works as well, is to my knowledge unique in its detail concerning perception, yet strangely it does not mention Whitelaw at all, despite the fact that her kind of acting figures hugely in the process described.

In *Rockaby* a woman, dressed in black and "Prematurely old," sits in a rocking chair alone on a dark stage.[2] Though her feet do not touch the floor, the chair rocks on its own to the soothing regular rhythm of tape-recorded lines spoken in the woman's voice. As the play opens she says "More," and the rocking begins, seemingly in response to her word. During the next fifteen minutes, the play's approximate length, the rocking slows to a stop four times and the woman reacts each time but the last by saying "More," after which the rocking immediately starts again; the final time her head slowly sinks as the taped voice echoes more and more faintly. The recorded text, separated by the "Mores" into four sections, is repetitive, like a litany, and tells of a woman who goes "to and fro," looking "for another/another like herself," until "in the end/the day came . . . when she said/to herself/ whom else/time she stopped"; on some repetitions of "time she stopped" the woman speaks along with the tape. The voice goes on to describe her going "back in" (presumably she was outside) to sit at her window "facing other windows/other only windows" looking for "another like herself/a little like/ another living soul," but finding "all blinds down/never one up." In the final section we hear that she "went down . . . down the steep stair . . . into the old rocker/mother rocker/where mother rocked/all the years/all in black . . . off

9

her head they said . . . and rocked." Thus "in the end," as she rocked "off" seemingly toward death, she "was her own other/own other living soul" – "other" asserting itself in the theater as a rhyme for "mother."

The action is richly ambiguous. We hear a moving, almost sentimental tale but are not sure what the action onstage has to do with it; we are given insufficient evidence to determine either who the stage character is or if she has really died. We hear near the end that she ultimately came to function as "her own other," so we naturally reconsider the preceding story in that light and suspect that its third person point of view is a result of her having become that "other" at some point; like the narrator in *Company*, she "speaks of [her]self as of another." This possible split in the character is suggested to us in very conventional terms, similar to the age-old practice of suddenly unveiling new information about a character's background near the end of a drama, but it is more unsettling than that because it raises the possibility that the voice is lying – in the sense that many Beckett narrators lie (in *The Unnamable, Company, Cascando,* and many other works), by making up tales that seem somehow connected to their survival while also functioning as pastimes.

The mention of "mother" rocking permits several different responses: we may conflate mother and daughter, viewing the woman as a composite character who incarnates certain tendencies passed down through all generations; we may continue to view her as a singular character whose self-objectification has taken the form of identifying with her mother; or we may even speculate that the voice belongs to a true other, perhaps a daughter telling a story to "rock her [mother] off," or some other alter ego (perhaps the mysterious force that rocks the chair) who happens to have a voice similar to the woman's. As in *Waiting for Godot, Play, Act Without Words II* and many other Beckett works, the action seems to be a section of an endlessly repeated cycle – i.e. a process the daughter's daughter will also go through, etc. – but no confirmation is given that such repetitions ever occurred or will occur, and the story heard about the past may or may not be a narration of events leading up to the action seen onstage.

Lyons feels that this unverifiability is the essence of Beckett's originality as a dramatist.

Many of the moments that we witness in the theater encompass two kinds of significance: they enact a unique moment in time and, simultaneously, they function as representations of typical moments in the complete lives of the characters. In other terms, they operate both as complete or self-sufficient representations of a temporal unit and as metonyms of a larger temporal unit (an illusory wholeness that cannot be represented). I make this point to suggest that Beckett's use of partial or fragmented temporal units builds upon a fundamental convention of dramatic structure: the use of isolated or discrete moments in time as the expression of the quality of a larger section of the total narrative. Beckett's innovation is not the use of a brief episode as a metonym of an extended narrative unit; on the contrary, his drama appears unusual or original because he leaves the relationship between the individual episode and the larger implied narrative unverified and, therefore, equivocal.

(p. 306)

It is equivocal, he goes on to say, both for the characters in the dramas and for us as spectators.

We exercise our tendency to build up a narrative whole out of the fragments displayed and, at the same time, recognize that this created history is a product of our imagination – ephemeral and unverifiable. In that sense, our futile struggle to deal with the intangibility of the experience duplicates the struggle of Beckett's characters as they grapple with their images of the past in the baffling environments of the present.   (p. 306)

The only drawback to these excellent observations is their implication that such intellectual struggles might be primary experiences for spectators. Lyons stresses the fact of equivocation at the cost, to some extent, of delineating its variables: exactly how is the environment baffling to spectators and characters alike? Exactly what struggle or struggles are duplicated? He writes:

We see almost nothing of the woman's present processes of consciousness other than her decision to sustain the text by the command "More" and her agreement with the notion *"time she stopped."* We interpret the physical behavior of rocking as a compulsive rhythmic act. While we extrapolate from the details of the narrative to see her behavior as a self-conscious re-enactment of her mother's final pattern of action, no material exists in the text by which we can test the validity of our interpretation.

   We may speculate that the gradual cessation of rocking and the final silence of the diminishing voice represent the character's death, but that speculation is, ultimately, unverifiable.   (p. 304)

In Whitelaw's performances, however, we see quite a lot of "the woman's present processes of consciousness," processes that activate her motivations as variables in the text's transaction with spectators; the clues she gives to her character's motivations can and do change the terms of the play's ambiguity. The play in performance is subtler even than Lyons makes it seem; indeed, in light of Whitelaw's acting choices some of his carefully wrought phrases (such as "decision to sustain" and "compulsive rhythmic act") seem like hasty assumptions. It is important to understand the extent to which acting (and directing, and designing) affects theories of audience perception, for, unlike textual interpretations, they depend on particular performers and performances. And in Whitelaw's *Rockaby*, the experience of watching the woman rock, perhaps listen, utter her "Mores" and finally drop her head is at least as powerful and significant as the experience Lyons describes of struggling to verify information in the taped text.[3]

The primary experience of *Rockaby* is that of a lullaby, an unchanging rhythm of words that lulls us into tranquillity until we are startled by the words "Fuck life" near the end, which make us perceive, at least in the woman's final moments, much more canniness than her previous near-catatonia has suggested. Before that we are kept from nodding like the woman by a sense of verbal expectation, a natural desire for predication that makes us await the end of the text's long sentence as much as the character's end. The narrative is like an extended predicate that refuses to resolve; we wait and wait for an active verb but keep hearing appositives ("all eyes/all sides"), new participles ("saying to herself," "facing other windows"), and what seem like new subordinate clauses ("till in the end") until the last section finally releases us with "and rocked" and the words following, which include "Fuck life." Like the Listener's toothless smile at the end of *That Time*, the "Fuck life" deliberately comments on the rest of the action, carrying the unnerving implication that the unblinking character may have been fully conscious all along.

The operative phrase here is "may have been," because a definite decision either way – toward consciousness or unconsciousness – would simplify the play to the level of melodrama. Though she may not have thought about it in these terms, Whitelaw took pains in rehearsal to preserve this "may have been," and her performance actually builds on the ambiguities Beckett wrote into his text. Significantly, Whitelaw's character never seems weak or unsure, yet her lines, live and recorded, clearly manifest the central uncertainty regarding active and passive consciousness. Her speech seems unquestionably driven by a clear mental purpose (which of course is never shared with us) that succeeds in projecting ambiguity without ambivalence.

When rehearsing and recording the tape with Alan Schneider Whitelaw regulated herself by moving her right hand back and forth like a soundless metronome, which allowed her to keep to a given rhythm while inflecting the lines in various ways. As with Mouth in *Not I*, she colored some of her lines in *Rockaby*, filling them out with diverse tones of voice and insinuations instead of leaving them neutral and with "no color" as Beckett requested. For example: the first several times she says "whom else" she pauses before the phrase and then emphasizes it as an irritable question – i.e. "whom else could I possibly be talking to?" – which implies self-awareness; in contrast, during repetitions of "a little like" she lets her voice trail up and down seemingly without direction as if she were singing to amuse herself and did not really understand her words. This variation creates an impression of a woman who is sometimes "off her head" and sometimes not, and leads the audience to expect only certain kinds of breaks in the median tone. Thus in the end when

1 Billie Whitelaw in *Rockaby*, directed by Alan Schneider, Samuel Beckett Theatre, NYC, 1984. (Photo: Martha Swope)

she slips by "Fuck life" without altering her tone in the slightest from that used in the lines before and after it, she shatters the sense of verbal innocuousness built up throughout the recitation. The impact comes not only from the shocking nature of the words themselves, but also from the earlier impression that lines spoken in that tone were "safe," free from active consciousness. The moment has unexpected power precisely because it is delivered as one passing item in a series; if it were separated in any way from the surrounding lines, or at all emphasized, it would jar as a melodramatic judgment on all we have seen and heard.

A recorded tape, however, even one containing effective surprises, can engage an audience only to a limited extent because they know the words on it were really spoken in the past.[4] A living woman, even one with only four one-word lines, potentially commands more attention than a canned symphony juxtaposed with her, and Whitelaw exploits that potential to the fullest. She performs masterfully the text's "unblinking gaze" by calmly and patiently shutting her eyes for irregular intervals and then opening them wide all at once, and she waits at least ten seconds before each of her lines, turning that progression of "Mores" into a series of eloquent statements about her inner state. Her first "More," which opens the action, is frightened and unambiguously inflected as a request, yet behind its slight panic one senses strong determination; this woman knows what she's asking for, though we may not. The second is higher pitched, very plaintive, and infirmly inflected as a question, like a word heard not quite clearly from a distance. The third is elongated, savored with a clearly pronounced "r," and has a slight tremolo as if she were afraid, or becoming hoarse. And the fourth is less an articulated word than an abstract utterance – "Ah" or "Ahr" – as if the woman remembered when to speak but not how. Within the limits of Beckett's single instruction, "W's 'more' a little softer each time," Whitelaw realizes this great range of variation, the effect of which is to assert the pre-rational quality of the lines, their effectiveness as music, before implying any rational significances.

Those significances do seep through, but only after we register a response to the vocal virtuosity, to the fact that such clear, complex utterances have emerged at all from this seemingly passive woman. Subsequently, questions of meaning are inevitable. What, if anything, is her intention? Who is she and to whom is she speaking? Onstage Whitelaw uses a voice more raspy and fatigued than the one on the tape, suggesting that the woman is older than the voice, but that is impossible if the two are synchronous and the tape represents her present thoughts. Of course she may be dissembling, consciously acting two parts, but that possibility is not fully supported by the "Mores." The first and second "Mores," inflected as questions, imply two possible purposes: she may be instructing the voice to continue and manifesting what Lyons calls her "decision to sustain the text," which implies that its progress is under her control, or she may be pleading for the voice to stop, implying that it has a source outside her, or at least that she cannot stop it. The third and fourth "Mores," which sound like automatic responses, lines recited mindlessly on cue, raise other possibilities – that her words are unconnected to any clear volition, or that they progressively lose such connection as she rocks off.

Anyone who thinks that points such as these are minor or irrelevant to the dominant experience of watching *Rockaby* should compare the two taped performances of the play on file in the New York Public Library's Theater Collection at Lincoln Center. The performance I have been describing, which took place in Buffalo, New York, in 1981 and was recorded at the end of D. A. Pennebaker and Chris Hegedus' television documentary on the making of *Rockaby*, is very different from the one recorded in 1984 at the Samuel Beckett Theatre in New York City. The differences between these tapes can be used to demonstrate the significant effect of certain performer choices.

The first thing one notices in the latter performance is that Whitelaw's make-up is different; more age lines have been added to her forehead and wide brown patches to each cheekbone, creating a deeply sunken, ancient look almost like that of a corpse. When asked about this difference, the actress told me that she believes the former film is of a dress rehearsal, not only because of the lighter make-up but also because her hands do not grasp the armrests as specified in the text (the latter detail reportedly a source of annoyance to Beckett when he saw the documentary). Despite this disclaimer, however, the earlier tape is in some respects praiseworthy, and more interesting than the later one.

In the 1981 performance Whitelaw's face was not necessarily old; she used dark-gray coloring that accentuated her eye sockets and a few lines beside her nose, but moderately so that one could not be sure what age she really was. Only when I saw the second tape did I realize how Beckett's costume and stage directions contribute to the ambiguity described above. The phrase "Prematurely old" raises the question, without answering it, of whether the woman is mother or daughter, and so does the character's dress. The high-necked evening gown looks very old, like something that belonged to one's grandmother, yet its sequins and those on the extravagantly trimmed head-dress, ever prominent as they reflect the stage lights, suggest youth and newness. In the earlier performance Whitelaw's make-up succeeds in communicating the idea of premature aging, but in the latter she actually looks old, like an indigent parent tricked up in clothes that may not be hers. It is a subtle difference – between age and premature aging – but it contributes to a general quality of definiteness, or quasi-realism, that lessens the impact of the text's ambiguities.

The woman in this performance is weaker, less independent and more nervous than the other. Her arms grasp the front of the armrests tightly, as if she were resisting the chair's motherly embrace. (In the performance I saw live in New York City, she grasped them loosely.) Throughout the action she seems determined not to acquiesce, determined to counteract some invisible pressure, which strongly suggests a force outside her. This quality is particularly apparent during her "Mores," before all of which she lifts her head off the back of the chair, straining in a way that bespeaks fragility and panic. Her first "More" is breathy, forceful, and inflected as a command, leaving an impression of a testy dotard making demands on her child. The second is slightly impatient and feeble, she is not at all sure that more will come, and in her doubtfulness she blinks a few times. The third, inflected as a question, is much more airy than the previous two, and though it is almost a whisper she thrusts it out from her diaphragm more forcefully than any other word in both performances. And the fourth is still softer and articulated distinctly as a word, but in a sad, almost tearful tone with a slight wobble of the head.

Just these few small changes shift the emphasis of the performance toward the notion that the stage character is fully conscious. This woman's "Fuck life" seems like an angry outburst, confirming what we already know about her attitude, instead of a creative and surprising act of defiance in the context of highly constricting circumstances, like the Protagonist's raised head at the end of *Catastrophe*. And when Whitelaw blinks, no doubt accidentally, during her second "More," she startles us because the rest of the time she is mostly unblinking in obedience to Beckett's directions. The moment interrupts the prevailing air of uncanniness, briefly transporting us to an atextual reality where people blink. Only one other moment even approaches this jarring quality: when her head sinks before the final fade out. In the former performance, its descent is completely smooth and conducted with an uncanny slowness that seems if not mechanical then at least weirdly controlled, allowing for symbolic interpretations of the event. In the latter performance, the head simply drops, albeit slowly but with an ending bump that leaves an impression of control relinquished and releases us prematurely from this world in which chairs rock themselves and laws like gravity are discretionary.

Despite all these discrepancies between the two tapes, however, my high opinion of Whitelaw's ability was in no way shaken. The live performance I saw late in the run at the Samuel Beckett Theatre was every bit as finely tuned as the one in the documentary and, to me, the astonishing fact, the one that sticks indelibly in memory, is that Whitelaw can evoke so much with so little physical freedom. To have seen her perform in *Not I*, *Happy Days*, *Footfalls* and *Rockaby* convinces one that she is a great Beckett interpreter.

How could anyone, you ask yourself, create those subtleties of meaning in the taped text and the "Mores" without understanding clearly what is at stake in each of her choices? That question, however, and others like it, turns out to involve a fallacy, for Whitelaw denies that she understands the text better than everyone else.

Like many other Beckett actors, she insists that questions of interpretation have nothing to do with her work. She says in the documentary, "People think that because I do this I am well read and knowledgeable and I know what it means. I have almost no education at all and no idea what it means." Elsewhere she comments, "I'm not interested in what the plays are about, to be absolutely honest. That's an academic's job. I get a bit nervous when people get too reverent about Beckett's work."[5] She makes a point in the documentary of stating that she left school at fifteen and still has little interest in books, reading only what she is working on. She has never read *Waiting for Godot*, though she has seen it in German, and doesn't know *Endgame* or the novels at all. Any understanding of her acting must begin with respect for these statements, but they must also be treated with circumspection. Whitelaw is neither a philistine nor a literary Know-Nothing, and one can be just as misled by believing that hermeneutics are irrelevant to her intricate, often hypnotic Beckett performances as by believing that they control her.

She begins her roles by listening to Beckett read his texts. Her metronome-like hand movements seen in the documentary are an old habit from her meetings with the author prior to each opening, at which they conduct one another like musicians. She says, "When I work with Sam we don't analyze the plays at all. My first task is to find the music of it. At first you don't know if it goes fast or slow, or where to put the metronome . . . What on earth people do trying to tackle Beckett without having Beckett at their side I don't know. I've always had the man close to me. I've never done any of his plays without him" (*VV*).[6] That those meetings help her a great deal can be seen by comparing her performance in the plays with her dramatic reading of the prose piece *Enough*, which Beckett did not rehearse with her, and which he disapproved of from the outset.[7]

She reads *Enough* without a trace of implied commentary on the story's events, except for a few sentences emphasized with a raised hand that recalls a stereotypical gesture of strident feminism and, if intended interpretively, would indeed constitute a misguided approach to this text. But the most prominent quality is her wilful flatness and lack of embellishment or illustration. When she sweeps blithely past a word like "geodesy," making the audience wonder if they are supposed to know what it means, one thinks of the way Jack MacGowran, in performing Beckett's prose, could keep even the most erudite passages from sounding pretentious by changing the tone of

2 Billie Whitelaw, reading *Enough*, directed by Alan Schneider, Samuel Beckett Theatre, NYC, 1984. (Photo: Martha Swope)

certain words to sarcasm, making funny faces, and assuming ridiculous postures. We must take Whitelaw seriously, then, when she says she does not read the texts for rational meanings, and that she works with Beckett musically. (I use the word *music* only in the simple sense of rhythmic sound and not in reference to specific composers or compositional structures; a book could be written about classical analogies to the musical structures in Beckett's works.)

Beckett, however, could read his texts the same way to hundreds of other actresses and never prompt a performance like Whitelaw's. (And alternatively, as with David Warrilow, his readings do not always elicit an actor's best work.) To see her onstage is to be instantly convinced that her performance comes from inside her, and it is not quite fair to say, as does David Edelstein, that she is "plugged straight into Beckett" (*VV*), despite the fact that she may sometimes believe that herself. She says in the documentary, "Beckett blows the notes. I want them to come out of me and create feeling in whoever's sitting out front." But if she sees herself as an instrument Beckett plays and denies any intellectual participation in the creation of the final artwork, that tells us more about why Beckett chooses to work with her – the attitude is similar to the tractability and perfectionism he has admired in German actors – than it does about her acting.[8] Whitelaw herself is responsible for internalizing what she hears from Beckett and transforming it into her own music, and she does that through an emotional process usually very painful for her: "nine times out of ten, in order to play a part I've got to dig out a piece of myself that I'd rather not know about" (documentary). Furthermore, the music of the plays, being composed of words, can never be wholly abstract because words carry rational meaning; performers like Whitelaw can make the music primary but never exclusive.

When asked about her preparation for roles Whitelaw usually gives two types of answers. She speaks about music, as in these comments on *Footfalls*:

... there's one little cry, one sort of Schoenberg type – I hope this doesn't sound too pretentious – one Schoenberg type note when she asks how old she is, and the mother says, "never mind how old I am," and she says what age again, and the mother says 40, and it seems to me to be in that awful monotonous endless ongoing situation just going backwards and forwards and to still only be 40 and perhaps have another ... if mom's 90 then another 50 years to go. That is a nightmare, to think that I have to live with this hell. And she says two words: "So little." But actually that isn't like somebody answering another character. It's a cry from the heart which creates a certain note ... and a certain sound comes out of my mouth. I don't just say, "so little," there's a sound, and then I go back into this dead, monotonous plod. (*VV*)

And she speaks about experiences in her life:

For about five years before my mother died [several months before *Rockaby* rehearsals], she had Parkinson's syndrome. She would sit with a blank staring face, hour after hour. I used to sit and watch her. I would think, "Oh, God in heaven, what's going on inside your mind?" When I do "Rockaby," I have a picture in my mind – I think in pictures – of someone staring out a window at a skyscraper block. Perhaps there may be one other person out there. How awful it must be to sit there waiting for death.[9]

She used to pace up and down, like Sam's mother actually, and you couldn't get through to her, and then she'd come out of it. And perhaps things like this were going on in her head . . . There's something in that that one can use; otherwise it's just a waste.   (documentary)

I quote her at length because these statements show that, despite her meetings with Beckett, Whitelaw does not work purely by sound; like most of us, she applies the plays to herself and comes to some understanding of them, or at least of moments within them. Which is not to say that music is less important to her than she claims; on the contrary, the way she savors certain words such as "carpeted" in *Footfalls* (as Krapp does his "Spooool"), the way she expands others into more syllables than they really possess, such as "rocked" in *Rockaby*, often succeeds in directing our attention away from meaning and toward rhythm. But we should recognize that her Beckett work is also significantly informed by a coincidence of natures, a natural affinity with the author's creations, involving her particular life experiences, personal mannerisms and emotional pains – which of course always vary from actor to actor, and spectator to spectator.

Even beyond those affinities, though, there are a few times in the documentary when she directly discusses meaning. In one scene, her hairdresser suggests that the character's wig be left untended like the hair of someone neglected in a nursing home, saying, "I think she's the woman, but the hat and dress are her mother's." Whitelaw answers, "Well, I don't know. We'll ask Alan. But I think, you see, that it *has* been done but like three hundred years ago. Ideally, it should decay a little more with each section." And in another context she says concerning her "Mores":

. . . I'm in the chair, and I feel that as long as I can hear my own thoughts, then I'm still there. And when the thoughts stop it's terrifying. It feels quite terrifying in that chair when the words stop. But whenever I say "more" the "mores" become weaker because she is fading into . . . whatever. And so whenever I say "more" it's like, "Don't let me go yet."   (VV)

At the risk of attributing undue importance to what are really passing comments, I want to point out that these thoughts are interpretive, though not of course in any academic sense; they are clear evidence of heuristic thinking. Whitelaw implies a symbolic reading of the character by situating her in a time continuum far longer than a human life span, and she suggests an understanding of the character's duality by saying that the voice reports her thoughts but is nevertheless capable of letting her go. My point is to show that she has an understanding of the play that is probably more sophisticated than most. She makes definite decisions that lead to confident actions onstage, but none of them resolves important ambiguities in the text; because her imagination is not limited to a particular identity or situation, she is equipped to give performances both purposeful and profound.

Whitelaw's approach to Beckett might be summarized as follows. She listens to the music of the text in Beckett's reading and uses it as a guide to meter, tempo and phrasing. Then, as she herself reads the words over and over in rehearsal, they affect her internally, first as music but later also as language. She allows those words to evoke visual images, sometimes from her own life, and in the end arrives at ideas about the play's meaning despite her aversion to analysis and her continuing emphasis on melody in her delivery. Thus her performances benefit from ideas through the avenue of music. One might well ask whether someone who works so much with subjective response can be called a Beckett "interpreter" at all, but in a way the semantic ambiguity of that appellation illuminates her approach.

When we say that an actor or musician *interprets* a text, we use the word neutrally to describe a more or less physical process of learning, and then speaking or playing, words or notes. But when we say that a critic *interprets*, we refer to a huge and problematic tradition of assigning meanings, in which most actors prefer not to participate. The truth is that although actors such as Whitelaw may not set out to, or wish to, interpret in the latter sense, and neither may audiences, interpretation happens anyway because some type of understanding is an inevitable part of anyone's significant entry into an imaginative work. As Richard Gilman once said to me about Susan Sontag's *Against Interpretation*, to ask for an erotics of art is itself an interpretation; we should question not the spectator's ability to feel but the denigration of mind implicit in drawing simplistic thought/feeling polarities. Thus, let us for the sake of argument call Whitelaw an inadvertent Beckett interpreter, and use that to facilitate a parallel with Beckett's spectators.

At the beginning of this chapter I quoted a passage from Charles Lyons stating that the participatory nature of Beckett's drama consists in the audience's "futile struggle to deal with the intangibility of the experience," which he says "duplicates" the characters' struggles to apprehend their pasts. For Lyons, these struggles have to do with incompleteness, with "the baffling environments of the present" and the unverifiability of information about the past, but one has only to see these plays in the theater to notice immediately that his model skips a step. It neglects the music of the plays and other aspects of their intense affect in the present, and assumes that the most sophisticated viewer is the one who pays closest attention to the words, which is too intellectual a process to account satisfactorily for either the characters' or most spectators' responses.[10] The woman in the chair is not just baffled by her surroundings, she is also lulled to sleep, and who can say to what degree she is affected by each stimulus? Similarly, spectators do not just wonder about plot information; they are also enveloped by a prominent sound pattern and a startling *live* stage picture. Thus, Whitelaw's approach to acting might be seen as a much more convincing metaphor than Lyons' model for watching a Beckett play, for it takes into account the fact that we sometimes come to see in oblique ways the literary values Lyons describes. We attend first perhaps to the text's music or the subtly changing tableau, and only later realize the poetry's implications and become inadvertent interpreters.

It would take a large-scale scientific study of audience reaction at many different productions to prove this point conclusively, but to an extent it is supported by Beckett's success in the theater: his plays would never have attracted more than coterie audiences if their primary contact with spectators was intellectual.[11] The intellectual is only one of several faculties called into play by Beckett performances, and usually not the first one. Martin Esslin suggests that most spectators' entire reaction (to later Beckett) is to "the *overall impact* of a single overwhelmingly powerful image," and perhaps that is true, but I suspect that for many this is merely an initial reaction; afterwards they remember bits of the haunting text despite what they think is their lack of understanding, and allow meaning to accrue to the play as its overwhelming effect wears off.[12] Shortly before his death, Alan Schneider said this about recent Beckett audiences:

What's interesting to me is that the ellipses of *Godot* are now transparently clear to college freshmen, where before they were baffling to all these great critics and philosophy professors. That's a matter of rules changing, and that the language of our perception is sufficient to take him in. The audiences that come to the Beckett plays at the Harold Clurman [*Ohio Impromptu, Catastrophe* and *What Where*] now are absolutely middle class, nonintellectual, nonaficionados. They get much more out of Beckett than the experts. I go once a week and listen to the conversations, they're fabulous. Beckett's very pleased by that.[13]

It is very easy to dismiss such comments as irrelevant to criticism, as referring to modes of apprehension less important than those of the trained mind, but that is an elitist position justified neither by the plays nor by their theater histories. Textual criticism of Beckett would do well to reconcile itself to some "illegitimate" responses. My answer, then, to the question asked at the outset – on what level should spectators be expected to understand? – is this: at the very deepest level, deeper even than the most sophisticated textual criticism, which all too often omits mention of the primary routes to the spectator's understanding.

Several years after the New York City production of *Rockaby* I saw a play that in some ways reminded me of it – Heiner Müller's *Quartet*, in which two characters play a series of sexually charged games that involve exchanging roles, adopting other personas, and dropping a host of literary allusions, all of which are familiar (from other dramas in the tradition of Brecht) as *Verfremdungseffekte*. The spectator, however, is never wholly dissuaded from emotional involvement because a simple, immediate action takes place against the background of all the literary games: a progression of raw, unexplained power shifts between the characters, culminating in one of them murdering the other. Müller shows that his background may grow as complicated as he likes, the audience will not be lost, so long as two breathing, speaking humans have something vital to resolve between them onstage. The play's final scene is surprisingly powerful because the audience realizes the essential point that the man in front of them, *whoever* he is, is dead. The whole huge allusive machine with all its ambiguous roles holds together because of the fascination we reserve for the ineluctable fact of death.

This same simple truth, I think, applies to *Rockaby*, about which Schneider, in a rare moment of disclosure, said to Whitelaw:

I know what this play's about. I'll tell you. It's not about dying, not about coming to die. It's about accepting death . . . It's coming to terms with m-o-t-h-e-r, "mother rocker," if you will. I'm not sure Sam would put it that way, but you're not dead by the end. You've accepted the inevitability of dying. You've accepted.

(documentary)

The voice's suspected mendacity understood, the narrative's unverifiability notwithstanding, there is a woman in front of us who appears to die. The ending may not be actual death, and may not even represent death unequivocally, but all its possible meanings refer to the idea of death. It is, at least, the end of the lullaby and "time she stopped," whoever she is. As in *Breath*, where the duration of the play represents the length of a life and the final curtain is the moment of greatest impact, the end of *Rockaby* stops time for a certain "she" and stuns the audience by not resuming the rocking and the rhythmic voice. For we spectators, all textual ambiguities recede as background to the fact of that final fade out, and all fictions and truths coalesce in our reluctant acceptance of it.

3 Considerations of acting in the early plays

In 1957, Alain Robbe-Grillet wrote about Didi and Gogo:

The dramatic character, in most cases, merely *plays a role*, like the people around us who evade their own existence. In Beckett's play, on the contrary, everything happens as if the two tramps were on stage *without having a role*.

They *are there*; they must explain themselves. But they do not seem to have a text prepared beforehand and scrupulously learned by heart, to support them. They must invent. They are free.[1]

This comment was made about the characters, but it has been frequently applied to the actor's challenge, the aspect of early Beckett involving "pure performance," which has continued to attract some of the world's greatest clowns. If a typical character actor works predominantly through intensive study of the script, in search of his personal history, a typical clown loves nothing better than dramatic freedom, the opportunity to hold an audience with nothing but a few props and his trusted charisma, on an empty stage.

Consider his dilemma, however, once he is cast in this play whose dialogue at first seems so much like Laurel and Hardy's. He must perform in a serious plot that both blocks unequivocal understanding of its serious meanings and undercuts the humor of his slapstick. He is under a continual obligation to create with the same sense of excitement and hope for spontaneous applause he would carry onto a music hall stage, except that he is not on such a stage, and is performing in a play that continually disappoints those expectations. His clowning takes place not against a noisy background of other clowning, as it does in circus or vaudeville, but rather against silence. His jokes and gags may be perfectly executed yet not provoke laughs at any of the points he expects; they may provoke delayed laughter, or laughter which the script will not allow him to treat as an end in itself. He portrays a clown *manqué*, a performer unsure even whether anyone is watching him, and in such a characterization too much conventional clown-success is failure. His "freedom," as Robbe-Grillet wrote, "is without any use."

Again and again in productions not only of *Godot* but of all Beckett's early works, difficulties have arisen like the one described in this scenario. Most prominently, both Bert Lahr as Estragon in the American premiere of *Godot* in Miami and Buster Keaton as O in *Film* (a character with marked similarities to Didi and Gogo) repeatedly tried to pad their scripts with trademark routines. Lahr's attitude, especially, created a conflict with the director, Alan Schneider, which significantly affected the play's meaning in performance, and which has since become legendary as an actor/director ego battle instead of as the excellent practical lesson it might have been.

In his autobiography, *Entrances*, Schneider tells of his frustration with Lahr's constant desire, in his own words, to be "top banana":

Bert soon discovered that what I called "Ping-Pong games" between Estragon and Vladimir were very much like vaudeville routines, and began to have a little fun . . . Every two minutes, Bert would smile and say, "It's all opening up, kid. It's opening up!" I would feel good for a couple of minutes, until Bert would come up with the idea of replacing the end of the "Let's go./We can't./Why not?/We're waiting for Godot" sequence with his old vaudeville "Ohnnnnggggg" instead of Beckett's "Ah." Or ask me to cut the Lucky speech because no one understood it. And, anyhow, the audience was coming to see him and not the guy playing Lucky, wasn't it? . . . I was afraid to tell him that perhaps the character of Vladimir was slightly more central to the play's thematic core than the character of Estragon.[2]

To Schneider, characterization of Didi and Gogo as straight-man and fool created a structural imbalance, distorting the play's atmosphere by preventing the representation of an equilateral tension between types of humanity.

In his biography of his father, *Notes on a Cowardly Lion*, John Lahr tells the actor's side of this story, speaking of it as a complex disagreement about approach instead of a clash of professionalism and childishness.

If Lahr's demands for textual changes were unreasonable, his instincts for the tragicomic had a potential that Schneider's own uncertainties kept him from exploring. While Schneider insisted that the play was a partnership, the melding of mind and body, privately he saw the mind dominating the belly ("The play is not about Estragon, but Vladimir"), a moot distinction that shades the comedy toward tragedy rather than vice versa.

Lahr's insight was from the gut. He knew that laughter would complement Beckett's poetry. Schneider leaned toward the poetry, but was afraid laughter would turn it into a romp.[3]

Unfortunately, even years later, this situation was filled with enough animosity to cloud its real issues.[4] With benefit of hindsight, however, we can distill it into several specific questions which still arise in every production of *Godot*. Superficially, the conflict concerns a differer~~t~~ opinion about the dominance of one character over the other, but behin~~d~~

is a more fundamental conflict concerning the presence of and emphasis on clowning.

The question of whether one character ought to dominate the other may or may not be interesting to critics, but it is certainly a moot point for actors. It has often seemed more problematic in rehearsal than it ought to be because Schneider asserted on numerous occasions that Beckett once told him he considers Vladimir the main character.[5] Whatever Beckett may have meant by that statement, in his own 1975 production of the play at the Schiller Theater in West Berlin, Vladimir and Estragon had equal prominence, so we may assume that, critical interpretation aside, his dramatic intention is to present two fictional tramps trapped in identical ways by the same predicament; and in that context one has no more power or significance than the other. Jack MacGowran once warned against tipping scales that Beckett took pains to balance:

I think sometimes the roles are reversed. I think Estragon is the one who has read and known everything and thrown it away and become completely cynical. Vladimir, who appears to be the brighter of the two, is in fact the half-schooled one, madly trying to find out answers and pestering Estragon the whole time. Otherwise, Estragon couldn't quote Shelley as he does and misquote him deliberately: "Pale for weariness of climbing the heavens and gazing at the likes of us." This gives you the impression that Estragon has read everything and dismissed it.[6]

The other Schneider/Lahr question – how much clowning can the play sustain? – raises much more fundamental questions about performance context; for clowning can consist of both externally and internally focused actions. To what degree should the actors understand their relationship in a naturalistic way, from within, and refer all clowning to it? Or more comprehensively, for whom does the Beckett actor in general perform in the early plays, and what responses can he expect from his audiences? To what degree should he concern himself with the play's disclosure of its theatricality, and how should that concern affect his characterization?

Beckett's critics seem to have satisfied themselves with answers to these questions much more often than his actors and directors. The simultaneous authenticity and histrionism in Beckett's theater has been used by numerous commentators, for example, as a ground for associating Beckett with Bertolt Brecht – as typified by this statement of Enoch Brater's: "in a fundamental sense Beckett parallels Brecht's dramatic technique: the actor in his theater is as consistently 'alienated' from the role he is playing as he is meant to be in Brecht's repertory."[7] As I will discuss at more length, however, this is a highly misleading view that not only underrates the specificity of Beckett's theater but also unwittingly projects a certain style onto it. Among practitioners there is actually little consensus on a "correct" approach to Beckett, nor is Beckett acting the same today as it was two or three decades ago (a topic discussed by Bernard Dort in a recent article).[8] What is possible, however, is to compare a number of different styles and attitudes in order to identify common elements in the productions that seem most effective.

I begin with two subsequent Schneider *Godots*: one produced for television in 1961 and now distributed by Grove Press as a film, the other produced at the Sheridan Square Playhouse in 1971 and available on video at Lincoln Center. Because it was a television project, the earlier production was subject to a number of practical limitations – e.g. short rehearsal period, cutting of all lines construable as profane – so it may be the least letter-faithful effort of this letter-faithful director.[9] Nevertheless, it assembled an extremely talented cast whose ability to clarify the internal action for themselves compensated a great deal for the restrictions of the medium.

One of the television screen's effects is to make the play's world seem magical and marvelous. The action is played on a cartoon-like set that resembles a fairy-tale illustration: a few beautifully rendered, wispy clouds interrupt the emptiness of the sky; ridiculous pillowy hills, all about chair height, flank the road as it winds gently for at least thirty feet upstage, and a flagrantly artificial tree awaits the characters downstage like a jungle-gym in a playground. It would not seem at all out of place for an occasional sprite or troll to flitter through this beautiful space, which is only to say that it feels more benevolent than disquieting. Beckett once commented that it is essential for the characters in *Godot* to appear trapped, yet this environment, like all fantasy, implies a potential for escape.

At the same time, however, it has an orienting effect that helps the actors make choices. As Ruby Cohn points out, this setting is different from that in most *Godots* because it is deeper than it is wide, which means that the audience sees characters entering from upstage long before they are close enough to join the dialogue, and the effect is to call attention to the specific location of the action on a road.[10] A road is, at the very least, a way directing people to and from somewhere, and one especially notices in this production the importance of that notion of direction to the portrayal of directionlessness in Didi and Gogo. The atmosphere functions, figuratively, as a means of direction, because we sense that the actors exist in a comic reality that is different from our everyday one, but that justifies everything they do and say in its own terms. We feel we have entered a special world – different from both its vaudeville and cartoon components – whose rules of operation we do not know precisely, but we see the characters obeying them and we learn more about them as the play goes on. By making a whole-hearted commitment to illusionism, in other words, the production gives its actors a stable environment in which to develop clear and definite character actions.

The relationship between Burgess Meredith (Vladimir) and Zero Mostel

(Estragon) is a good demonstration of the kind of comic symbiosis necessary to focus the audience's interest on both characters, even though it develops in a fantastic world where less seems to be at risk than is usual in stage productions of this play. Meredith's Didi is an extremely interested, truly sympathetic man who asks questions such as "How's your foot?" or "Like to finish it?" with a smile of genuine kindness. He becomes intensely involved in everything that occurs, which exacerbates his repeated disappointment when he fails to find the meanings he craves, and he has a parental impulse to handle all really important matters personally, which often backfires on him because, other than Gogo, no one in his world responds to parental qualities such as infinite patience. After shooing his indelicate friend away, he speaks to the Boy in act I in the softest voice he can muster, but learns no more than Mostel/Gogo would have by speaking harshly. The friends end the act hand in hand, that physical contact evidence of a neediness neither makes any effort to disguise.

Mostel's Gogo is, as might be expected, a jolly and very good-natured fellow who uses his humor to fill the many moments when nothing else happens. He does employ classic Mostel mannerisms, but never to change the text. For example, during the insult exchange in act II – "Moron!/ Vermin!/Abortion!" – he and Meredith walk away from each other, back to back, like mock-duelists. Mostel, wearing a huge smile, turns his face to the camera and shows his paunch in full profile as he walks on tiptoe, twiddling his fingers in punctuation of each barb. Because Meredith behaves similarly and is included in the game, however, the impression is not primarily of a star-clown performing for the audience; it is rather of two friends clowning for each other, and only incidentally for whomever else might be looking on.

One of the most memorable parts of the production is Alvin Epstein's portrayal of Lucky, which bears a striking resemblance to Klaus Herm's in Beckett's production fourteen years later. Epstein pants constantly for air with his eyes bugged out and raised to heaven, his stringy white hair protruding from under his hat like the pieces of a broken umbrella. His dance is very simple and thus effective at communicating a lost artistic skill instead of merely dumb humor: he spreads his arms grandly like wings, then draws them together close to his chest as if wrenched in agony, suddenly screwing up his face and tentatively raising one leg. And his delivery of the speech, though hectic, is probably the most sensible that English-speaking audiences have seen. Because of his varied hand gestures and frequent changes of pace, one is sure throughout that all his words make perfect sense to him, so his internal plot motivation – to impress Pozzo and avoid being sold at the fair – becomes unusually clear.[11]

The production's illusionistic self-sufficiency, then, is at once its greatest delight and its greatest drawback. The stage is like an aquarium, a too neatly packaged world that fascinates us partly because we could not live there, forming a mysterious, highly crafted casing for wholly realistic, self-enclosed events. *Waiting for Godot* holds the potential to impose its theatricality, its metaphoric staginess, far more strongly than that on spectators' consciousnesses. The frame of the television screen emphasizes this innocuous quality, but it is also a result of the acting.[12] Mostel, for example, who usually speaks unabashedly in a New York Jewish accent, is surprisingly adept at compensating for what many critics have described as the intellectual quality in Didi and Gogo's lines. Vivian Mercier writes:

I once remarked to Samuel Beckett that I thought it odd of him to translate the colloquial French "Ce serait un moyen de bander" as "We'd get an erection." It seemed to me, I said, that here and elsewhere in the English version of *En attendant Godot* he made Didi and Gogo sound as if they had earned Ph.D's. "How do you know they hadn't?" was his answer.[13]

Beckett's response is interesting because it implies that he wants his characters to use unexpected words to make us unsure about their histories, which, among other things, reminds us that they are acting. Beckett *intends* his language to assert itself by sounding beautifully aphoristic and artificial; thus Mostel compensates for what should never have been treated as a problem. He speaks French ("Que voulez-vous") gruffly with no perceptible change in accent, as an American might imagine a crude Frenchman talks (not to be confused with how a crude Frenchman actually talks). And he delivers introspective or philosophical lines, such as "We always find something, eh Didi, to give us the impression we exist?," matter of factly, as if no mental effort were necessary to arrive at such thoughts. The result is a clear impression of a strange fictional character to whom those statements constitute concrete experience, not abstract ideas, but a very thin impression of an actor acting.

The Sheridan Square Playhouse production also renders a fictional world that is different from ours, but one with far less mysterious trappings and rules. Ten years after his television version, Schneider seems to have gone out of his way to produce a *Godot* that was free from any hints of the atextual stylizations to which Beckett objected. He wanted this one to be funnier, quicker, more lively than the typical *Godot*, and he started by stripping it of anything that could be considered embellishment. In the process of paring down, however, he removed some of what he himself had always said was the Beckett actor's most important tool, concrete circumstance. This comment, made shortly after the production opened, betrays some of his thoughts at the time about abstracting the characters' situation:

This is the fourth time I've done *Godot*, not the second . . . And it's not that I have four different concepts; I have one that I'm continually moving toward. The concept is: to see if I can get a sense of waiting, of unfulfilled, unredeemed waiting.[14]

The action takes place on a level stage of wooden planks, completely bare except for a real tree upstage, behind which are black curtains – no mound or rock. Henderson Forsythe and Paul B. Price are a very young-looking, young-behaving Didi and Gogo, and they wear badly tattered everyday suits rather than the old formal attire of Mostel/Meredith and many other early casts. From the opening business with Gogo's boot, which is like a gymnastic stunt, they are both unexplainably enthusiastic and energetic; Price especially never tires at all. And though the vocal deliveries are often intentionally grating – people seem always to be shouting – the audience laughs frequently, delighted by what appears to be a play about games. Eventually, though, the ever-present physical activity comes to seem all but irrelevant to the action because it is given no emotional basis, no justification in the characters' relationship. This Didi and Gogo are so busy rushing to play that they haven't time to develop their bond beyond a simple mutual opportunism; they are like Bowery bums who stay together in order to leech more efficiently on passers-by. Unlike Mostel and Meredith, they need each other only for exigencies.

Such an interpretation is not exactly atextual, but the acting and directing choices that communicate it all seem to be smaller in scope, less resonant and memorable than those in Schneider's previous productions. Consider, for example, the quality of play during several exchanges. After Pozzo offers Gogo his handkerchief to wipe away Lucky's tears, the script reads:

> *Estragon hesitates.*
> VLADIMIR: Here, give it to me, I'll do it.
> *Estragon refuses to give the handkerchief.*
> *Childish gestures.*

Price/Gogo's hesitation consists of wiping his own bald head with the cloth, which makes Forsythe/Didi think he wants to keep it for himself, and prompts the line above and a struggle for possession of the prize; whereupon Lucky and any potential sympathy for him are forgotten. The stage direction "Childish gestures" certainly permits such a reading, but its effect in performance is to stress the characters' selfishness instead of their camaraderie. Later, the episode where Didi gives Gogo a carrot that turns out to be a turnip starts with Price spitting out the turnip rhythmically (milking a laugh on each bit), and ends with he and Forsythe nose to nose in an unprovoked argument. In his production, Beckett also allowed the actors freedom of play during these sections, but their games left the impression of real psychological exchange, not of two performers competing for laughs.

Anthony Holland's performance as Lucky also contributes to the production's impersonality. He delivers the speech as fast as he can, pausing only briefly when breath becomes absolutely necessary, implying that it is all utter nonsense while concentrating on creating a funny spectacle. This is the

3 Henderson Forsythe as Vladimir and Paul B. Price as Estragon in *Waiting for Godot*, directed by Alan Schneider, Sheridan Square Playhouse, NYC, 1971. (Photo: © 1971 Alix Jeffrey/Harvard Theater Collection)

most commonplace short-cut taken with this role: actors and directors fill out with grotesquerie what does not make immediate rational sense. At the Long Wharf Theatre in New Haven (in the 1981 South African *Godot* discussed in the following chapter), I saw Peter Piccolo captivate an entire audience by suspending a five-foot string of drool from his mouth for fifteen minutes; from his entrance until his dance, spectators watched no one else. In the 1977 Los Angeles Actors' Theatre production, Bruce French played Lucky with shiny silver hair sprayed to retain the shape of his bowler, his mouth permanently stuck in an "oh" position, and a white hangman's noose around his badly disfigured neck (shown in close-up many times in the PBS television version). Holland's lightning-fast pace really amounts to one of these grotesque *coups de théâtre* which overweigh the internal situation and make Lucky seem to exist in his own play.

In the interests of emphasizing acting qua acting, the performers in this production sacrifice the integrity of their fictional relationships, giving the action in essence the opposite bias to Mostel/Meredith's; instead of seeming fanciful, this production seems blunt and empty. Yet one hastens to add that the biases are not equally objectionable; when one compares specific moments, it becomes apparent that the later cast is outclassed by the earlier. For instance, when Forsythe asks if he should tell the story about the two thieves and Price says, "No," his answer means, flatly, no; he wishes Didi would be quiet. Mostel's answer to the same question means yes, his "No" being just an impish game that Didi recognizes as part of their affectionate playing technique. The certainty of the first reading stifles the audience's curiosity about their relationship while the second nourishes it – a point that could be made equally well with direct comparisons of countless other specific moments. As act 1 ends, despite the nearly sentimental nature of the lines immediately preceding the curtain, Forsythe and Price sit Indian style beside one another, hands folded, staring straight ahead, and there is neither warmth nor coldness between them, no sense of emotional connection whatsoever.

It is worth mentioning that the coarse atmosphere in this spare, angry production is typical of the no-nonsense theatrical style that prevailed in the early 1970s, so many of its significances, like those of other performance events from that era, are time-bound. I refer to a general pugnacity in American culture as a whole during the final years of the Vietnam War, expressed in the work of Richard Schechner, Joseph Chaikin and Megan Terry, to mention only a few. The surface of this *Godot* is a gruff, up-front, biting humor that thinly covers an unmistakable underlying violence. The ubiquitous laughter is neither generous nor compassionate, but rather sardonic and mean-spirited, either at the expense of a couple of too-familiar New York bums, or in anger at some invisible authority. Thus, the characters' frequent expressions of puzzlement generate little sense of wonder in us; we are made to feel we know exactly what is going on at all times.

More significantly, what these two Schneider productions demonstrate is the difficulty of blending Beckett's internal and external actions. Mostel/Meredith favored the beautifully theatrical over the metatheatrical and ended up creating a fantastic form of fourth-wall realism. Forsythe/Price emphasized cynical metatheatrical playing at the expense of theatrical illusion and ended up losing the play's emotional center and, hence, justification for their physical activity. Perhaps the most difficult question of all for both actors and directors is how to combine these approaches – how to reconcile authentic realism with authentic artificiality – and some of that question's most satisfactory answers have come from Beckett himself, who directs with what he calls "physical themes."

Beckett's 1975 Schiller Theater production of *Warten auf Godot* takes place on a raked stage so huge that it dwarfs the stone and tree, which are at least forty feet apart and contrasted visually by a dully colored backdrop.[15] The audience sees the action occurring in a nearly empty space, which discourages perceptions of theatrical illusion. Didi (Stefan Wigger) and Gogo (Horst Bollmann) are both onstage at the outset – one of many changes from the published text – and the audience immediately laughs at the way Beckett takes advantage of their different physiques. The tall and lean Wigger wears striped pants with a black jacket that is too small for him, and the short, chubby Bollmann wears black pants and a striped jacket too large for him; when they appear in act II they have exchanged clothes. The effect of their clownish appearance is to eliminate the possibility of spectators imagining real-life histories for them, as was so easy with Forsythe and Price, and to call attention to their complementary senses of humor: one responds to the other's jokes so quickly and cleverly that it sometimes appears as if they have access to a common mind.[16] They are unabashed performers very obviously taking the stage in order to tell us a story.

As in all Beckett's productions, the stage movement is extremely calculated and non-naturalistic. Walter Asmus, Beckett's Assistant Director for *Godot* and many other productions, describes a typical piece of direction in his rehearsal diary:

Beckett walks on the stage, his eyes fixed on the ground, and shows the movement as he speaks Estragon's lines; "You had something to say to me? . . . You're angry? . . . Forgive me . . . Come, Didi. Give me your hand . . ." With each sentence Beckett makes a step towards the imaginary partner. Always a step then the line. Beckett calls this step-by-step approach a physical theme; it comes up five, six or seven times, and has got to be done very exactly. This is the element of ballet.[17]

Almost any section of the production could be used as an example of these graceful, highly polished gestures, which usually become part of some visual symmetry, and which are usually executed in silence because of Beckett's rule about separation of speech and movement. Didi and Gogo make their stage crossings in long, arched paths and frequently stop to pose for tableaux – e.g. the heights of Bollmann, Wigger and tree in identical proportion (apparently one of Beckett's favorites). At one point they walk arm in arm across the vast stage, which takes at least fifteen seconds, keeping in perfect step the whole time, only to turn around when they reach the other side and return. And at another point Bollmann travels toward Wigger by means of a standing broad jump, after which they clasp hands and broad jump together in another direction.

In description this type of activity sounds contrived, but in the theater it actually turns out to be strikingly natural. Like the 1961 Schneider production, this world defines its own sense of the natural, only without a full

4 *Warten auf Godot* (*Waiting for Godot*), directed by Samuel Beckett,
Schiller Theater, West Berlin, 1975. Klaus Herm as Lucky, Horst
Bollmann as Estragon, Carl Raddatz as Pozzo, Stefan Wigger as
Vladimir. (Photo: Ilse Buhs)

commitment to illusionism. Wigger/Didi and Bollmann/Gogo's world *is* a
staged performance, and they express their emotions, so to speak, geometri-
cally: it seems completely reasonable to us that Bollmann might do something like a standing broad jump just to entertain himself, and find Wigger
joining him a moment later; the more surprising the invention the better
because surprise breaks monotony. Since those geometric expressions are in
no way arbitrary – Beckett's *Regiebücher* for all his productions contain
hundreds of detailed notes for systematic activities intended as "subliminal
stage imagery" – Didi and Gogo's movement is like a shared code that serves
to entertain, primarily them but also others.[18] And that code creates an
atmosphere onstage in which different degrees of realism make no sense. In
most *Godot* productions, as in Brecht, some lines are directed outward, or
addressed to the audience, in the context of all others being directed inward in

a quasi-normal fashion, but no such distinction exists here. Any action, any line, any gesture, can be interpreted two different ways: as a performance, or as a "real" event in the characters' fictional lives.

Again the role of Lucky offers a good illustration.[19] Like Alvin Epstein, Klaus Herm is especially good at communicating the idea that Lucky was once a clever man. He appears crazed, but one senses him constantly thinking; it's as if his nervous tension were a physical impairment that diverts perfectly rational thoughts away from their proper outlet. When he begins the speech, his voice is slow and clear as in a lecture, but he soon becomes emotionally involved and gestures wildly; at this point, however, unlike in most other *Godots*, Didi and Gogo edge closer to him, and he grows more humanly animated, not more machine-like. The speech is not done as a single forward charge, but with long (up to five-second) pauses inserted at various points, which imply that he thinks he is doing well until the final section.

Herm/Lucky's successful portrayal of the character's former lucidity makes us wonder why he stays voluntarily bound to Pozzo, which in turn makes us reflect on the voluntary nature of all his ties. Since he is free at any time to relinquish his post as actor, both in the theater and within the play, "it follows that he doesn't want to" (Pozzo's words). This may be obvious, but what becomes unusually clear in this production is that the same is true about Didi and Gogo in their context of waiting for Godot. Wigger/Didi and Bollmann/Gogo seem especially disturbed by Lucky because they perceive a resemblance between themselves and him which their mockery cannot mitigate. They have been reminding us all along that they are performers, and their theatrical gesture when they try to stop his speech – an extremely unreal, non-violent pummeling – appears as a poignant moment of con-naturality with this scapegoat-actor.

What Beckett's production shows clearly, then, is that the two realms of meaning, presentational and representational, can be blended into a consistent atmosphere of ambiguity without the actors having to make constant shifts back and forth between them. Because it commits to an internal logic of clowning, his *Godot* is light-spirited, physical, and sensible. And because it is choreographed with such a firm hand, it transcends that simple clown-sense without forcing its clowns to act as authorial mouthpieces. From a stance of simplicity and humility it succeeds where countless slick and intellectually ambitious productions have failed, eventually leading the spectator's mind toward questions of presentational action without destroying the integrity of its representational action. One's thoughts quickly finish with local questions – Who is Godot and why doesn't he arrive? Why do Didi and Gogo stay together and keep returning? – moving presently, almost automatically, on to more comprehensive ones: for whom is any performance given and with what expectations? Why am I in the theater, and what am I waiting for?

Moreover, the same seamless blending of realms seen in this *Godot* is also

5 Rehearsal for *Warten auf Godot* (*Waiting for Godot*), directed by Samuel Beckett, Schiller Theater, West Berlin, 1975. Samuel Beckett (back to camera). Actors (from left to right): Stefan Wigger, Carl Raddatz, Horst Bollmann, Klaus Herm. (Photo: Anneliese Heuer)

found in the most effective productions of *Endgame* (which I discuss presently), *Krapp's Last Tape*, and *Happy Days*. Krapp speaks ostensibly to his tape recorder, urgently fetching it, fondling it as if alone with the girl in the punt, yet also slipping on a banana skin like a music hall Fool. And Winnie speaks ostensibly to Willie, even though he remains invisible behind her until the end and we sit in front watching her soliloquize from a flagrantly metaphorical lodgement. In each case, the actor faces a similar challenge: to appear to play simultaneously with two different consciousnesses, *in* the play and *of* the play.

There is an extremely broad spectrum of possible solutions to this problem, recognition of which does not entail any particular type or degree of clowning but rather an acceptance of multiple audiences. In fact, two of the most masterful solutions I have seen, both by French actors, have come from opposite ends of the clowning spectrum. One is a production of *La dernière bande*, directed by Mario Gonzalez at the Théâtre de la Tempête in Paris in 1987, in which Stuart Seide performed all the movement as a painstakingly practiced mime. Wearing thickly caked, light-gray make-up brushed back into his hair, accentuating an unnaturally purple nose, Seide moves in such a bizarrely comic manner (torso bolt upright in a perfect vertical, legs severely bent, traveling two feet ahead of the torso) that his movement alone creates and sustains an atmosphere halfway between circus performance and clownish naturalism. In other words, he blends two realms of action by making the quotidian seem otherworldly.

The other example is Madeleine Renaud's *Oh les beaux jours* which Beckett helped direct in 1963. What particularly distinguishes Renaud is precisely her ability to make the quotidian theatrical without using demonstrative techniques, or indeed any strategy of exaggeration or amplification whatever. She takes what might be considered the opposite approach, using the character's boredom to project tranquillity. Instead of flaunting Winnie's indomitability, as do most actresses, she understates it and makes spectators feel as if she were talking casually with them in her living room while occasionally attending to distasteful but unavoidable household matters such as Willie's spitting. In other words, she establishes an imaginary link between two audiences by creating an impression of chatting with an unseen yet specific partner.

Perhaps the greatest confusion about Beckett's theater has always been the taxonomical one – what kind of animal is it? What is its theatrical genus? Of all the performances I have seen in the course of researching this book, none answers those questions more authoritatively than the ones the author directed. Beckett is not a great director in the sense of Meyerhold or Stanislavsky, and could not be, since with one exception (Robert Pinget's *L'Hypothèse*) he has directed only his own works. He has not developed unique staging techniques that will gather followers and blossom into an aesthetic movement, he has not published any extended theory of theater or drama, and has not established an authorized style of acting for his plays – like, say, the one Brecht developed with the Berliner Ensemble.

Nevertheless, his productions do bring into full actuality ideas about staging that he had while writing yet left unsaid in the published plays. They are the best examples we have of how he intends his work to appear in the theater, and thus they are uniquely capable of pointing up distinctive theatrical values in the texts that some performance styles serve better than others. The polyvalence of the works itself, for instance, can be seen to support a standard of judgment: styles that imply choice among meanings, or among realms of meaning, are inferior to those that do not. And that simple standard, that idea of considering ambiguity as a positive performance value, is really all the critical raw material one needs to discuss a poetics of Beckett performance.

Despite the fact that he did not make his career as a director, Beckett has succeeded through playwriting and occasional directing in inventing a new *kind* of theater, one involving a type of audience/stage transaction that does not fit either side of the traditional Stanislavsky/Brecht dichotomy.[20] Many critics have pointed out shared characteristics with one or the other or both of these, but few have gone on to draw the obvious conclusion: that Beckett really represents a third category situated between Stanislavsky and Brecht because of the way he renders the presentational and representational indistinguishable. In a lucid analysis, Michael Goldman explains:

It is the combination of subtexts, then, that produces the effect, with one important proviso: *that no subtext be treated as privileged.* This is in sharp contrast to the standard convention of modern subtexts before Beckett, in which the subtext is understood to represent the authentic source of the text. The character may not be in touch with the source, but the actor is. In the Stanislavskian system, the character may not be aware of the drives or inhibitions that run beneath the text of a Hedda or a Lopakhin, but the actor makes them available to the audience as a truth in terms of which the text can be located. In the Brechtian system, this privileged truth lies in the actor's commitment to the social interpretation of the character, which gives the gestus its effect. But it would contradict Beckett's vision to offer such a possibility of authentication. Thus, our engagement with the actors, though it can be intense, must not be confidently located. We must not be allowed to feel, "Yes, I can get behind these appearances."[21]

Stated more simply, the theatrical model of Stanislavsky – which in mutated form still dominates the American stage – is based on the inviolability of an internal fiction, whereas Brecht's model is based on the inviolability of selected social truths external to fictions that function as vehicles. Beckett accepts neither of those bases, rejecting the very idea that an audience should hold *anything* inviolable, unless that anything be uncertainty itself.

Beckett's theater might be seen loosely as a combination of the other two that results in conflict between them, the opposing philosophies so to speak canceling each other out, but the result is a completely new and independent synthesis rather than a void of unfulfilled potentialities.[22] The Beckett actor does preparatory work similar to what is required in both the Stanislavskian and Brechtian systems but does not receive the satisfactions associated with following either process to completion. He reads the text closely in the interests of researching his character's background, but his investigation is frustrating from the outset because Beckett inevitably reports character histories in disparate fragments, the veracity of which is unreliable. The actor also invents extra-textual activities to keep the audience interested in the action, in effect commenting on the text, but he must perform them without for a moment implying that he is free from the text, or from the way the fictional situation traps his character. As Bud Thorpe, who played Vladimir in the San Quentin Drama Workshop's 1984 production of *Godot*, said in an interview:

It's a fine line we have to tread, working so hard to give the character a human quality, and yet move the left foot on the tightrope and you realize you are an actor delivering poetic prose in play form.[23]

The only satisfaction possible for such an actor is a specifically Beckettian type that depends neither on the profundity of the original analysis nor on the psychological depth of the ultimate portrayal.

According to most of the actors I have interviewed, satisfaction in early Beckett comes from sources similar to those Whitelaw mentions with respect to *Rockaby*: from what is achieved through vocalization and physicalization (inadvertent interpretation notwithstanding), judged technically in terms of music and dance. Which is not to say that actors can focus on movement and vocal quality to the exclusion of psychological characterization. It is true, however, that a surprising number of excellent performances develop, as it were, backwards – beginning with external physical techniques and working inward toward psychological centers – in the manner of Meyerhold's Biomechanics.

Of course, a clear distinction must be made between physical techniques that succeed in leading the actor to a workable psychology and techniques that remain techniques; and in the early plays this difference is most often perceivable through the relationships between characters. I touched on this issue earlier when discussing the way Bollmann and Wigger's walking and jumping, etc., became an active part of their characters' friendship. Any discussion of this kind of stage movement, however, ought eventually to focus on *Endgame*, which Beckett has said he prefers to *Godot* because of the greater exactitude with which its physical activity is planned.

Hamm and Clov are even more isolated than Didi and Gogo – since all roads, fairs, sources of chicken bones, carrots and turnips, all useful interactions with a world outside the stage scene, are gone – which amplifies their relationship by enclosing it as in a Joseph Cornell box. And as Pierre Chabert notes, the stage movement is also magnified, partly because Clov's activity is seen against the other characters' immobility.

Just as there is an intrinsic tension between silence and words, so there is an intrinsic tension between immobility and movement. Words emanate from silence and return to it; movement emanates from immobility and returns to it. All movements, all gestures move, so to speak, within immobility, are a victory over immobility and have value only in the tension they maintain in relationship to immobility: "There I'll be, in the old shelter, alone against the silence . . . (*he hesitates*) . . . the stillness. If I can hold my peace, and sit quiet, it will be all over with sound, and motion, all over and done with."[24]

In performance, movement and emotional action are inseparable. Like a rubber band nailed to a central point, Clov moves from Hamm to window to kitchen to ashcans, but always eventually back to Hamm again, just as he must return to the words Hamm taught him (complaining, "If they don't mean anything any more, teach me others. Or let me be silent"), and continually wonder whether Hamm is lying about his lack of alternatives ("Outside of here it's death!").

Endgame in a way epitomizes the transaction all Beckett's plays make with their audiences in that its internal action is nearly opaque to those who do not question its external action, the movement and the fact of the play itself. When a character called "Hamm" lifts a "handkerchief" (read "curtain") from his face and then says "Me – to play," word joins gesture in a blatant presentationalism that is not even metaphor, since it cannot be understood in other than theatrical terms. The play's only real plot question, in a conventional sense, is whether Clov will leave, yet that question gradually takes on unexpected enormity as we realize that, Nagg and Nell notwithstanding, Clov's departure would leave Hamm-the-actor without an audience, which is, in Beckett, figurative death. Unlike *Godot*, which can be played badly and still have limited impact as a disturbing tale, *Endgame* almost does not exist even as a story if actors and director fail to realize that its histrionic movements and gestures are the propulsive force of its action, and not embellishments to it.

In Joseph Chaikin's 1979 production at the Manhattan Theatre Club, for example (available on video at Lincoln Center), the internal relationships are smothered by several broadly disconnected and frontal physical characterizations.[25] Dan Seltzer plays Hamm as a caricature huckster who, by delivering many of his lines without sharp consonants ("Meedaplay"), implies that he might be more comfortable in a wide-lapelled madras jacket than an actor's dressing-gown. And Michael Gross uses an explicit imitation of Stan Laurel for Clov, standing heels together and toes apart while twiddling his fingers next to his chin, and speaking in a saccharine, babyish manner as if to say "this makes sense" in response to everything. Seltzer and Gross seem to realize that their characters are actors, but not that they act for each other as well as for the audience; they deliver many exchanges with faces staring straight out to the house. Like Forsythe and Price, they are performers competing for spectator attention, but they lack even the former pair's limited opportunistic relationship, which results in a nonsensical action line and makes the dialogue sound like a string of non-sequiturs – similar to the

6 Peter Evans as Clov and Alvin Epstein as Hamm in *Endgame*, directed by Alvin Epstein, Samuel Beckett Theatre, NYC, 1984. (Photo: Martha Swope)

way Shakespeare can be made to sound like randomly chosen quotations from Bartlett's.

Alvin Epstein's 1984 production at the Samuel Beckett Theatre (also available at Lincoln Center) achieves the opposite effect. The relationship between Epstein's Hamm and Peter Evans' Clov is built on a clarity – or rather a clarity of ambiguity – to which all gestures can refer, and Evans exploits that "reference potential" to the utmost, as does Seide, by means of a distinctive walk invented for the role: with knees bent and legs apart, he shuffles rhythmically on tiptoe in a very practiced movement that manages to convey the idea of pain without resembling any familiar type of limp. It is like a danced abstraction of cripplehood, and thus appears simultaneously presentational and representational; Evans seems to perform it both for the audience and as an interactive part of his dealings with Hamm. For example, when he is suddenly stopped by an order – "Time enough. (*Clov halts.*)" – he freezes on the spot and loses his balance (recall he is standing only on his toes), swaying precariously as if on a tight-rope for several seconds, which becomes a gestural expression of his irritation at being halted. Like Wigger and Bollmann's geometric movements, Seide's walk, or Renaud's tranquillity, this physical characterization creates an atmosphere that allows the play's major relationship to suggest meanings simultaneously on several different levels without suggesting that any one is more important than the others.

Considering Evans' success as Clov, I was surprised when I interviewed him to learn that even though his training and working habits are firmly rooted in the tradition of American realism, his most significant progress with the role occurred when he departed from his usual process.

I try to formulate a lot of questions in my head, either beforehand or during the rehearsal period, to make an emotional background for whatever character I'm playing. Call it what you want, the "spine" of the character – I'm sure you know that Clurman term . . . I find that a very helpful way to work . . . But it became clear after a while that it wasn't working for the play, and I had to make some kind of leap . . . I mean, I always thought that those kind of external things were dangerous. But in *Endgame* . . . as soon as I made up that crazy voice and the extreme physicalness of it, it freed me to make choices that before I couldn't make, because I was locked into my own given physical self . . . It's funny, imposing this leap of faith. When you create a character not just through intellectual means but through real physical things, it opens up all kinds of doors that you could never have foreseen.[26]

What he describes as a "leap of faith" is actually his independent discovery of the approach used by most actors when working with the author as director. Because Beckett is so reluctant to discuss the psychological motivations of his characters, generally communicating his wishes through line-readings and the highly specific blocking already described, his actors *must* work from external considerations inward. Though he sometimes gives conceptual images as general explanations (e.g. "Gogo belongs to the stone, Didi to the tree"), Beckett will not spend any rehearsal time on intimate conversations about personal feelings and experiences; in Asmus' words, "he tries to go the direct way" whenever possible.[27] And what is most unusual about that approach is that in using it he rarely encounters the same problems other directors would.

That is, of course, partly a result of his worldwide fame, which causes unusually cooperative rehearsal atmospheres, but it is also because of the quality of his demonstrations. Asmus explains:

As a director I know you are always tempted to give line-readings, because it *is* the direct way. But when I give a line-reading, I cannot be sure – I know that by experience – that the way I speak the line is exactly what I mean, because I am not talented enough, or not good enough to give the exact reading. Beckett . . . I haven't experienced one play with him where at some point in the work, somebody (an actor, or whoever) wouldn't say, "Why don't you play this part?" – because his line-readings are so fabulous, so inspiring, so true. It's a matter of truthfulness that you sense is there; he is at that moment what any actor should be, simple and true at the same time.[28]

Although Beckett always remains open to suggestions, his rehearsals are largely times for actors to learn certain dictated behaviors, it being understood that any "Stanislavskian" explorations must be done on their own. As in Biomechanics, however, those behaviors eventually help bring about inner motivation. (The rehearsals are like proofs of the James-Lange theory – simultaneously developed in the 1880s by three psychologists working independently on three different continents, William James, Carl Georg Lange and Alexander Sutherland – which holds that particular muscle movements actually cause corresponding emotional states. The roots of this idea reach back to Descartes.) Indeed many actors come to depend on Beckett's instructions as much as does Whitelaw, as if they were sources of character information as rich and indispensable as the written texts.

The example of the author's direction, then, is not only atypical but also difficult to consider at all as a model process; for what other director could reproduce his working atmosphere? One could say, for instance, that Beckett the auteur, by revising *Godot* with so much new "writing" about stage movement, eluded the whole problem of talented clowns wanting to use gags to fill time on what they see as an empty stage. Having acknowledged this discrepancy, however, we can still recognize that the unconditional trust Beckett has earned again and again from actors has contributed significantly to the creation of performances that clarify his dramatic purposes.

Furthermore, we do well to remember that these are, in most cases, extremely talented and experienced performers making conscious judgments about the value of Beckett's choices on the basis of strong (not to say headstrong) opinions and stage instincts.

But the text is so beautiful, so evocative, that I don't concern myself with gestures while acting, or with objects, or the position of my arms – aren't I turning my neck a little too much to the right, a little too much to the left? – or the shutting of the eyes . . . I don't worry about it. I'm easy. Because I have only to let Beckett speak.

I have worked on this text by sublimating it. I do not distinguish between speech, gestures, objects. For me it is a whole; it is the interior state that matters. And what dominates is joy, a gift of total self.   (Renaud)

Beckett is already the director long before he takes charge of the rehearsals and works with the actors. In this way he is unique in theatrical history, imposing an ultimate limitation on the work. The direction is always written into his texts in the most literal way, showing itself in a theatrical language where the word is never dissociated from the place where it is spoken or from the concrete language of the stage, where the word is never conceived outside the framework of the accompanying gesture, the movement, place, the physical stance and the bodily posture.   (Chabert)[29]

Because they trust him enough not to question the physical and tonal frameworks he gives them, Beckett is able to persuade his actors to concentrate on what Alan Schneider called their "local situations," and to let everything else come by itself from gestures and verbal music.

The most salient result of that is that unlike many performers in his plays, the ones Beckett directs never *act* a double function onstage, for their characters do not distinguish between living and performing. They distinguish only between spontaneous and rehearsed action: spontaneity makes them feel momentarily free from the dulling effect of the repetition that is their actorly fate. In *Godot*, for example, all references to the audience ("that bog") and to the fact that a performance is occurring ("the Board") have meaning within the action as fleeting attempts at spontaneity, as if delivered behind an imaginary fourth wall. And all similar references in *Endgame*, such as "I see a multitude in transports of joy," were cut from Beckett's 1967 Schiller Theater production of *Endspiel*. Which brings me back to my comments at the outset about direct comparisons between Beckett and Brecht.

What is sometimes referred to as the "alienation" of Beckett's actors from their characters is actually a new and complex phenomenon for which critics have simply borrowed a received term that seems to fit. Brecht's theories are commonly seen as relevant to Beckett's theater because at first glance affinities do indeed appear to exist between the authors, but when one looks closer the superficiality of those affinities is glaring. "The danger is in the neatness of identifications," wrote Beckett about Joyce.[30] And, ultimately, the attempt to use Brecht's theories to help understand Beckett's theater is a neat "identification." It amounts to yet another effort to pin down an infuriatingly elusive aesthetic.[31]

Consider this statement, made without further analysis by Martin Esslin in his review of Beckett's *Godot*:

> I have in the past, from purely theoretical premises, argued that the Absurdist Theatre, although starting from quite different assumptions from those which Brecht postulated from a Marxist point of view, ultimately also arrives at a genuine *Verfremdungseffekt*. Here Beckett's direction of *Warten auf Godot* brilliantly demonstrates that assumption in practice. And if Brecht regarded Charlie Chaplin as the perfect embodiment of *verfremdet* acting, Beckett's production emerges as wholly Chaplinesque in concept.[32]

As should be clear from the foregoing discussion, it is not at all self-evident that this production has anything to do with Brecht. Nor do I find the acting particularly "Chaplinesque," if what Esslin means by that term is that the performers subtly communicate information to the audience apart from their characters. As has been frequently observed, Chaplin-as-Chaplin always remains to a certain extent visible behind his roles, but that is exactly what does *not* happen on Beckett's stage. His actors play characters who are fully aware that such self-irony is possible but who hold unappeasable doubts about whether it has any effect, whether it is worth their trouble, or whether they are "as much as being seen." If anything, the production calls to mind that other great clown, known for his enigmatic deadpans. "The preference is for Keaton's style over Chaplin's," writes Goldman about Beckett in general.[33]

There are two usual bases for associations of Beckett with Brecht, apparently separate but actually related, the first of which is their shared interest in clowns. That interest in itself, however, proves nothing since almost every original dramatic thinker of this century has had it in common with them. (Clowns are mentioned explicitly, for one thing, in the programs of all the major historical avant-garde movements.) It would only be significant if the clowns happened to have similar metatheatrical respon-sibilities – e.g. as satirists commenting on their fictional situations – which indeed numerous critics have sought to demonstrate by pointing out the reflexivity in Brecht and Beckett's dramas. In this way, the issue of clowning leads into the second basis for association: the fact that the plays of both sometimes call attention to the machinery of the stage.

Here again, though, the common structural device in itself proves nothing. One can take a broad literary-historical stance and use the coincidence to view the authors as coadjutants in the great modernist effort to dismantle Naturalism, but in the end that approach robs both theaters of specificity by lumping them together with innumerable others supposedly rebelling against the same nineteenth-century enemy. The simple fact of an author employing reflexivity means very little, and indeed Beckett and Brecht's reasons for employing it are almost opposite. Brecht recommended *Verfremdungseffekte* not for their own sake but so that audiences would attend more closely to his messages. His actors occasionally break the illusion of their ongoing Naturalistic fictions in order to teach us something about them. Beckett's plays are neither didactic nor even, in Brecht's sense, opinionated – as Harold Pinter once said, they are "not selling me anything I don't want to buy" – so his actors have no pedagogical obligations.[34] Beckett values not the message, but the *Effekt* itself, the "shape" of the idea.

I am interested in the shape of ideas even if I do not believe them. There is a wonderful sentence in Augustine. I wish I could remember the Latin. It is even finer in Latin than in English. "Do not despair; one of the thieves was saved. Do not presume; one of the thieves was damned." That sentence has a wonderful shape. It is the shape that matters.[35]

Critics such as Esslin and Brater generally do begin by acknowledging these differences between Brecht and Beckett – as can be seen from Esslin's disclaimers in the quotation above – but invariably they then go on to emphasize what appear to be similarities of technique. Brater, for example, says that "one can speak of precedence and possible borrowing, similarities in the orchestration of dramatic structure, but not similar reasons for manipulating it in comparable ways"; but he then lists a number of confining actor's circumstances (such as the isolation of performers in *Not I*, *Play*, and *Breath*) as proof that Beckett "introduces a new dimension of alienation into Brecht's epic theories, a level of physical estrangement on stage in the very process of performance."[36] Despite initial disclaimers, such a conclusion involves several false assumptions: (1) similarity of purpose – that physical discomfort and other situational necessities beyond the actor's control are intensifications of voluntary activities motivated by political savvy; and (2) similarity of result – that any distance between actors and characters has the same effect in Beckett's plays as it does in Brecht's.

Brecht thought that stage activity should be distanced from spectators in order to prevent empathy, which supposedly hinders objective thought, and he often achieved that distance through various applications of clear, explanatory language (in songs, placards, etc.): "A representation that alienates is one which allows us to recognize its subject, but at the same time makes it seem unfamiliar."[37] Beckett's actors cannot use their language for that purpose, because their words allow neither them nor us to recognize paraphrasable subjects in the plays. Any activities separating the actors from their characters, such as asides or non-realistic physical predicaments, are part of the internal fictions and require no conscious shifts of context on the performers' parts. A Beckett play's only identifiable subject, if you will, is the impossibility of naming a subject – which is a dilemma moreover with which spectators empathize. Even in poorly acted productions, they empathize with the actor's obviously painful circumstances.

The physical plights of Beckett's actors are not acted in the sense of being feigned; they are authentic, and provide little cause for spectators to respond more intellectually than emotionally. They are part of the subject matter – the basis of theater events about uncertainty and not vehicles of certain messages. One could say that all Beckett's plays are concerned with the impossibility of recognizing clean subject/object distinctions like the ones Brecht wanted to emphasize. He uses performance circumstances to dramatize the impossibility of escaping the proscenium frame, and hence of transcending life's theatrical circumstances, and recognition of that impossibility is necessarily grave. In Beckett, it is meaningless to say that empathy hinders objective thought, for the ideal path to such thought (to understanding the metaphorical relationships between spectators and characters/actors) consists of the sensory and emotional experience of recognizing that one is, to use Robbe-Grillet's phrase, as "irremediably present" as the actors. "As for Gogo and Didi . . . their situation is summed up in this simple observation, beyond which it does not seem possible to advance: they are *there*, they are on the stage."[38]

Robbe-Grillet, one of Beckett's earliest critics, recognized this central point about "Presence" onstage in the very first production of *Godot*, realizing that the originality of this author's drama consists not in any particular technical innovations or stylistic preoccupations but rather in the invention of a new type of audience/stage transaction. One could hardly exaggerate the importance to theater history of this new performance model which, as I will argue in my conclusion, has had enormous impact partly *because* it is not Brechtian. From the 1960s one thinks particularly of the German writer, Peter Handke, who in a play called *Kaspar* introduces his audience to a clown who does not know he is a *Kasper*, and who becomes entangled in an action much more serious and disturbing than anything one would expect in *Kasperletheater*, or even *Kabarett* – an action, moreover, that implicates the audience as abettors of its inexorability, since it takes place on a stage set designed to represent nothing but the stage of the theater giving the performance. But I am getting ahead of myself. The question of Beckett's historical context is best addressed at the end.

4   Considerations of acting in the late plays

Though critics often refer to a comprehensive Beckett aesthetic, the author's oeuvre is in fact not at all uniform regarding matters of theater practice, and any general statements about approach should be reconsidered and refined with respect to the specific demands of the later plays (and of the media plays as well, which I take up in chapter 6). Having spoken about reluctance among theater practitioners to accept ambiguity as a positive value, I must also acknowledge that acceptance of it is no guarantee of success, especially in works such as *Rockaby* and *Ohio Impromptu*. It does not necessarily follow that an actor who is effective in early works will also be so in the late ones, or the other way round. And furthermore, it is possible for two actors of comparable vocal and physical talent to have equal sensitivity to Beckett's ambiguities and for one of them to be far more effective in a late role.

Trying to find reasons for such discrepancies can, of course, be as complicated as trying to articulate the differences between two human beings, but it is not an utterly quixotic effort when one focuses on the closely circumscribed circumstances of the short, late plays. In chapter 2, I used the example of Billie Whitelaw to demonstrate that a certain kind of acting significantly affects and effects meaning in these works, despite their severely delimited physical conditions, and I want now to situate that kind of acting in the context of the audience/stage transaction described in both preceding chapters, in the interests of characterizing a performance sensibility specific to late Beckett.[1]

In 1984 I had a rare chance to see, within one month of each other, two veteran Beckett actors play the same role in a late play, when Alvin Epstein replaced David Warrilow as Reader in Alan Schneider's production of *Ohio Impromptu* at the Harold Clurman Theatre in New York. The two performances were very different, as might be expected with actors of such disparate backgrounds and experiences. (Epstein made his Beckett reputation in the 1950s for roles such as Lucky and Clov, whereas Warrilow became known in the 1970s for nameless characters in works such as *That Time* and *A Piece of Monologue*.) Entirely unexpected, however, was the sharpness of the contrast between them, the way they seemed to stand as representatives of opposing schools of thought in Beckett acting, as if conducting an undeclared debate whose outcome would determine how the late works would subsequently be performed. And when one examines the performances closely, the implications of their differences do indeed extend beyond matters of style and personality to much more basic issues of audience perception and the very aesthetic form of the later plays.

Ohio Impromptu is about twenty minutes long and written in the general style of *Rockaby, Not I* and *Play;* that is, a meticulously sculpted tableau remains nearly motionless the entire time, allowing spectators to meditate on its metaphoric significance while a flow of words emanates from the stage, guiding meditation. Two identically dressed characters ("Long black coat. Long white hair"), Reader and Listener, sit at a large table in exactly the same posture while one reads to the other, and a wide-brimmed black hat "sits" at the table's center.[2] Reader recites a story of a man who moves away from a place where he was "so long alone together" with a companion – probably a lover ("the dear name"), who may or may not have died – to a "single room on the far bank" from whose "single window he could see the downstream extremity of the Isle of Swans." Subsequently, the man is visited from time to time by a stranger, who may or may not have been "sent" by the lover. Each time he visits, the stranger spends the night reading a "sad tale" to the man and then leaves at dawn.

As in all of Beckett, as soon as one attempts any explanation of the physical situation, its various levels of significance interconnect ironically and lead to a multiplicity of meanings. And as in *A Piece of Monologue, That Time, Rockaby* and most of the other late works, spectators are simultaneously soothed by the music of the language and perplexed by a series of logical questions. Are the characters onstage the characters in Reader's story? Are the two men wholly distinct or really different images of the same character? Why is there only one hat, and what does the hat's presence mean about the singularity or duality of the character(s)? Is Reader the author of the "sad tale" and, if so, what else in the play's world does he control, and what is his relationship to that other controlling author, Beckett? These are perhaps only the driest, most formalistic and obvious of the possible questions – which also include issues of biography (Beckett and Joyce are known to have walked together on Paris' Isle of Swans), literary allusions (the text is replete with Shakespearean formulations), and questions about truth or falsehood (similar to those raised before with *Rockaby*) in the moving story about an apparently bereaved lover – and none of these, of course, is answerable in any final way. Once again, however, different performances can be compared in terms of the way they affect formulation of the questions.

After the lights come up, a few moments pass as one's eyes adjust to glaring reflections from the white table and white hair. Warrilow makes his first, simple gesture: slowly, with a tired hand, he turns a page in the huge book before him. In the script it is just an ordinary stage direction ("R turns page") but he transforms it into choreography, the hand's stillness and gracefulness conveying pure exhaustion, as if the sheer number of times the page had been turned had caused it to gain weight at each new turning. Warrilow has not yet said a word, and already the scene is filled with mystery about the past.

He reads, eyes ever intent on the book, with a voice at once raspy and guttural, in a monotone so low one imagines it coming from somewhere below the stage: "Little is left to tell" – and Listener (played by Rand Mitchell in both performances) knocks on the table, cutting him off. Warrilow pauses, takes a breath, repeats the preceding phrase and then pauses again; after a few seconds, Listener knocks again, and the reading continues. This knock-repeat-knock sequence, which recurs six times in the play, is the only evidence, before the end, of contact or exchange between the characters, but Warrilow handles its pauses in such a way that he actually develops that slim evidence of contact into intimations of depth and complexity in the characters' relationship.

The first knocks are timed so that they fall just slightly before Reader's next word is expected, as if Listener were commenting on what has been said, or asking a question, or acting as a kind of literary athletic coach who is drilling Reader in the practice of telling tales. One can read Warrilow's subsequent breath as an eloquent counter-response to Listener's interruption. Strangely, the actual taking of the breath seems never to vary in the slightest, yet one's impression of its meaning ranges widely over the six recurrences, changing according to the context of the repeated phrase – from good-natured patience at the beginning of the play to resigned exasperation near the end. The question of *why* the knock must come and *why* the phrase must be repeated is, so to speak, asked anew every time Warrilow takes his barely audible breath. The knock sequences never appear to be mere rehearsed patterns (though that may be one of their aspects) but are always rare opportunities to "express" within incredibly constricting circumstances. It's as if the characters cleverly steal brief moments of human contact while constrained to a physical situation which prohibits such exchange.

Warrilow continues reading at a slow, soothing tempo whose relentless regularity is itself a source of character information, conveying the sense that one of his purposes is simply to fill in time. The story reaches the point where the man in it reconsiders his decision to move, and decides to stay where he is.

In this extremity his old terror of night laid hold on him again. After so long a lapse that as if never been (*Pause. Looks closer.*) Yes, after so long a lapse that as if never been. Now with redoubled force the fearful symptoms described at length page forty paragraph four. (*Starts to turn back the pages. Checked by L's left hand. Resumes relinquished page.*)

Warrilow's interpretation here is one of balanced and confident indeterminacy; his actions are specific, but enigmatically undefined. He pauses to look closer, grumbles, and then draws his "Ye-e-es" into a subtextual comment similar to his intake of breath in the knock pattern. But it is not limited to the obvious comment, i.e. "Yes" as a word not printed in the book, an expression of Reader's own thought that his first reading of the line was correct. It is much broader, commenting clearly only on the fact that Reader has stopped reading, and unclearly on other matters; it provides evidence of self-consciousness without eliminating the possibility that "Yes" is in fact printed in the book. Thus, by avoiding an overly practical reading of the line, Warrilow preserves the possibility of opposing interpretations of the scene. For example, if he really were unsure of the sentence, it might well be his first reading of the book, in which case he could not be the stranger in the story, who reads his book many times; alternatively, his pause and repetition of the previous line – without the sanction of a knock! – might be inserted in order to tease or otherwise provoke Listener, a game played on the assumption that both characters know precisely what words are in the book.

For me, the most astonishing part of Warrilow's performance begins two sentences later, when he tries matter-of-factly to turn back the book's pages and Listener checks his hand. Warrilow starts the activity by calmly licking his lips and readjusting his shoulders, as if glad of a short break between two very familiar, tedious tasks, but as soon as he is stopped the whole mood shifts. With just an infinitesimal change in the quality of his grumbles, a minute difference in the length of his pauses, Warrilow invests all the rest of the play with a weird tension. Why was he stopped, and what was so terrible about that? Questions suddenly cease to be passive and forcefully assert themselves. What exactly has been violated? An urgency in the present about the tension between the characters combines with, among other things, a tension between metaphors, or rather between two sides of a literary reference both comic and sad. Beckett simultaneously pokes fun at himself and figuratively depicts his own death. He says, in effect, "no one wants to hear about 'the fearful symptoms' again (i.e. the subject of my whole oeuvre) so I shall continue on to my destined end." Instead of returning to "page forty," as the book supposedly instructs, and following the infinite cycle around yet again, as in *Play*, *Act Without Words II* and his many other circular works, he breaks the pattern and brings his (and Reader's) da capo to its fine.

Resolution of these tensions comes only in the play's final moments, and then not completely. Reader says "Nothing is left to tell" and closes the book, after which he and Listener slowly lower their hands, raise their heads, and look at one another, as if for the first time. It is both a direct confrontation, suggesting mutual recognition, and, because of its exact symmetry of movement, a denial of the possibility of confrontation or difference, suggesting mirror-like mimicry. It can be both of these simultaneously because Warrilow's performance has left the play open to several different interpretations. He renders the basic situation – one man reading to another – realistic enough to justify an anecdotal approach: meaning taken only from the story (e.g. once upon a time two men had this strange encounter in a Gothic tower). And he remains poker-faced enough

7 David Warrilow as Reader and Rand Mitchell as Listener in *Ohio Impromptu*, directed by Alan Schneider, Harold Clurman Theatre, NYC, 1983. (Photo: Martha Swope)

(almost completely expressionless) to justify symbolic approaches: meaning taken from metaphors drawn from the situation. His acting choices, like Whitelaw's, admit both interpretive extremes, causing them to combine in a way that permits spectators freedom to choose among possibilities of meaning. By simultaneously embracing several positions, his performance causes his character to appear as both a metaphor and a personality.

When the lights come up on Alvin Epstein when he plays Reader, he looks almost exactly like Warrilow; the gray-white facial make-up, the long bristly wig and thick black coat buttoned to the neck are quite depersonalizing. After ten seconds, however, he raises his hand to turn a page and it is clear that this performance is very different from its predecessor. The hand performs its task crisply, unexpressively, efficiently. One feels that the play actually begins when Epstein starts reading, that its introductory silent section is only filler instead of inactivity pregnant with mystery.

He speaks in a gruff, hoarse voice that occasionally drops into low gutturality; it sounds like a young man imitating an old man. This Reader is unquestionably dissembling: he raises his eyes from the book while he reads, glancing about the stage, out at the audience – clever, clear acting choices, but perhaps they are a little too clear, too specific. One result of Epstein's "theatricality" is the impression that Reader has memorized the book. Because the possibility is immediately eliminated that it is his first reading of it, one begins to look for meaning more in the fact of his memorization than in the story's words. Of course, such meaning is not forthcoming, because Beckett remains ambiguous in the issue.

Epstein's Reader has a very specific personality – sarcastic, slightly affected, impatient, sententious – which sometimes substitutes itself for textual significance. The knock sequences, for example, do not interrupt him; he anticipates them. Reaching a point in the book where a knock belongs, he stops to wait for it. He keeps the pauses after each first knock very brief and uniform, and hardly waits at all to continue speaking after the second ones. The play is at least five minutes shorter with Epstein. None of the first knocks come as surprises; they are given by rote, as if completely planned, creating only the most minimal sense of connection or relationship between the characters. This Reader is simply eager to go on. The knock sequences are particularly bothersome parts of a compulsory business with which he became bored long ago. Perhaps they are especially annoying or worrisome to him because Listener theoretically has the option to control part of their timing; such is the depth of relationship between this Reader and Listener, intimations of egocentricity.

The more Epstein's character distances himself from his actions, the more everything in the play must be understood as "acting." Nothing in the script actually contradicts such a view of things, but it does prove quite limited at certain points. For example, when Epstein reaches the section quoted above where Reader pauses and looks more closely, he stops abruptly and glares down with knitted brow, then continues in a slightly peevish tone with a short, clipped "Yes." It is a firm, easily intelligible action: while reciting a long speech, he finds himself unsure if he has correctly memorized a line and stops to verify it in his script. Such clarity is usually the mark of confident, intelligent acting – effective with much of Beckett and most other writers – but in the context of *Ohio Impromptu*, this particular clear action is reductive because it is too specific. It actually cuts off aspects of meaning in the text, such as the question of whether "Yes" is printed in the book, or whether the repetition of "after so long a lapse . . ." is some sort of gibe at Listener. As with many exchanges in Schneider's 1971 *Godot*, it is such an overtly naturalistic action that it denies the moment symbolic value.

Another example is Epstein's attempted return to "page forty paragraph four." He raises one end of the book very slowly in a stylized movement wholly distinct from all his others, and then Listener stops him in similar slow motion. It is one of the few moments in the performance that allows for the symbolic, but its value as a metaphor is limited indeed. The result of stylizing the sequence is the implication that this same thing has happened every time, that Reader has never before been allowed to turn back to page forty, and that his being checked by Listener is only a part of their familiar routine. As in the silent opening, Reader's hand seems to move without resonance, like an artisan's, not an artist's. There is no urgency in the present, there are no echoes of other endless life-cycles, just one more rehearsed activity in the life of this sardonic actor. And since Reader is not shocked at being stopped, the ending has no more reference to the hand-check sequence than to any other part of the play. Instead of with unspoken horror, the two men ultimately look at each other with understandable numbness. Their final encounter is the rehearsed action that comes after all previously rehearsed actions.

A bit of textual interpretation will help to place the differences between the performances in a literary context. After seeing Warrilow, *Ohio Impromptu* appeared to me an extremely complex composition. Beyond the incomparable beauty of the surface love story, I saw a multi-layered exploration of paradoxes specific to writerly existence. The play begins with a Pirandello-like vision of overlapping illusion and reality (or illusion and illusion) and, through the mechanism of a story about several degenerated past lives, progresses to an unflinchingly honest study of alienation from oneself, as happens in *Enrico IV*. Beckett, however, infuses the study with his own peculiar brand of paranoia, essentialized, acutely aimed at himself.

The idea of self-as-listener in *Ohio Impromptu* recalls, perhaps more than any other Beckett work, *Krapp's Last Tape*, as if the two plays were written as parallel inquiries into narcissism; that is, the writer's special strain of that malady. Like Narcissus, Krapp is obsessed with himself, an obsession that ultimately leaves him bereft of any stable identity. The self cannot be located or defined simply by searching through past selves; for they function only as self-mocking mirrors, never as independent entities or images capable of providing parameters for the self's definition. Beckett, the great poet of loneliness, turns this theme upon his own profession in *Ohio Impromptu*, musing upon a lifetime spent at one of the loneliest of human activities, writing.

What is the value of "the works," as *What Where* asks?[3] Can they alleviate some of life's loneliness, perhaps even speak back to him like independent minds, as does the narrator-as-"other" in "Text for Nothing 4"? Or can they assert their immortality so as to make thoughts of death less terrifying? It's as if the writer (Reader) only exists among his creations, which are reflections of himself. Inasmuch as those creations deny their connection to him as reflections and act independently like separate "lives," he can rest and consider his life worthwhile. Inasmuch as they lie inert or merely mimic him, they have no permanence and reflect onto his life their complexion of death, understandable in this context as a series of indistinguishable moments. This idea of death in fiction's unchangeableness is hardly new in Beckett's work. It is a variation on what motivates O's horror of "perceivedness" at the end of *Film*. And it is what Malone has in mind when he exclaims about his storytelling, "If this continues it is myself I shall lose and the thousand ways that lead there. And I shall resemble the wretches famed in fable, crushed beneath the weight of their wish come true."[4]

Epstein's performance suggested to me none of these types of resonances, but instead left me preoccupied with the ostensible story, perhaps the merest of the play's many aspects. I felt dissatisfied, the way one does after reading those modern translations of Shakespeare ("Blow out, blow out, you short candle of life!"), for I knew the play meant much more than could be seen in this version. References outside the "realistic" world dropped away, and questions about distinctions between illusion and reality, correspondences between Reader and writer, were all either muted or eliminated altogether. Reader-as-actor appeared to be encountering Listener for his own neurotic amusement. He exhibited a kind of hypochondriacal narcissism; i.e. he *thought* he suffered from that disease, and acted as if he did, when all he really suffered from was fear of and impatience with Listener for scattered breaches of mimicry or obedience, e.g. the knocks. His condition might more properly be termed arrogance or egotism and, in any case, it rendered the play's range of meaning indefensibly small.

How to account for this discrepancy? Epstein is not an incompetent actor. He is, for one thing, a seasoned professional who deserves a measure of praise for consistently refusing the attitude, common among actors, that sees Beckett's highly prescriptive directions (especially in the late plays) contemptuously as cook-book recipes for stage behavior. As Alan Schneider described the problem in 1975:

After all these years, there are a number of actors (and directors) who still do not respond to Beckett, or avoid doing his plays. They feel he limits them too severely as artists, removes their creativity and individuality, constricts them too rigidly in their physical and vocal resources. They tell me that he must hate actors because he denies them the use of their own impulses, as well as more and more of their physical selves. After all, if they can not move freely about the stage, can not use their voices and bodies – their very means of reaching their audiences – what are they but impersonal or even disembodied puppets of his will?[5]

And, what is more, Epstein created some of the most memorable early Beckett characterizations in America, such as the Lucky described in chapter 3. His talent and experience with this author are undeniable. When I spoke with him, however, I learned much about his acting techniques that proved very helpful in understanding the differences between these two Readers.

"I've never approached any of the roles in Beckett differently from the way I approach any other role," he said in the interview included in part three. "I never considered them special in that sense – that there was a *way* to do Beckett differently from the way you do anything . . . every role is different from every other role, and you find a way to do every role." Speaking at one point about his work on Lucky, I mentioned that I didn't expect a Method-like approach could be of much use, and he responded:

But [it] is. I mean, you sit down and try to figure out: who is this character? Why is he behaving this way? Why is he saying what he's saying? I did do that. Now I might not describe that as the Method approach, but it has to do with it. I had to figure out what his relationship was to Pozzo, why was he on the end of a rope, what did Pozzo mean in his description of Lucky when he said, "So I took a knook"? What is a "knook"? Pozzo doesn't explain it; he doesn't explain it to Gogo and Didi. And why does Lucky carry the baggage, and the stool, and why does he obey orders? Those questions are easy to answer. What was really hard to figure out was the significance of his abject slavery, and what I discovered gave color to the simplistic and obvious explanation that he's a servant. He obeys everything, every order, and is rather cruelly treated but doesn't protest. That's clear, but what kind of slave, and how long has this been going on?

Epstein got his answers to these types of questions from the speech, which he worked on by "break[ing] it down into memorizable, understandable phrases," eventually developing a specific personality to fit the decisions about character relationships made by him and the other actors.

In other words, his approach to Lucky was to treat it as a conventional character role, involving logical present actions informed by extensive background research – which, incidentally, has proved the most effective avenue for most actors embarking on roles such as Hamm, Clov, Didi and Gogo. As I have already discussed, those characters are hardly naturalistic, but they are rooted in a kind of naturalism because they exist in certain recognizable landscapes and engage in a kind of playing recognizable from life. Not so in the later works, however, as Ben Barnes points out in a rare essay on directing Beckett:

> . . . as Beckett continued to write for the theater the problem of production became . . . one of convincing the actor to forfeit the notion of character in the service of poetic stage images born out of a vision which has honed itself into something limpid, austere, simple, where the trappings of the theatre are shed and the emphasis is on language accompanied by a single stage image.[6]

Epstein's comments make clear that he understands this development in Beckett's work very well, but what to do about it as an actor is another question. What indeed is left after one "forfeits the notion of character"?

When I asked Epstein what sort of reality an actor playing Reader must create for himself, he answered as follows:

> I would say that it's much more ambiguous than Hamm or Clov or Lucky. Those characters exist in an identifiable reality – the reality of the play. In *Endgame* there are two men who live shut up in a room with two old people in ashcans, and one is the master and one is the servant, one is older and blind, the other is younger and crippled. So you know who they are and you know where they are. In *Ohio Impromptu* there are no such easy answers. But again you get them from the text, because the text is a perfect receptacle for Beckett's vision, for what he's writing about. The identity of the two men becomes clear; one seems to be a figment of the other's imagination, and then toward the end of the play you're not sure which is the real one and which is the figment. But as long as you know that possibility exists, that's already something you can deal with, that you can act.

His technique, in other words, is to find a kernel within the play that *is* like the "clear" identities in the earlier dramas: since one cannot act the idea of the character's duality, or indeed any *idea* of ambiguity at all, one chooses a singular understanding of the action and plays that firmly. He specifies further: "The possibility that's awakened in my imagination is that, out of extreme loneliness, the man who is alone and bereaved invents a companion who is himself, a sort of alter ego who comes and reads the sad tale over, to have company, and to have someone share the grief."

But then who or what carries the burden of communicating the text's ambiguities? The stage picture alone, without any help from the actor's understanding? Epstein answers:

> There are different schools of thought about this. Some people won't even consider

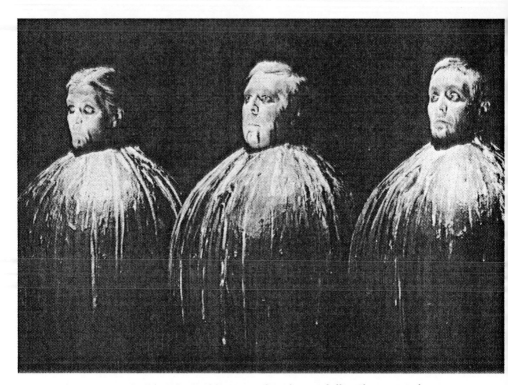

8 *Spiel* (*Play*), directed by Samuel Beckett, Schiller Theater Werkstatt, West Berlin, 1978. Actors (from left to right): Hildegard Schmahl, Klaus Herm and Sibylle Gilles. (Photo: Ilse Buhs)

such questions as legitimate. They say Beckett is pure poetry and just music, and that you don't ask yourself these questions, but I think that's a load. Somewhere in themselves they had to have asked those questions, and they had to have answered them. That they don't want to talk about it is perfectly legitimate . . . But no matter how abstract and disconnected you want to keep yourself from the meaning of the text, it still has meaning; it's not notes in music, where you can keep your distance . . . And so I think that it isn't quite sincere to call it "music." On the other hand I don't think there's any hard-and-fast rule about it. You find certain questions that you feel, for personal reasons, need to be answered or decided upon, and others that you don't want to answer. I come down more on the side of ambiguity. I certainly, as I said before, don't think we should answer questions Beckett doesn't answer.

If you decide that something is an ambiguity that mustn't be resolved, then it's also something you ignore. The question of whose story it is becomes moot, it doesn't matter – I mean, if you identify with the character. I'm reading a story, and whether or not it's mine, I identify with it . . . So you know that you're not just reading a story about somebody else that means nothing to you; the grief is real, whether it's yours or his. You characterize a man to whom this has happened.

These statements are wholly honest, and they reach to the center of the problem. Epstein insists, as I did with Whitelaw, that the mind becomes engaged in the play's uncertainties, despite others' claims to the contrary. But he goes on to say that that engagement to some extent necessitates answers to questions recognized by the intellect. And in the end he admits that he must abandon the indeterminate and ground his performance in naturalistic motivations, such as the psychological identification of one man with another. In other words, he retains at least the fundamental framework of the Stanislavsky system by, in Goldman's words, treating one subtext as privileged, thus implying the existence of "a truth in terms of which the text can be located" and encouraging the audience to interpret the play advertently, to try to decode it logically as if seeking the answer to a riddle.

Like Epstein, Warrilow too says, in the interview in part three, that the "process of working on [Beckett's] material is no different from working on any other writing, great writing, in terms of the way one sets about the work," but one must view that comment in the context of his uncustomary acting process.[7] Warrilow also acknowledges the relevance of *Ohio Impromptu*'s enigmas and the importance of not explaining them, but unlike Epstein he does not look to them for character motivations; in fact, he says he does not need psychological ballast at all. I quote several passages from our conversation because he makes some of his more significant points in the course of exchanges.

DW: When I'm being totally honest I have to tell audiences that I do not understand what it is I am doing. I don't understand the writing. I'm not a stupid person, but if somebody were to say to me, "What is *Ohio Impromptu* about?" I either cannot give a true answer or I don't want to. I don't know quite which it is. I think it really is, I can't. I don't know how. I did have a short discussion about that play with a young director in Paris, and his attitude (and maybe it's Beckett's as well, I don't know) was that it's totally simple and straightforward, not complicated at all, and the questions I have about it are irrelevant and have no bearing on anything. That is not my experience. My experience of that piece is that there are questions but no answers to any of them, that it is on a level of mysteriousness which defies entry except on a soul level. The questions I have, the sort of academic questions – Who is this person? What is this book? What is this story? When is this taking place? How many times has it taken place? – none of them is answered. There are no answers to those things. One can make assumptions, but those are only assumptions, that's all. It's just like opinion.

JK: How much do you, as an actor playing Reader, have to decide where you are, what the book is *for you*, etc.?

DW: What's *your* answer to that question?

JK: Well, I'm not acting it; I'm just watching.

DW: How much do I need to decide those things for you to have an experience of the play?

JK: How much?

DW: Well, I'm telling you I made none of those decisions.

JK: What kinds of decisions do you make?

DW: That I will read the text. And that I will read at a certain pace, using a certain kind of voice, and that there will be an intention.

Warrilow's primary concern is theatrical effectiveness ("What's *your* answer to that question?"), and not fidelity to a fictional reality that he feels is beyond his understanding. And in order to judge that effectiveness, he performs with a kind of double consciousness – of speaking and listening – like a musician. Psychological intentions are not completely excluded from his work, but the ones he uses are sometimes peripheral, as can be seen in the following comments about his 1986 production of *L'Impromptu d'Ohio* in Paris, which Beckett helped direct.

DW: Now, the most useful intention that Beckett gave me early on in the *Ohio Impromptu* experience was to treat it like a bedtime story and let it be soothing. It wasn't always that way in performance. But I do think that that can be a very satisfactory way of approaching the text. It's also a very beautiful idea, for Reader to be telling Listener a bedtime story.

JK: It sounds like *Rockaby*.

DW: Yes, very much like that. And, incidentally, the way Samuel Beckett reads it is very much the way the actresses do *Rockaby*; there's a similar lilt.

JK: It sounds as though all of the issues for you are musical issues . . .

DW: Yes, they are.

JK: . . . and none of them is within any reality of a character.

DW: Right. I barely deal with psychological reality. I don't have to. I mean, I can have ideas about that but it isn't what works. What works is finding what musicians have called the "right tone." By "right" I mean what works for me. I then have to trust that it'll work for somebody else – that if I get it right, if I sing it "on key," "in tune," it's going to vibrate properly for somebody else.

JK: How do you know when something's "working"?

DW: It pleases me, and makes me listen harder and pleasurably to myself. When the note is not quite "on," it makes me physically uncomfortable, it makes me nervous, it doesn't sit right, I start to get negative feedback from my system.

Even in his relationship with Listener, Warrilow avoids fictional psychological involvement, as revealed in these comments about why he "became attached" to doing the piece with Rand Mitchell.

His total devotion to the work. His ability to surrender ego to the piece. You know, there are not many actors who are willing to give of themselves, of their time and their energy, to so seemingly thankless a task: sitting at a table with their head down, hidden, saying nothing, from time to time knocking on the table . . . And he was tireless in his attention, in his concern that everything be just right. I mean, I'm sure that in many ways we just went overboard about this; one can just go crazy about these things. But, you see, I want people to care about the work as much as I do; that's important to me. What I personally feel about the relationship between those two men is unimportant. I *feel* it's unimportant.

Warrilow values the other actor onstage inasmuch as his concentration improves the quality of the music by helping Reader concentrate.

We are back to the issue of inadvertent interpretation. How could Warrilow's performance be so illuminating of the play's logical questions if he really had no thoughts about them? As Epstein points out, the play is not only about music, it also has subject matter, as do most compositions with words, and Epstein is as skilled as any actor at the task of culling "sense," useful performance material, from verbal texts. How could Warrilow, who claims not to bother about meaning at all, give a performance more relevant to "sense" than Epstein, who studied the text closely? One answer to both questions is that Warrilow *does* think about text, but does not use those thoughts consciously to motivate his performance. He internalizes them, makes them a part of his general attitude toward the play; one might say that he translates them, in a way, into musical terms, becoming a kind of informed instrument. This is not a minor point; for even if one has a beautifully resonant voice, omitting this step of inform-ation can lead to a dull performance – as occurred with Whitelaw's reading of *Enough*.

The more difficult task, however, is to relinquish understanding once one has it, in Barnes' words, "to forfeit the notion of character." It's as if actors were required to undergo a two-step process in which the second step cancels the first: analyze the text as a conventional play, and then push that knowledge to the back of your mind in order to concentrate on the verbal music. But that description is more rigid and premeditated than the actual techniques of Whitelaw and Warrilow, whose acts of analysis are so automatic that they do not even acknowledge them as part of rehearsing. They do not need to work at forfeiting character because they never consciously adopt recognizable personalities to fit decided-upon ideas about text. Actors such as Epstein, on the other hand, work on the basis of their text analyses, and thus have difficulty freeing themselves of its natural consequence: psychological motivation.

To reiterate for the sake of emphasis, there is no question here of good and bad acting, but rather of different types of acting, both done well. Epstein's skills were undoubtedly central to his success with Lucky and Clov; for those roles demand that an actor excel at conventional character research, in order to fill out the human dispositions that Beckett's unconventional milieus leave sketchy. In *Godot*, *Endgame* and the other early works, the actor may adopt a specific, eccentric personality, justify all his activities with realistic motivations, and be assured that his character's, and the play's, metaphoric aspects will come through – depending, of course, on the competency of the director. In late plays like *Ohio Impromptu*, however, that same acting technique seems to have the opposite effect of limiting the spectator's access to metaphor, as if these works lose significance in proportion to the extent that actors engage in analysis, and gain significance to the extent that they forego it.[8] (I choose the word "forego" instead of, say, "ignore" or "disregard," because both Whitelaw and Warrilow, instead of repudiating intellect altogether, rather use it passively and then move away from it before it begins to control them.)

Lest I leave the impression, however, that these plays can be performed effectively only by actors whose techniques are as idiosyncratic as Warrilow's, let me append an example of an actress whose usual approach to character is similar to Epstein's but who was eventually able to overcome her habits and give a brilliant performance as May in the German premiere of *Tritte*, directed by Beckett. The story of Hildegard Schmahl's frustrating but eventually successful efforts to approach this "strange, mysterious" character is the focus of Asmus' rehearsal diary for the production: "In Berlin, Beckett was confronted with an actress . . . whose work in the theatre is based on the search for realistic concrete motivations and who is not willing or not able automatically to work in an intuitively structural way."[9] Schmahl's difficulties began on the first day of rehearsals, when she announced that she did not "understand the play" and received a response from Beckett to the effect that she should emphasize her footsteps. The play originated in his mind with the activity of pacing, he said, and the text "only built up around this picture." "But how is the figure of May to be understood then?," Schmahl immediately rejoined.

Throughout the following weeks, the actress struggled to fulfill the author's wishes, to imitate the cold, conspiratorial quality of his monotone line-readings while going through the motions of pacing in the slumped, infolded posture he demonstrated. "I can't do it mechanically," she would say. "I must understand it first and then think." But her vocal deliveries remained scattered, unconvincing and laden with superfluous "color."

A serious performer, deeply dedicated to solving the problem of inhabiting this play's universe, she conducted a kind of heroic search for realistic

9 Hildegard Schmahl in *Tritte* (*Footfalls*), directed by Samuel Beckett, Schiller Theater Werkstatt, West Berlin, 1976. (Photo: Anneliese Heuer)

intentions that could produce the external qualities described to her, even visiting a psychiatric clinic at one point to consult a doctor about female patients with obsessions. Beckett did not encourage her at all in that direction and continued to stress the importance of physicalization – "The position of the body will help to find the right voice" – but the actress, at least at first, could not trust that advice. What did Beckett mean when he said that the posture should not express fear but rather "that May is there exclusively for herself"? How is the actress to understand and make use of the description of her goal as "the absolute encapsulation of the figure in itself"?

Answers to those questions eventually came to Schmahl almost passively through exactly the route she fought at the start of rehearsals, and then only after she had exhausted all possibilities of finding them "the hard way," through active, conscious means. As Beckett told her explicitly after several weeks, the process of understanding cannot be forced:

When you feel yourself too far away from the right tone, you have already failed. You are looking in your acting for the right *tone*, that is fatal. You are acting in too healthy a way . . . Try gradually, while you speak the words, to see the whole inwardly. It has a visionary character . . . it is an image which develops gradually.

Her most significant leap with the role coincided with her decision to make the primary ground for her performance physical and not psychic. In Asmus' words, once she relinquished the attempt to "produce the images from the inside," all the "more or less unconscious movements of the body, especially of the head" that inevitably accompanied her psychological intentions disappeared. She was able to hold her body stiffly, avoiding all uncalculated movement, and that new tautness in turn affected her articulation.

May stands independent of her surroundings as a concentrated bundle on the strip of light. No superfluous movement distracts, the tension communicates itself to the observer, one is drawn into the undertow of her story – the concentration is passed on and challenges the observer to an absolute concentration. Beckett is satisfied with the result. "You have found the trick" is his comment.

Schmahl ultimately succeeded by means of a radical self-denial. By opening her psyche to the play through calculated physical behaviors – a kind of intensification of the process Peter Evans used with his painful walk in *Endgame* – she essentially forewent active use of the psychological research over which she had taken so much trouble, her grueling attempts to find a privileged subtext. That research may have continued to inform her performance but no longer in a conscious sense, for she eventually came to adopt the author's view of her task as primarily sculptural. To Beckett, the character as stated in the play is fully self-sufficient, her posture less an indication of isolatable emotions of the moment than a metaphor for a

10 Klaus Herm in *Damals* (*That Time*), directed by Samuel Beckett, Schiller Theater Werkstatt, West Berlin, 1976. (Photo: Ilse Buhs)

chronic ontological condition; thus, a nearly exclusive concentration on corporeality *is* the natural way to portray her.

This is obviously an author's viewpoint, as distinct from a director's, since it identifies an aesthetic goal without providing much practical information about how to achieve it. The important point here, however, is that it did turn out to be reachable for an actress whose experience and talents lay mostly in conventional drama. Despite her proclivity to inquiry, Schmahl managed to become an informed instrument like Whitelaw and Warrilow through a long and troublesome process of learning to trust the text. Having made that point, though, we may go on to ask whether it was indeed necessary that the process be as torturous as it was.

In his interview with me, Asmus, who has directed all of Beckett's plays in addition to assisting at his productions, said unequivocally, "No": with directors who are not Beckett the actor's break from his/her habitual working method need not be so radical as Schmahl's.

Later on when I directed [*Footfalls*] it struck me that there is a real hate relationship with the mother, which is very realistic and which you can really discuss with an actress, who has her own mother experiences and so on . . . there is a real social story behind it, which we can find if we talk about our lives and our relationships to our parents . . . [but Beckett] would never have this private discussion as we have.

In Asmus' opinion, this familiar type of intimate exchange with actors, while perhaps useless in the Stanislavskian sense of unearthing emotions and memories for conscious recall onstage, is nevertheless sometimes useful for the simple purpose of making performers more comfortable with the physical and vocal tasks demanded of them. And the fact that Beckett will "never" engage in it probably does stem partly from his unwillingness fully to adopt the director's viewpoint in lieu of the author's.

In the last analysis, however, I suspect that there is more to Beckett's insistence on "external" rehearsal techniques than what can be attributed to conflict between an author's and a director's visions. One could interpret his almost complete refusal to discuss internal situations as a tacit admission that the actor's physical dilemmas onstage *are* the significant situations. As discussed earlier in connection with Robbe-Grillet's idea of "presence" onstage in *Godot*, the simple fact of a performer standing before us can itself present enough of a psychological circumstance to keep an audience interested, and the late plays intensify that circumstance by making actors into spectacles of painful vulnerability.

If Didi and Gogo were trapped because they could not make use of their freedom, then characters such as W (in *Rockaby*), Reader and May are trapped still more literally inside confining physical predicaments, thus urging thoughts about their "presence" onstage all the more strongly onto spectators' consciousnesses. As elaborated above with Whitelaw, it is the live actor, the fact of life in the actor, that finally animates Beckett's stage pictures and amplifies the impact of their disturbing, melancholy beauty – even though that animation gains expression only through the most highly calculated sounds and movements. And every bit of psychological characterization, every hint of a complex nonfictional life extending beyond the simple picture, weakens the effect of that sense of pure existence.[10]

This dramatic value, as much as any shyness or lack of directing experience, seems to me the reason why Beckett arrives at rehearsals with such extremely precise, pre-formed ideas, and why he does his best to elude questions from actors, sometimes even dispensing with verbal directions and using a piano to communicate his wishes.[11] Both musically and visually, he sees his later works as compositions in "gray," tiny worlds drained of color, and thus the actor's challenge in them is to achieve ideal shades of colorlessness. There is something quixotic in that expectation, given the compromising realities of actual stage rehearsals, but like all Quixotes, Beckett piques our curiosity to see how close he can come to his ideal.

PART TWO

Directing

5 Underground staging in perspective

> I detest this modern school of directing. To these directors the text is just a pretext for their own ingenuity.
>
> (Samuel Beckett)[1]

> "Don't all of [pause . . .] Samuel Beckett's plays have very elaborate and detailed stage directions?" one of my friendly neighborhood critics asked me the evening my latest Beckett trio opened in Washington.
>
> "Yes, they [pause . . .] certainly do."
>
> "And those three heads stuck in those, uh, marvelous-looking urns? . . . That means that you didn't have to think about any actual movements?"
>
> "That's, uh, right."
>
> "Well, excuse my asking, Alan, but what do you *do*?"
>
> (Alan Schneider)[2]

To the extent that most acting problems are in some fashion also directing problems I have been dealing all along with the task of directing Beckett, at least with the part of it that relates to character development. As is well known, however, there is another side to directing involving the problematic exercise of interpretation, which does not primarily concern actors.

Even more than with other authors, the subject of directing Beckett is inextricably bound up with questions of faithfulness to text, mostly because this ordinarily reticent author has been extraordinarily vocal in his objections to faithlessness. Not entirely by accident, he had the good fortune of seeing many of his premieres staged by two paradigms of loyalty – Roger Blin and Alan Schneider – who not only adhered to the very specific instructions in his scripts but also made frequent public comments about the propriety of that strictness.

BLIN: As far as I'm concerned, I don't have any specific personal theatrical style. With writers of this standing, I simply try to push them as far as they will go. By stressing what they are. But I don't try to put on what could be identified as a "Blin" play.[3]

Directors with this attitude were once common, but since World War II they have grown rarer every year. Thus, as he nears the end of his life, Beckett has fewer and fewer spokesmen *in the theater* for his point of view. Among younger directors, his preference for his scripts to be performed as written, stage directions included, is commonly seen as old-fashioned conservatism, as if the very idea of respecting texts had become some sort of Victorian prudery.

Over the years, his publishers have made various efforts to enforce his wishes, but at one time or another all the plays have been altered by directors thinking to improve them, and much has been written about the unethicalness of these dismissals of a living author's express preference. The fact is, however, that for better or worse concept productions occur, have occurred for some time, and by now have a history of their own. Of course, the fact that a phenomenon has a history does not necessarily legitimize it, and my experience has been that, with rare exceptions, these productions actually serve to prove Beckett right, at least aesthetically. It becomes obvious from them that the directors might have looked much more closely at the creative possibilities of what was already written in the texts. To make that judgment on principle without looking at actual productions, however, is unfair.

At the end of 1984, a minor scandal occurred in Cambridge, Massachusetts, when Beckett's American publisher, Grove Press, tried to stop performances of the American Repertory Theatre production of *Endgame*, directed by Mabou Mines member JoAnne Akalaitis, because it departed from the published stage directions by including a subway setting and incidental music. In this chapter I situate that now infamous production in the context of the history of "altered Beckett" and then use it and numerous other examples to discuss the question asked by Schneider in the epigraph above: given the restrictions imposed by the texts, how is the Beckett director's task to be defined?

To clarify my position on the Akalaitis affair from the outset, I am, unlike most commentators, less interested in her legal and ethical right to do what she did than in the consequences of her aesthetic choices for spectators' perceptions of the play. Many critics have avoided serious discussion of this and other productions that obviously run counter to Beckett's wishes, perhaps out of fear of his ire, but that critical attitude has always seemed to me just as irresponsible as the directors' alterations of lines and stage directions. When I first met him, I took the opportunity to apologize to Beckett in advance for not complying with this unwritten rule, and his response was in fact quite sympathetic. He told me that it was essential "to visualize a play on your mental stage while you're writing," and went on to explain that the reason he preferred *Endgame* to *Godot* was that it was better visualized in that way and is thus "a more complete and coherent movement." He then stated that, although he does not see how his plays "can work with any other stage directions," he does not deny that "people can make improvements" and is in fact willing to listen to anyone who thinks he can explain to him "how it's better another way."[4] Let us see, then, what has been offered in the way of "improvements" during the thirty-six years since Blin's production of *Godot*.

Because his plays take place in what Bert States calls "generic times and places," Beckett has frequently been accused of social irrelevance.[5] In the 1950s and 1960s, it became fashionable among certain literary critics, particularly from Eastern Europe, to see his works as whining portraits of hopelessness, overly formalistic and elitist proofs of the futility of the Cartesian/Capitalist tradition of Individualism they culminated. Martin Esslin's grouping of Beckett with Ionesco, Adamov and other Western writers under the classification "absurd" only served to supply such criticism with ammunition.

The end of the bourgeois world, which the absurd authors want to persuade us is the end of the world and of human beings, letting both die in their plays, is reflected in these bourgeois dramas in an astonishing, complete self-disintegration. Beyond Beckett's nameless crippled creatures, reduced to voices, you cannot go. All later drama, then, can only return to the society of human beings. After the absurd drama has run its course ad absurdum and has explained its bankruptcy, it must be produced again as drama, because it will have no other choice but to breathe new life into its corpse or to cease, to exist.[6]

Western Marxists were scarcely less harsh in the beginning, though their denunciations appeared much more seldom after Theodor Adorno, leading exponent of the Frankfurt School, defended Beckett in the famous essay "Trying to Understand *Endgame*." Adorno, on whom Beckett was an important influence, argued that the apparent meaninglessness in the latter's work stemmed from an unrelenting realism that carried the most precise social relevance:

The irrationality of bourgeois society on the wane resists being understood: those were the good old days when a critique of political economy could be written which took this society by its own *ratio*. For in the meantime it has thrown this *ratio* on the junk-heap and virtually replaced it with direct control. The interpretive word, therefore, cannot recuperate Beckett, while his dramaturgy – precisely by virtue of its limitation to exploded facticity – twitches beyond it, pointing toward interpretation in its essence as riddle. One could almost designate as the criterion of relevant philosophy today whether it is up to that task.[7]

Theater practitioners, few of whom read Adorno, even in Germany, have not been so easily convinced. Brecht was the first of many whose initial response to Beckett's work was that it needed to be doctored, somehow fixed or rather completed, by filling in the "missing" specifics. Toward the end of his life he had two ideas for adapting *Godot*. One employed numerous cuts and stylistic revisions to make the dialogue more colloquial, and specified social roles for the characters: Estragon, *"ein Prolet,"* Vladimir, *"ein Intellektueller,"* Lucky, *"ein Esel oder Polizist,"* and *"von"* Pozzo, *"ein Gutsbesitzer."* The other divided the action into scenes in which the tramps wait for Godot while music plays and films are projected behind them depicting revolutionary movements in the Soviet Union, China, Asia and Africa.[8] In each case the intention was clearly to historicize the action, ground it in a definite time and place, in order to concretize the ambiguous notion of Godot as the socialist millennium.

Brecht himself did not live to realize these plans, and it remains unclear whether he dropped them because of failing health or flagging interest. In 1971, however, a Stuttgart production influenced by them was mounted by one of his students, Peter Palitzsch, who commented at the time that it helped him to think of Didi and Gogo as unemployed workers: "If I could bring that kind of social connection into the play, I would feel better."[9] Today in East Germany, where Beckett's underground influence has been very strong and very complicated, an effort is made to mention Brecht's intended rectifications whenever Beckett's name comes up, giving the plans the sentimental air of unfinished masterpieces. For example, in the 1986 GDR premiere of *Das letze Band*, twenty-seven years after its West German premiere, the famous Brecht actor Ekkehard Schall played Beckett in a double-bill with a musical version of Brecht's *Die Erziehung der Hirse* (*The Education of Millet*). In an interview with me, included in part three, Schall denied that this coupling was made for any political reasons.

I don't think at all about playing Brecht off Beckett or Beckett off Brecht, using them that way. I polemicize with the contents of the texts about my experiences with reality; that's enough. The confrontation in the theater of socialism/capitalism doesn't interest me.

The theater program, however, contained lengthy notes about Brecht's *Godot* and Beckett's lack of interest in "improving" or "instructing" people, and Schall performed Krapp with the same casual style he uses for all his Brecht roles, indicating the idea of "sluggish old man" with broad, obvious gestures instead of developing a visceral relationship either with the tape recorder or his words – which made the play boring and superficial.

Of course, the people who come to my performance expecting a sensation to emerge, or to be shown suddenly how Beckett and his way of writing now overturns the whole theater world here, they're not satisfied. That's also not my intention. I find it a wonderful play, he is a wonderful writer, but I don't say, "That is now the way to an absolutely new land." I can perform this play with my methods.

My sense of the evening was that it succeeded in assuring spectators that nothing wonderful had been kept from them during years of censorship.[10]

With similar polemical intention to Brecht, the Yugoslavian playwright Miodrag Bulatovic borrowed Beckett's characters in 1966 in order to show their reactions to a Godot who did come. To Bulatovic, Godot is a universal, quasi-religious character whom Beckett "embezzled," and his freely symbolic, somewhat haphazardly structured drama, *Godot Came*, may be understood as an act of repossession. His Godot is a baker whom the other characters do not recognize as a savior, and whom they eventually sentence to death; discovering that they cannot kill him, however, they banish him from their company, and in the end he leaves behind immense quantities of bread for them to eat when they will. Despite this author's public statement that he intended to speak neither for nor against Beckett (to whom *Godot*

11 Ekkehard Schall in *Das letzte Band* (*Krapp's Last Tape*), directed by David Leveaux, Theater im Palast, East Berlin, 1986. (Photo: Maria Steinfeldt)

Came is dedicated), his play, like Brecht's planned revisions, is a judgment in a tacit sense, because it implies that Beckett's original is falsely pessimistic due to insufficient clarifying details. Clas Zilliacus writes:

Miodrag Bulatovic calls his *Godot* a play of ideas. It is not; its author's talent is not suited to encode his ideas lucidly enough to get across. Neither does it have the firm political contours Brecht's *Godot* would have had, if we may extrapolate from his plans and from the finished oeuvre. Yet both stand united against Beckett, taking sides for those two-thirds of mankind who have other things to think about than existential anguish . . . They are looking for a way out. And they share an important premise: they regard Beckett's *Godot* as a political play with the wrong basis. [11]

Though they rarely frame their counter-arguments in socialist terms, Westerners interested in applying Beckett concretely also adopt this attitude.
   Zilliacus writes, quoting Esslin:

"When *Waiting for Godot* – a totally apolitical play in Britain or America – was first performed in Poland at the time of the thaw of 1956, the audience there immediately understood it as a portrayal of the frustration of life in a society which habitually explains away the hardships of the present by emphasizing that one day the millennium of plenty is bound to come." Returning the argument it might be suggested that even a Western audience inclined that way could take this play politically . . . [12]

Exactly what he suggests took place in 1979 when the black South African actors John Kani and Winston Ntshona performed as Didi and Gogo at the Long Wharf Theatre in New Haven, Connecticut. What was really a predominantly apolitical production, directed by Donald Howarth, with two extraordinary actors from South Africa came to be seen by reviewers and audiences as "the South African *Godot*." (Beckett has withheld production rights from all South African groups proposing to present his plays before segregated audiences.) A few elements could be construed as political, such as the fact that Pozzo (Bill Flynn) was white, dressed remotely like a Boer, and carried a milk-white whip, giving a particular bias to certain lines (e.g. "You are human beings none the less . . . Of the same species as myself," or "The road is free to all . . . It's a disgrace. But there you are"), but these were not at all emphasized and most of the action made no sense as direct political allegory. Lucky, for instance, Pozzo's slave, was played by a white man (Peter Piccolo). Of course, publicists looking for scandal are not necessarily even interested in actual productions, and this one was eventually subject to so much wilful politicizing that it was banned from the Baltimore International Theater Festival in 1981 after a protest from local black leaders. [13]
   In the West, instead of censoring or rewriting Beckett, we read into his plays the details of whatever timely social issues are at hand. Even theater

practitioners who consider themselves open-minded enough to accept frameworks of indecision sometimes end up pinning them down to particular
meanings out of fear that audiences will not understand. When the Off-
Broadway Roundabout Theatre produced *Endgame* in 1977, for instance, a
long, simplifying explanation of the action appeared in the program, from
which I quote a small section:

THE ANECDOTE: *Hamm* finds himself a survivor after a world holocaust. He
systematically refuses to aid fellow survivors and establishes himself in a shelter,
with his parents who have lost their legs in an accident. *Clov*, his slow-witted
companion, a child at the time of the disaster, has been exploited as his servant, clown,
and slave. He is the last human being with whom *Hamm* has any contact.

Though few avant-garde directors would admit it, the same process occurs
Off-Off Broadway and in countless European theaters, where directors
frequently express their love of and respect for Beckett's work by overlaying
their ingenious illustrative ideas on it. What begins as an attempt at creative
collaboration ends up as a private explanation of what was originally created
to resist explanation.

Endgame has suffered especially from this attitude.[14] In Western Europe,
where the ethic of the New is particularly strong among directors, an
undeclared can-you-top-this? contest began with the play after Beckett's
definitive production at the Schiller Theater Werkstatt in 1967 – which
infuriated many directors precisely because of its definitiveness. Director
Rolf-Harald Kiefer and dramaturg Peter Kleinschmidt, for example, pro-
posed to set the play in an old people's home in Cologne in 1973 and went
ahead with that production even after receiving a firm letter from Beckett
demanding that they perform it "in accordance with the stage directions,
nothing added and nothing left out" (the exchange of letters was published in
the program). And the next several years would witness, to list only a couple,
a Munich production set in an attic-like space cluttered with ruined columns,
old mattresses and other junk, and Nagg and Nell's bins wrapped in plastic
foil (director: Volker Hesse), and a Stuttgart production set in a padded room
resembling a mental ward with walls painted photorealistically (director:
Alfred Kirchner). In a 1978 *Theater heute* article whose title, "Das 'Endspiel'
immer weiterspielen?," might be translated "To play the 'Endgame' over
and over?," Peter von Becker discusses this phenomenon, wondering if
Endgame, which concerns the "end of all theater repertories," ought to be
treated as just one more play in the theater repertory. "Isn't it a folly, in our
Beckett Theater, which wants to put an end to the playing and the explaining
and the perpetual talking, so obviously to play further? When one can't play
further?"[15] Directors, of course, have continued to think they can, and their

tradition of looking for new settings is unbroken. In 1983, Marcel Delval flooded the Théâtre Varia in Brussels up to its first two rows of seats, in order to stage *Fin de partie* in knee-deep water.[16]

In America, where all Beckett's plays are performed less frequently than in Europe, one cannot speak of a deluge of concept *Endgames*, but Akalaitis' interpretation does have precedents. The "Bare interior" specified in the script has been rendered variously as a skull, a womb, a fallout shelter and, in a particularly unrestrained production by Andre Gregory, a cage. In his 1973 version with the Manhattan Project, Gregory seated the spectators in cubicles of four (the number of characters in the play) separated from each other and from the hexagonal arena stage by chicken wire. One saw the playing area only blurrily through this wire and a covering scrim, which was flooded with bright light reflected off a shiny metal floor. Certain details nevertheless did appear clearly, e.g. the location of Nell in a refrigerator box and Nagg in a laundry hamper, inside which he later hangs himself. And many liberties were also taken with Beckett's language, seemingly in the interests of humor. Walter Kerr's description is worth quoting at length:

[Hamm and Clov] are scarcely capable of getting a phrase out without decorating it. The decoration includes cock-crows, halloos, clucks, brrs, burbles, bugle sounds, imitations of automobiles and rockets, screeches, machine-gun rat-a-tat-tats, interpolated "yucks" to express disgust, and innumerable repetitions of that sound that is made by bringing tongue and teeth together while blowing out the cheeks.

Thus, if Clov is threatening to leave Hamm and Hamm is protesting, the Beckett dialogue is turned into, "I'm going to leave you bong bong!" followed by an equally hearty, "No bong bong." If Hamm, in his despair over the universal silence, murmurs "No phone calls" without expecting an answer, he gets an answer: Clov instantly launches into a telephone bell-shrill rendition of "Hello Ma Baby, Hello Ma Honey," having already exhausted "Stars and Stripes Forever," "My Merry Oldsmobile" and "Give My Regards to Broadway." I am not at all certain that Beckett requires this relevance to matters American.

(*New York Times*, Feb. 11, 1973, Section II, p. 20)

After a production like this one, and after Brecht, Hesse, Kirchner, Delval, Kiefer and many others at least as unmindful of the published texts, it was difficult to understand why Beckett and Grove Press chose to take such severe action against Akalaitis in 1984. I did have the chance to ask Beckett directly about this matter during one of our meetings, and his answer was particularly enlightening in that it wasn't confined to intellectual or political considerations. At first, he spoke about ART being a reputable theater, Akalaitis being a well-known director, and mentioned his indignation that the production was dedicated to Alan Schneider. But his thoughts presently moved on to the idea of directors preferring to work with dead authors. "But I'm not dead yet," he said. "Not quite. I'm a dying author, certainly." I then asked him why it was less important to respect an author's text after he's dead, and he answered, "Well, just because then you can't hurt his feelings."

Akalaitis' *Endgame* was not the first example of such a reaction from Beckett or one of his publishers, but it was the most public.[17] The scandal began when Grove objected to the production before seeing it, and then responded to a preview invitation from ART by sending the producer/director Jack Garfein, whose objectivity was considered questionable since he was producing another *Endgame* in the New England area at the time. Relations between theater and publisher then grew hostile and extended beyond letter-writing to an attempt at legal injunction against the production's opening. At the eleventh hour, matters were settled out of court through common agreement on a program insert. Spectators received the following statement by Beckett and rebuttal from Robert Brustein (excerpts only), page one of the published text and a statement by Barney Rosset.

Any production of *Endgame* which ignores my stage directions is completely unacceptable to me. My play requires an empty room and two small windows. The American Repertory Theater production which dismisses my directions is a complete parody of the play as conceived by me. Anybody who cares for the work couldn't fail to be disgusted by this.   (Beckett)

. . . Like all works of theatre, productions of E N D G A M E depend upon the collective conbributions of directors, actors, and designers to realize them effectively, and normal rights of interpretation are essential in order to free the full energy and meaning of the play . . . We believe that this production, despite hearsay representations to the contrary, observes the spirit and the text of Mr. Beckett's great play – far more so, in fact, than a number of past productions, which to our knowledge evoked no public protests from Mr. Beckett's agents . . . Indeed, when directing his work, Mr. Beckett makes significant revisions in his own text and stage directions, suggesting that even he recognizes the need for changes with the passage of time . . . To threaten any deviations from a purist rendering of this or any other play – to insist on strict adherence to each parenthesis of the published text – not only robs collaborating artists of their interpretive freedom but threatens to turn the theatre into a waxworks. Mr. Beckett's agents do no service either to theatrical art or to the great artist they represent by pursuing such rigorous controls.   (Brustein)

As Akalaitis told me in an interview, this settlement had little to do with artistic matters; it was actually based on the reluctance of both Grove Press and ART to pay for a trial. In fact, the actual object of fury, her production, eventually became beside the point. Under dispute was the very *idea* of departing from Beckett's published stage directions, which is precisely the issue one must push aside in order to concentrate on the object. Unless we are prepared to say that no production that fails to follow every original stage direction deserves critical attention, then this *Endgame* ought to be examined and allowed to speak for itself – especially in light of Akalaitis' (and Mabou Mines') considerable reputation for producing, interpreting and adapting Beckett texts.

The script specifies: "Bare interior. Grey light. Left and right back, high up, two small windows, curtains drawn. Front right, a door. Hanging near door, its face to wall, a picture." Douglas Stein's set is a burned-out subway tunnel with implied windows high up, but no picture. The script contains no mention of music. At ART, a score by Philip Glass is played while the audience enters the theater and during selected bits of dialogue: a steel drum and guitar pulse in quick syncopation as a deep, repeating electric bass line creates an ominous, epic undertone and a zither-like instrument builds a sense of progression with a treble melody. It sounds like a rock and roll tribal rite. To the average audience member ignorant of Beckett, objections to this set and music must have seemed very odd; for both elements are powerful as pure theatrics.

Broken steel girders outline the top of the back wall, which is about twenty feet high and made of metal plates. Thus, each time Clov needs to look out a

12 Setting for *Endgame*, directed by JoAnne Akalaitis, American Repertory Theatre, Cambridge, MA, 1984. (Photo: ART/Richard Feldman)

window, he must climb all the way up this wall on two tall structural ladders. To the left and right are partial life-size subway cars, situated diagonally, no track in sight, as if strewn there by a tremendous explosion. Their windows have no glass and are charred at the top edges, indicating a fire. The electric lights on the cars are unaccountably illuminated, as is a line of theater striplights offhandedly lying in a rubbish pile in front of Nagg and Nell's ashbins. Centered in the floor of black mud is a large puddle that reflects the various stage lights, and beside the puddle is a charred human body.

As a visual composition, this stage picture is breathtaking, but theatricality is not the main issue; we must ask whether the design serves the play. It unquestionably suggests a specific time and place – an American city, probably New York, after nuclear holocaust – which, in the beginning, heightens spectators' involvement by dredging up emotional baggage about the arms race and making it difficult to push the production away to a safe, objective distance. Like Brecht's plans for *Godot*, however, it also limits the action to a single field of reference, blocking off differing approaches to meaning in the text. Interestingly, Adorno foresaw this form of reductivity in 1958, before any concept productions had even been tried.

The *dramatis personae* [of *Endgame*] resemble those who dream their own death, in a "shelter" where "it's time it ended." The end of the world is discounted as if it were a matter of course. Every supposed drama of the atomic age would mock itself, if only because its fable would hopelessly falsify the horror of historical anonymity by shoving it into the characters and actions of humans, and possibly by gaping at the "prominents" who decide whether the button will be pushed. The violence of the unspeakable is mimicked by the timidity to mention it. Beckett keeps it nebulous. One can only speak euphemistically about what is incommensurate with all experience, just as one speaks in Germany of the murder of the Jews. It has become a total *a priori*, so that bombed-out consciousness no longer has any position from which it could reflect on that fact. The desperate state of things supplies – with gruesome irony – a means of stylization that protects that pragmatic precondition from any contamination by childish science fiction.[18]

Endgame, in other words, is not about life after nuclear holocaust, which neither Beckett nor anyone else could possibly depict; it is about *our* lives, which are lived under the threat of disaster, nuclear and otherwise. Adorno describes the play's lack of specificity as a "taboo on history":

History is excluded, because it itself has dehydrated the power of consciousness to think history, the power of remembrance. Drama falls silent and becomes gesture, frozen amid the dialogues. Only the result of history appears – as decline.[19]

By breaking this taboo and providing her own historical "means of stylization," Akalaitis in effect transforms brutal realism into science fiction.

In her interview in part three she explains her reasons for taking such action, and I quote some of her points here.

JA: When people say, "Why did you choose that setting?," it seems so obvious to me. We had another kind of set before; we had a kind of underground tunnel. It was vaguer; it was a vaguer place, very primitive. But then I thought it looked like a set for *King Lear* or *Macbeth*, and Doug [Stein] did too; it was a muddy cave that didn't seem urban. And I wanted something that *was* urban, that could touch us, refer to our lives. Something that was not European, not arid, that had a kind of energy and funkiness. I was interested in all those values. We started with the idea of tunnel, and slightly behind that the idea of post-nuclear, but that was never a major consideration . . .

JK: I'm sure by now you've heard the argument against specificity – that it was setting it in a specific, recognizable place that annoyed people, not just the subway. What do you think about that argument?

JA: I think it's idiotic. I mean, everything onstage is in a specific place. At least it's in the theater. At least it's in Cambridge at the American Repertory Theatre. If you have it in a black box and put a chair onstage, the audience does not walk in and say, "We are in no-man's-land, we are in a vague, abstract, Platonic space." I mean, that's the thing about theater; it doesn't happen in your mind, it doesn't happen on the page, it happens in a place. And frankly I find that so irritating. It's very academic, that whole idea that directors can't be specific. Everything is specific. I mean if you put a chair onstage it is chosen by someone and it means something.

It is not clear from these or her other comments whether Akalaitis understands the objection to specificity – she does not acknowledge that its application to Beckett may be different from specificity applied to other drama – yet she does state explicitly that she thinks it unimportant. Candidly admitting that she does not "understand the meaning of the play," she nevertheless thinks it needs contemporizing, or at least Americanizing, and thus she uses it to pursue her own artistic agendas, the most pressing being consciousness of present time and place in the theater event. Text, interpreted to mean only lines and not stage directions, must stand or fall on its own, it would seem, in juxtaposition with an impressionistically applied director's vision.

We must momentarily forget, then, what we know about the play's perfectly balanced ambiguities – "Understanding it can mean nothing other than understanding its incomprehensibility" (Adorno) – in order to consider soberly other values in her production.[20] This *Endgame* is really a collage-work – a label that proves fitting despite the fact that Akalaitis would disclaim it – whose effects are often wholly distinct from Beckett's.[21]

The production has a specific stop-start rhythm, traceable both to the bursts of music and to the actors' frequent, abrupt shifts between mechanistic and naturalistic vocal deliveries. One immediately recognizes the stylistic choice of frontality as the signature of the New York avant-garde, common to Mabou Mines, Richard Foreman, the Wooster Group, the late Charles Ludlam and many others, but here that style is made to serve a quasi-classical reference: Clov (John Bottoms) behaves throughout like a running slave, playing the Fool to Hamm's Master (Ben Halley, Jr.). There is a cruel *burla* of Clov hitting his head on the low transom each time he runs out to the kitchen, and there are various verbal *lazzi* including repetition of the following lines five or six times in quick succession.

> HAMM: Go and get the oilcan.
> CLOV: What for?
> HAMM: To oil the castors.
> CLOV: I oiled them yesterday.

Almost all of these "bits" seem like expressions of aggression, released in spurts as by a manic-depressive personality, despite the fact that they may not have been intended that way (see Akalaitis' comments in her interview on the lines just quoted). One moment nothing whatsoever seems to matter to the characters, the next moment they are in such a panic that they almost step out of their roles. They seem always to be trembling from some fundamental restlessness, which crystalized in my mind as a feeling of would-be primitivism.[22]

This feeling is worth elaborating on because it constitutes the production's most plausible claim to interacting fruitfully with the *Endgame* text. The score is central to the primitivism, as are the set and lights. The music plays at top volume during all of Clov's initial activity – which Bottoms performs frenetically, bare-chested, like a primitive dance – but then it stops suddenly, returning only briefly during wistful moments, and the characters seem to long for it, as for regression to a pre-human form. They would like to be animals and avoid their human crisis, but the technical elements around them – the mostly broken machinery, the light and sound cues, the play's script – force their humanness, their species' clever modes of invention, back upon them, thus rendering weak-kneed and unconvincing any attempt they might make at primitive behavior. They have all the drawbacks of animalism (dirt, disease, hunger) but none of the benefits (unconsciousness of death).

Like the subway setting, this vision of failed primitivism is very theatrical and engaging. For instance, the lighting changes severely each time the music returns, and once during a nostalgic exchange between Hamm and Clov played as a voice-over, momentarily stunning the characters. It seems to force upon them the idea that they are trapped inside a play, as do the illuminated car lights and the ludicrous line of "discarded" striplights, which also mock them and undermine any dignity they might feel even as actors.

Thus Akalaitis does build on the work's widely discussed reflexivity. Her actors seem rushed through scriptural repetitions by a cosmic theatrical director with a macabre sense of humor; when Hamm says, "Our revels now are ended," plaster falls from the ceiling. The characters/actors seem weighed down by the force of *Endgame* itself, as if the play's monumental critical and production history hovered over them like the massive set on the huge ART stage, and each time they perform the text, snarling at its enslavement of them, they only add to their burden and make it more contemporary.

The trouble is, the play's American production history is not as monumental or overwhelming as this production implies; a spokesman at Grove Press estimates that fewer than ten professional U.S. productions were authorized in the decade before 1985. Thus, very few spectators could possibly have entered the ART auditorium convinced that *Endgame* is a tired classic in need of renovation. Clever as they are, then, Akalaitis' renovations are reduced to functioning as images in tandem with the text's concerns, which ultimately lessens their interest and impact even as parts of a collage. Consider, for example, the use Akalaitis makes of the interracial casting. According to Halley, the production was originally conceived as a project for him and Bottoms, whom Brustein cast before hiring Akalaitis as director. Akalaitis, in Halley's opinion, then built her concept partly around the fact that he was black, dressing him in a dreadlock wig, casting the black actor, Rodney Hudson, as Nagg, and asking both to speak in black dialect.

> I didn't understand what was the purpose of it. Why the direction to keep saying things like a black American? What does that mean? I'm an English-speaking actor . . . Well, what it means is: "Let's be racial-political here, let's draw some sort of Mason–Dixon line in art." And I don't feel that's correct.
>
> (Interview on March 13, 1986)

As was seen in Kani and Ntshona's *Godot*, interracial casting in Beckett is not socially loaded unless one acts to direct spectators' attention that way. By itself, the fact that Halley and Hudson are black and Bottoms and Shirley Wilbur (Nell) are white actively implies nothing, but in the context of these particular costumes, voices and setting it becomes loaded, implying that these four people are arbitrary survivors who happened to be trapped together when the bomb exploded. These choices doubtless relate to Akalaitis' desire, quoted above, to make the play relevant to anyone and everyone, here and now, but one is finally left with the feeling that she went to great trouble to solve a non-problem. The program notes, for example, focus on social issues such as miscegenation and urban homelessness, leaving an impression of straining to demonstrate the current relevance of this twenty-seven-year-old (in 1984) classic. It must have been evident even to spectators unfamiliar with Beckett that neither the play nor the world required such introduction, and the interracial casting would have been accepted in more general terms had it been left undiscussed.

One irony of Akalaitis' effort to contemporize this presumably old-fashioned and foreign text is that the play ultimately exposes the needlessness of her contemporizing. The writing proves stronger than the directing, and teaches us an important lesson about its resilience and resistance to "obvious" (Akalaitis' word) improvement. During the controversy before the opening, Beckett's representatives were particularly worried that Cambridge audiences would be offered a distorted view of Beckett's writing; hence the inclusion of his first page in the program insert. Anyone who saw the production, however, can testify to the fact that the setting's effect was not powerful enough to present such a serious threat to audience perceptions.

Suppose, for instance, that the main perceived violation relates to Beckett's intentional indeterminacy of time, which Richard Goldman describes succinctly: "All references to the past in his plays never convince us that the characters or their world were ever different."[23] One could even go further

13 Ben Halley, Jr. as Hamm and John Bottoms as Clov in *Endgame*, directed by JoAnne Akalaitis, American Repertory Theatre, Cambridge, MA, 1984. (Photo: ART/Richard Feldman)

and say that *Endgame* militates against spectators believing information about the past. For example, Nell's, "It was on Lake Como . . . One April afternoon," is followed immediately by the question, "Can you believe it?" If there ever was a different past, one more like our world, complete with "forests" and "bicycles," then the action would represent a hypothetical future. And if things were never different, then the action would represent a metaphorical present whose primary quality was its stasis. As it happens, of course, Beckett makes no decision, but rather insists upon the impossibility of anyone (characters, director or spectators) knowing the answer for certain.

If the script of *Endgame* is performed intact, as it is at ART except for the repetition of the lines quoted above, this indeterminacy is not affected by simply changing the setting. Beckett's words preserve the essential ambiguity, and the action still occurs simultaneously in both a metaphorical present and a hypothetical future, just as it does when the stage directions are followed to the letter. Since the play implies that the characters' situation may never have been different, the metaphor of the setting, bare room or subway tunnel, is forced all the more strongly onto the world of the audience, because they cannot take comfort in knowing that the horrifying events depicted are from another era: i.e. perhaps the world is and always was, figuratively, a burned-out subway tunnel.

In other words, despite the fact that it is more specific, the new metaphor, the subway, does not succeed in historicizing the action. As I discuss further below, it does undercut the play's deeper resonances, because its profusion of visually striking details renders Beckett's strange and impeccably chosen props – gaff, clock, dog, stancher, steps – a bit too commonplace. As Thomas Kilroy writes, Beckett's generic landscapes work against the spectator remembering familiar contexts for props and set elements: "We identify objects on a . . . Beckett stage only at the expense of memory, or to put it another way, by surrender to the economy of action within the play, the only system in which the objects are usable."[24] The objects-as-symbols normally have a durability, a proud recalcitrance, that Akalaitis' "economy of action" lessens by making it too easy for spectators to take intellectual possession of them, directing associations toward the ordinary or banal. Mostly, though, the setting embarrasses itself by seeming peripheral – both physically and conceptually underutilized.

Clov, for instance, uses one of the cars as a place to toss the sheets at the beginning, and occasionally as a short-cut passage to upstage right, where it blocks his activity on one of the ladders; but otherwise the cars are ignored and do not affect the characters' behavior. And since no scriptural changes are introduced to localize the situation further, as they were with Andre Gregory, the actors seems always to be speaking a language that does not fit with their surroundings. Halley says that he felt this effect acutely even onstage, attributing it to his differences with Akalaitis over the characteriza-tion of Hamm. His understanding of the character as a writer whose relationship with Clov is literary/scholarly (his mental image was Joyce and Beckett), he says, clashed with her early direction: "not eloquent, not Lear and his Fool, not classical, really hysterical, really vulgar, violent." Thus we have a setting and a collection of political overtones that are left passive because they conflict with the playtext and a lead actor's instinct, leaving the production ultimately as apolitical as Beckett's unaltered works.

Strangely, this political ineffectuality of the setting leads one to notice that Akalaitis is actually more respectful of text – that is, verbal text – than many directors; as she herself comments, "every pause was, for me, almost sacred." Beckett's words are allowed to resound on her stage at nearly full strength because she does not intentionally eviscerate them for the greater glory of subjectively chosen theatrical moments, as is so common in "director's theater." (For example, Andrei Serban's 1984 *Uncle Vanya*, in which Chekhov's script was cut so severely that it actually *became* less interesting than the spectacle of the actors shouting their lines across fifty-foot distances on the all-wooden set.) Rather she juxtaposes those moments with Beckett's words in the hope of achieving effective collage. The resulting composition, however, already described as an image of failed primitivistic behavior, succeeds only sporadically in illuminating *Endgame*; most of the time, the audience observes the script struggling against an obviously unnecessary attempt to contemporize and politicize it.

One could wish that all directorial alterations of Beckett were as self-revealing as Akalaitis', but they are not. In 1986, for example, I saw a German television production of *Glückliche Tage* (*Happy Days*), directed by Roberto Ciulli (from the Theater an der Ruhr, Mühlheim), in which there was no mound, and Winnie (Veronika Bayer) walked around the theater calling to Willie (Rudolf Brand), who lurked in the wings and worked the stage machinery. This production was far more likely than Akalaitis' to give spectators a false impression of Beckett's work, because the new setting was actively utilized, as if the author had specified it, and the text was altered to fit a new action line about an old actress trapped in a theater building.[25] For example, during the act 1 section when Beckett says that Winnie raises her parasol, Bayer walks along the front wall of the mezzanine as if on a tight-rope, holding her parasol aloft for balance as circus music plays in the background. Then she verbally directs Willie back into the prompter's box – he emerged from there in order to set her parasol aflame by throwing a switch on the light panel – with lines taken from twenty pages earlier ("So ist's richtig . . . ganz herum . . . jetzt . . . rückwarts rein" ["That's it . . . right round . . . now . . . back in"]).[26] The Germans watching the broadcast with me had never seen *Glückliche Tage* before, did not miss the mound, the

hellish light, or anything else about Beckett's original situation, and thought
Bayer did an excellent job of portraying an aging woman who was under-
standably neurotic because she'd become superfluous in her profession. In
other words, the novel metaphor of the theater-as-prison was theatrically
effective despite being pedestrian and clichéd in comparison with Beckett's
astonishing image of a woman sinking into the earth.

Which raises several thorny questions about taking the author at his word
when he says he would accept other stage directions if shown that they are
"better." What if they are merely effective, and not "better"? As Bernard
Shaw never ceased to point out during his years as a drama critic, spectators
are often bludgeoned by theatrical effectiveness; it is no guarantee of
anything and frequently prettifies work that is philosophically superficial or
reprehensible. Furthermore, is it legitimate to try to show Beckett the worth
of an idea through a production? A director like Ciulli could never argue his
case convincingly beforehand, because his concept is plainly a weak substitute for the original. He must resort to the evidence of a mass audience
judgment made largely in ignorance of his alterations, and then ask Beckett
to "bow before the *fait accompli*" (Beckett's words in a 1978 letter to an Irish
actor).[27] As the ART representatives repeatedly pointed out in 1984, it is
difficult to argue morally or aesthetically against the *idea* of departing from
Beckett's directions, much easier to speak against the results. In either case,
though, Ciulli's production is vulnerable because on television it has the
pernicious result of giving hundreds of thousands of viewers an atextual
first-time experience of *Glückliche Tage* – a play, one might add, that has
counted some of the most independent-minded contemporary directors,
such as Serban and Giorgio Strehler, among its most textually faithful.

In fact, Serban's 1979 production of *Happy Days* at the Public-Newman
Theater, which was also broadcast on television, provides an excellent
example of how a certain kind of director comes to be textually faithful not
out of fear of Beckett or his agents but out of his own sense of what is most
effective. "It would be idiotic to change Beckett around," said Serban during
rehearsals with actress Irene Worth, and his *Happy Days* shows, among
other things, just how much there is for a director to "*do*" within a Beckett
text's confines.[28] I refer not only to Serban's character work with Worth but
to his technical choices as well. Winnie's mound is unusually high, perhaps
ten feet or more, and covered with a brown, mossy substance that looks more
like the "scorched grass" the script calls for than any other *Happy Days*
setting I've seen. The backdrop, also faithful to the text's description, "very
pompier trompe-l'oeil," is a happily blue, Magritte-like sky dotted with
small white clouds, except for a ring of cloudless space directly over Winnie,
forming a kind of halo. Worth is dressed very simply, as was Ruth White in
the 1961 world premiere, in an unpretentious pearl choker and a plain, pink

short-sleeved top that occasionally falls off her shoulders and accentuates the size and pendulousness of her breasts.

The effect of these choices is to emphasize the character's Earth-Mother aspect and, at the same time, place it in a humorous, enigmatic context. The steep symmetrical sides of the mound, which meet slightly above Worth's waist, suggest a giant skirt of earth, and her demeanor throughout is, to use the actress' phrase, "like a housewife."[29] The backdrop, because of its surrealist quality, both emphasizes a dream-like absurdity in the action and suggests its universality; as the critic Katharine Worth writes, " 'pompier' indicates just that kind of mixture of highly coloured and highly conventional that could appeal to large numbers of people besides women like Winnie."[30] In other words, the production makes a firm commitment to the portrayal of a specific, domestic, middle-aged personality and uses its setting, along with certain gestures, to comment on that portrayal. This is a very straightforward directorial approach and, partly because of its straightforwardness, it succeeds in illuminating the play. Moreover, it is very different from the approach of the author-as-director, though equally legitimate. In Beckett's production of *Happy Days* at the Royal Court Theatre, done at this same time in 1979, Billie Whitelaw played Winnie as a young seductress in a black-lace bustier, speaking precisely and rhythmically in front of a blank, luminous backdrop that offered no overt comment whatever on the action.

There is something peculiarly American about Serban's production, despite the fact that he is Rumanian-born and Worth, originally from Nebraska and California, has spent much of her career in London. This quality is difficult to pin down, but it has to do mostly with culture-specific gestures and speech patterns: associations, nebulous and distinct, that American spectators make with the way the actress puts words together, preens, expresses puzzlement and boredom, digs in her bag, makes funny faces – all of which would have counterparts in productions done in other cultures. Indeed, Beckett has always welcomed suggestions for Americanization of the Anglicisms and Irishisms in his plays; for instance, his and Asmus' replacement of "Macon" and "Cackon country" with "Napa" and "Crappa Valley" in the 1978 *Godot* at the Brooklyn Academy of Music.[31] To achieve the ultimate goal of this Americanization, though – i.e. rendering the play accessible on the profoundest possible level – one ought not to stop at switching certain words, but rather go on to arrange all language and gesture into a kind of "musical" composition that the audience can and wants to follow.

"Music" in this sense, as any good director knows, is not just a matter of sound; it must be understood more broadly as blending into dance and storytelling, including physical movements, bits of information, anything the director must "conduct." To me, Serban's most significant achievement with *Happy Days* has to do with his conducting of its music, or, stated another way, his editing of Worth's extraordinary range of physical and vocal mannerisms. Like the production's American quality, this musical aspect is almost impossible to describe. One could list example after example – such as the way Worth's deep, amoroso voice works in counterpoint with the guttural, benevolent grunting of George Voskovec's Willie; the way her shift to an extremely fast, unusually enunciated delivery during the "gabbled" section, beginning, "Bless you Willie I do appreciate your goodness," functions as a kind of scherzo; or the way silence functions, as always in Beckett, as a constant obbligato – but such a list could never even approximate the sense acquired in viewing a performance.

I recommend the PBS video recording of this production to anyone interested in how any play can work musically, and in particular how the musical nature of Beckett's drama may be preserved even where the acting has a naturalistic basis. My sense of this widely seen television version, unproven empirically but based on numerous conversations with viewers from different geographical areas, is that it did as much to promote Beckett's reputation in America as did the dozen or so Schneider premieres seen by relatively small audiences in the major theater centers. This video preserves extremely well what might be called the production's cumulative effect, the quality in it that seems to build on itself as the performance goes on, investing various recurring lines and activities, no matter how banal, with an increasing resonance, as happens in Schneider and Warrilow's *Ohio Impromptu*.

More difficult to see in the video version, however, is why the setting, Beckett's physical situation, is indespensable to the communication of the play-as-music. Serban pushes the mound downstage as far as possible so that Winnie is unusually close to the spectators, which amplifies the presentational impact of the actress talking directly to them and mutes the idea of Winnie as a respresentation of a fictional character in a distant place. These two realms are exquisitely blended, as described in chapter 3 with Beckett's Schiller Theater *Godot*, leaving a sense of unnerving honesty from which there is no escape, short of walking out, either for spectators or performers. The feeling of isolation created by the environment in *Happy Days*, as Katharine Worth writes, can be even more absolute than that in *Godot* and *Endgame*:

[The] backcloth does what none of the earlier plays had done, rules out the idea of change and chance, obliterates the off-stage; no unseen unpredictable vast here, no unrecorded vital darkness as in *Krapp's Last Tape*. No possibility of darkness at all.[32]

Language and gestures are isolated precisely because the background is "still," so to speak, free from change, recognizable histories, realities outside the stage frame. And only if it remains "still" will the director's musical composition be discernible, for any type of "movement" in the form of outside references or environmental variations becomes a distraction, deflecting spectators' attention away from the music like a subway train rumbling beneath a concert hall.

Are there no settings other than the ones Beckett specifies, then, that can possibly provide this requisite stillness? Perhaps, yes, but we cannot expect any to come from the imaginations of directors who fail to see how Beckett differs fundamentally from other playwrights. Again, *Endgame* provides the best example. Since, as Adorno writes, the play can have political meaning only through its ambiguities, which constitute its inexorable historyless-ness, the specificity of time and place in Akalaitis' production renders it incapable of commenting specifically on the urban reality it takes pains to evoke. In trying to shift the action onto a specific canvas, she comes face to face with the playwright's original refusal to paint on such a canvas, which on one important level represents his lack of faith in art dealing with actual political process. The essential problem not only with Akalaitis' approach but also with that of the other directors mentioned – Ciulli, Gregory, Delval, Palitzsch, Hesse, Kirchner, and even Brecht – is that they treat Beckett as if he were a pre-modern playwright, i.e. someone who provides words containing a message it is their job to deliver and illustrate.[33]

As I have explained in detail with a number of examples – *Waiting for Godot, Happy Days, Rockaby, Ohio Impromptu* – Beckett's plays are much more theatrically complete than that. Their physicalizations are "visualized on [Beckett's] mental stage" so precisely that the stage directions must be considered part of his texts, and anyone claiming faithfulness to those texts ought also to be faithful to the movement and settings. I want to stress that that statement does not stem from blind loyalty – indeed I considered the legal attempt to close down Akalaitis' production wrong, perhaps even unconstitutional – but from measured judgment about Beckett's achieve-ment; for the radical originality of his work, the aspect that has actually changed contemporary theater, is precisely what these directors deny in their stagings.

Only once have I come across a "concept" production in which the director made clear that he understood how Beckett's work departs from the representational norms of most other drama – George Tabori's 1984 *Warten auf Godot* at the Münchner Kammerspiele – and indeed this is the only altered setting I know of that Beckett expressly tolerated.[34] Using one of his favorite devices, Tabori staged *Godot* as a rehearsal: no illusionistic scenery whatsoever, the actors sitting around a plain table smoking and drinking coffee. At the start of each act, Thomas Holtzmann and Peter Lühr (Didi and Gogo) enter languidly in what could be slightly aged street clothes and read indifferently from their scripts, one of which is the Suhrkamp paperback edition of the play, as ubiquitous in Germany as the Grove edition is in America. Then they gradually work up to performance tempo, leaving their scripts for longer and longer intervals and becoming more and more spontaneous, until at some point the spectator realizes they have embodied the characters, though it is impossible to determine exactly when that transition occurred.

At first, the points when they drop their scripts seem like sections that the actors happen to have memorized, allowing them to experiment with movement, as often occurs at early rehearsals of a play. Later those sections seem like improvisations, the actors attempting to depart from the text, or at least to lose themselves sufficiently in the action that they may call it "theirs." But each time the familiar exchange arises, ending with, "Wir warten auf Godot," Holtzmann holds up his crumpled paperback as if to say that they cannot leave because of the play, *Waiting for Godot*, and not because of any fictional character named Godot. What holds them is the routine the script dictates, which they cannot escape no matter how hard they work toward spontaneity; for they must return tomorrow, speak again the very same words, and try to make that activity seem worth doing. The difference between this consciousness of routine and that, say, in Akalaitis' *Endgame* is like the difference between an Artaud play and a Grand Guignol performance; the ostensible content is similar but the former is by far the more intense experience because it eliminates superfluous representation.

Tabori's production, in other words, is not merely a mimesis, of an episode either on a "country road" or in a hypothetical theater, but a meditation on mimesis. And it is unusually compelling because it makes that meditation central instead of peripheral to a chosen dominant metaphor, such as a subway tunnel or an attic room. Recall the parallel between Beckett and Joyce drawn in the Introduction: "His writing is not *about* something; *it is that something itself*." The subject matter of Beckett's scenes is their duration in present time; his dramas are not *about* experiences; *they are those experiences themselves*. And, as States points out, you can easily destroy the potential for audiences to view them that way "by simply littering [the landscapes] with the content of a history (refuse, ruins, billboards), things heavy with a definite past and consequently destined for future use"; for you thereby lead viewers away from present-time experience, away from perceiving the play as music, and toward the refuge of older and more distanced viewing patterns, such as searching for social and political allegories.[35]

One could explain this point another way, by considering briefly why a writer of Adorno's intellectual disposition would value Beckett so highly. Adorno judged all artistic endeavor in terms of his own philosophical ideas

which, in the tradition of German Idealism, involved very strong opinions
about subject/object relationships. To summarize crudely one aspect of his
vastly complex thought: art has a negative responsibility not to follow the
mendacious ''bourgeois'' model of healthy, independent subjects (spectators) appreciating the organic wholeness of well-defined creative objects,
but it also has a positive responsibility to reflect *and* embody the alienation
and agony of subjects necessarily distant from utopian integration either
with each other (in society) or with creative objects. Again consistent with a
long tradition of German thought, music seemed to him the expressive mode
best equipped to fill these criteria, and Beckett offered a kind of literary
equivalent to music.

Differences in tone – between people who narrate and those who speak directly – pass
judgment on the principle of identity. Both alternate in Hamm's long speech, a kind
of inserted aria without music. At the transition points he pauses – the artistic pauses
of the veteran actor of heroic roles. For the norm of existential philosophy – people
should be themselves because they can no longer become anything else –, *Endgame*
posits the antithesis, that precisely this self is not a self but rather the aping imitation
of something non-existent. Hamm's mendacity exposes the lie concealed in saying
''I'' . . .[36]

Perhaps Beckett was of a similar mind when he wrote about *Endgame*: ''My
work is a matter of fundamental sounds (no joke intended) made as fully as
possible, and I accept responsibility for nothing else'' (letter to Alan
Schneider, December 29, 1957).

   Just as one need not be an exceptionally profound or experienced observer
to see that Serban's *Happy Days* (or Asmus' *Godot*, or Schneider's *Ohio
Impromptu*, etc.) functions as music, one need not look very deeply into
Akalaitis' *Endgame* (or Palitzsch's, or Kiefer's, or Gregory's, or Ciulli's
Glückliche Tage, etc.) to see that it does not, despite her use of actual music
and her assertion that ''a good handle into Beckett is the rhythm.'' These
productions function rather like Scribe, Zola, or for that matter Noel Coward
plays, spinning out once-upon-a-time, fictional tales in pleasing backgrounds that, for the most part, sit safely in their proscenium frames. Hugh
Kenner once described Hamm as ''the generic Actor, a creature all circum-
ference and no center''; and the emptiness of *Endgame*'s world is essential to
communicating the paradox of that centerlessness, which forces the audience
to wonder not only who he is, but also who all the other characters are.[37]
Every piece of decoration, every extrinsic bit of recognizable history, acts to
neutralize this paradox and turn the story into one of fully centered men
whose identity is clear from the added associations; and with minor
modifications that statement could apply as well to all the other plays.
   Thus, Beckett's strongest argument against accusations of conservatism

may well be *Tu Quoque*: "Physician, heal thyself!" The unfortunate truth is that, even after four decades, it still requires a certain courage to trust in his basic dramatic discoveries, in the unaided theatrical power of ambiguous identity, time and place. When one lacks that courage, or when one simply does not see any more than allegories in the plays, then one ends up filling in "missing" specifics in an effort to explain the unexplainable. The problem, sadly, is not complex but all too simple. What is often attributed to narcissism and monomania on the part of contemporary directors, particularly those calling themselves avant-garde, is frequently just bad old-fashioned conservatism – denial of newness to the truly new by blending it into the established – and yet another example of the theater's notorious resistance to fundamental change.

6   *Eh Joe, Dis Joe, He Joe*: toward a television icon

At the end of his book *Beckett/Beckett* (1977), Vivian Mercier writes:

I am prepared to argue that the brevity of the latter works is due not to any philosophical aspiration towards silence but to . . . perfectionism: the only perfectly finished piece of workmanship is the miniature.[1]

As discussed throughout the previous chapters, in his search for the perfect image, Beckett has inserted more and more precise stage directions into his texts, and sought more and more complete control over the action in productions he directs. In live theater, however, even with the most amicable rehearsal atmospheres, it is impossible to have total control because practical circumstances always necessitate some compromises. Only in the television studio, particularly at Süddeutscher Rundfunk (SDR) in Stuttgart, has he been able to wield a directorial baton sufficiently powerful to conduct performances exactly the way he wants and to record them for posterity in that form.

Beckett's five television plays are jewels of astonishing precision, masterpieces all but unknown even to most Beckett appreciators because of their practical inaccessibility. One occasionally comes across a stage adaptation of *Eh Joe* or *Quad*, but such productions do not provide the same experience as the works in their intended medium, which are rarely rebroadcast after their premieres and lie moldering in various video archives.[2] These works have played a significant role in the development of the author's late stage plays, but it is important to stress that they were written specifically for television and are not stage plays. Conceived within the compass of a particular medium, they have extended that compass, and ultimately transcended it by forming what Martin Esslin calls a new genre: "visual poetry."[3] Consider this example.

A gray-haired man dressed entirely in black sits, head bowed, resting his arms, at a small table. Behind him is a rectangle of light suggesting a window. A male voice rises, as if from far off in the darkness, humming and then singing the last line of a Schubert *Lied* – "Holde Träume, kehret wieder" ("Lovely dreams, come again") – an enchanting line of music, sung with deep devotion like an aria to a lover, which lulls the man to sleep.[4] As he

95

14 Rick Cluchey in his stage adaptation of *Eh Joe*, Goodman Theatre, Chicago, 1983. (Photo: Goodman Theatre)

sleeps, we see his dream in a square cloud above him where the light rectangle has now faded to black. It is himself, seated the same way but facing the other direction. A disembodied hand appears and touches him gently on the head, which he then raises; then the hand withdraws and returns first with a chalice, from which he drinks, and then with a cloth to wipe his brow. He gazes upward and extends his right hand, which is soon clasped by the disembodied hand, and then clasped again by his own left hand. The three joined hands sink slowly to the table, and he rests his head, which a fourth hand then gently touches.

The dream disappears, the window-rectangle returns, and the man awakens. Then the *Lied* is heard again, the light fades, and the dream returns. It is the same dream as before, but not identically presented. This time the camera pulls in close so that the square cloud takes up the entire screen. The image, now seen in much greater detail, moves more slowly than before, and has a weird glow that gives it a religious flavor. Moreover, the man, whose loose pony-tail looked like an eighteenth-century wig the first time, now resembles Christ, and his blank stare is somehow not expressionless, especially near the end, when it betrays an unmistakable feeling of gratitude. The head is cocked slightly to the side and is strangely (for Beckett) pious, like countless adoring figures in Renaissance paintings.[5] Finally the camera pulls back to recover the dreamer, the dream cloud disappears, and the picture fades to black.

This play, entitled *Nacht und Träume* (*Night and Dreams*), is in certain respects paradigmatic of Beckett's television work, not because of the dominant image of the man seated at a table, which reminds one more of *Ohio Impromptu* or *Krapp's Last Tape* than of most of the other television plays, but because of the structure of contrasting distant and near views of the same scene. Few details are visible in the dream's first appearance, which seems cold and somewhat trite, but its second appearance is saturated with emotion, even to the point of risking sentimentality. The expected sentimentality never arises, however, because Beckett eludes it through specificity and repetition, as he also does in *Eh Joe, Ghost Trio, Quad* and *. . . but the clouds . . .* The events seen in detail convey very specific actions and intentions, which make us reconsider any expectations of unearned emotion. The specificity disorients us, makes the action seem at once familiar and strange, and ultimately applies a peculiar forward pressure to it that makes the outcome seem, in retrospect, inevitable. All five of these works manifest an unnerving, dream-like self-sufficiency. They are like objects suddenly come across in the water after a long sea voyage, fragments telling a history more revealing, in its way, than what could have been told by any presumably lost whole. And we learn from such fragments only by observing them twice, three times, contemplating them, as if Beckett were saying, in effect, that everything can fall into cliché if examined superficially.

With the exception of *Eh Joe*, Beckett has reduced the spoken texts of these plays almost to nothing and conceived their stories (for there are still always stories) in terms of visual images, working more as a choreographer or painter than a traditional playwright. In fact, one could see the works collectively as an extended effort to move away from language; during the 1982 taping of *Nacht und Träume*, Beckett told his Stuttgart cameraman, Jim Lewis, "that it was difficult for him to keep writing words, without having the feeling that it was a lie."[6] And when he says he distrusts words, we must take him seriously, for his television scripts are sparing even with language not intended as speech.

Beckett provides neither the kind of descriptive stage directions given by other authors in their plays without speech (e.g. Kroetz's *Wunschkonzert*), nor even the degree of description found in his own earlier mimes (e.g. *Film, Act Without Words I* and *II*). The television scripts are largely numbered sets of camera directions that give little sense of the completed works' atmospheres, and in some respects they remind one of attempts by certain contemporary artists to delegate final construction of artworks to unknown hands; for example, Sol Lewitt's wall drawings, which consist of detailed directions to be followed by whomever wishes to display them. As Clas Zilliacus writes of *Eh Joe*, "It is less a work of art, in fact, than the key to the proper execution, as its author sees it, of that work of art."[7] When Beckett directs, however, these ground rules change because then the works are executed by the master and bear the stamp of his painterly hand.

That hand, in fact, has specific painterly qualities that could even be characterized by comparison with a particular painter. The action of the television plays typically takes place in a central area surrounded by darkness, which functions as a vessel for the "lighted" condition, the inner state, depicted in the stories; in art history the main proponent of obscure backgrounds used in this way is Caravaggio, whom, incidentally, Beckett admires. Beckett's instruction at the beginning of *Eh Joe*, "No need to record room as whole," could be an epigraph for a study of Caravaggio, who focused almost exclusively on foreground figures, surrounding them with darkness and lighting them with a single source that generates sharp shadows.[8] As in Beckett, the viewer is drawn immediately into the internal action of these figures since it is clear that the artist has no interest in providing the context of another whole.

Comparison with Caravaggio is bound to seem surprising at first, since he is in general so much more aggressive an artist than Beckett. If the analogy is not pushed too far, however, it can be useful in illuminating Beckett's intentions in the television plays – which are framed in rectangular screens and thus lend themselves well to the old simile of paintings as windows. Caravaggio's heavy chiaroscuro is a fillip to the High Renaissance ideal of windows looking outward on vast distances drawn in perfect perspective; he prefers windows looking inward on particular souls enveloped in sublime abysses of black and brown – the depiction of Man divorced from his traditional place in the perfect order, existing on his own in a kind of nothingness. And that preference recalls a comparison Beckett once made between himself and Joyce:

The more Joyce knew the more he could. He's tending toward omniscience and omnipotence as an artist. I'm working with impotence, ignorance . . . I think anyone nowadays who pays the slightest attention to his own experience finds it the experience of a non-knower, a non-can-er. The other type of artist – the Apollonian – is absolutely foreign to me.[9]

This declaration of humility might be seen as similar to Caravaggio's conviction that the made-up scene, the practice of "working from one's head," inevitably results in generalization and represents a kind of hubris. Unlike most of his contemporaries, the painter insisted on working from life

15 Klaus Herm in *. . . nur noch Gewölk . . .* (*. . . but the clouds . . .*), directed by Samuel Beckett, SDR, Stuttgart, 1977, © Süddeutscher Rundfunk Jehle. (Photo: SDR/Hugo Jehle)

because he believed he knew no more about truth than what could be learned from empirical observation. Beckett, too, in a way, prefers to work from life. His plays are a reaction not only against what might be called the "dramatic Mannerism" of his day – the habitual imitation of the *manieri* of established modern dramatists such as Ibsen and Chekhov – but also against the tendency in the movement known as postmodernism to reject everyday experience as a basis for stage action.[10] As Tom Driver writes, "Beckett suggests something more free [than dogmatism] – that life is to be seen, to be talked about, and that the way it is to be lived cannot be stated unambiguously but must come as a response to that which one encounters in 'the mess.' "[11]

Furthermore, Caravaggio's narratives, despite their realism, frequently vie for visual prominence with the geometries of his figures, so that it becomes difficult to trace causes for the sense of necessity in his works, the feeling that no other arrangements for them are thinkable. The seriousness of the religious subjects is undercut by a deeply ironic, almost sacrilegious, sense of humor. But since that humor often has a geometrical source – e.g. the folds in a saint's belly resembling certain folds in a robe beside him – the final impression is never ridiculous. The perfection, the seriousness so to speak, of the abstract compositions reflects a new kind of purposefulness back on the figures' expressions and the narratives. (In the *Doubting of St. Thomas*, for example, I am amused by a fleshy finger probing around in one of Jesus' wounds and by numerous rows of collateral wrinkles on the Saint's brow; the narrative at first seems silly, but as I continue looking I follow Thomas' finger back along a straight line that connects with a bent elbow opposite and then notice other similar structural lines forming a starburst with the wound at center. In the end the act of probing takes on a compositional necessity that makes me reconsider initial judgments of narrative silliness.)

Strangely, Beckett's television plays can also be analyzed like this, not only because their changing rectangular images have precise geometrical arrangements, but also because their situational ironies are revealed in similar ways. Beckett frames these plays as short tales with an initial appearance of simplicity, sentimentality, or humor, but in production those frames function as strategies to draw the spectator in and lead him to inspect the action more closely; one gradually notices, among other things, the repeated use of particular geometric shapes as external expressions of inner psychological states, and ultimately it becomes clear that the framing tales were not as sentimental as they first appeared. In other words, the psychological depth in these works, like that in Caravaggio's and many other great painters', becomes accessible through the lure of their illusorily simple psychological surfaces, and the use of geometry as a storytelling tool.

In *Ghost Trio*, for example, we see a plain gray room with a solitary man, F, seated to one side, and hear a female voice describe his "familiar chamber" banally as a series of rectangles (floor, wall, door, window, etc.), all of which are then shown serially in close-up. The voice says, not in an ironic tone but implying irony, "Having seen that specimen of floor you have seen it all," and then, "Knowing this, the kind of wall – . . . The kind of floor – . . . Look again" (p. 248). The close-ups are repeated several more times, and soon the spectator realizes the error of thinking of the room and action as banal: for one thing, there is a man in the space, a human life, which reflects a psychological complexity back on the simple shapes; and for another, the camera does not always obey the voice but sometimes acts on its own like an independent presence.

As Linda Ben-Zvi writes, "Like the art that makes Watt's pot less familiar the more it is described, Beckett's rectangular television world explodes 'the familiar room' of F and the viewer."[12] One could say that Beckett structures his play so that it actually teaches the viewer how to view it, as he did in his Schiller Theater *Godot*. He gently ridicules the attitude that automatically sees simplicity as simplistic, as Caravaggio ridicules the attitude that automatically sees a biblical scene as pious, or a scene from everyday life as base or mundane. Thus Beckett prepares us to "look again," not only at F's apparently sentimental situation of waiting for a woman while listening to music, but also at our own situation of sitting before a rectangular television set.

These qualities are all perceivable in the works regardless of who is directing, so long as the director respects Beckett's instructions, but when he himself directs, the author makes them even more prominent. Beckett tends to use the production process in Stuttgart as an opportunity to make final refinements in his scripts, and those changes usually have the effect of achieving more directly both the ironies just described and other purposes already apparent in the published texts. On several occasions, Beckett has mounted an SDR production of a play shortly after assisting at a BBC production of it, and as Martin Esslin writes, "the German [versions] are later and perhaps incorporate some of Beckett's own second thoughts about the first versions. Perhaps they are closer to the definitive images he was striving for."[13]

Beckett will not admit, at least to me, that he sees anything wrong with the BBC productions; he genuinely respects them, indeed was present on the set for most of them, and says that he undertook the SDR projects because he enjoys working there. To be frank, though, a major reason for that enjoyment is that, in Walter Asmus' words, "the working conditions in Stuttgart are absolutely singular in the world."[14] And Beckett did tell me that he considers the technical crew in Stuttgart "unique because they really

16 Klaus Herm in *Geistertrio* (*Ghost Trio*), directed by Samuel Beckett, SDR, Stuttgart, 1977, © Süddeutscher Rundfunk Jehle. (Photo: SDR/ Hugo Jehle)

are . . . concerned with what they're doing," and that the logistical circumstances at SDR, which permit more than ten days of rehearsal for a tenminute play such as *Was Wo*, are "absolutely unthinkable in London."[15] Ultimately, the SDR productions must be taken as his final statements, and they contain significant differences from their predecessors – differences worth observing closely not just for the sake of establishing "definitive" texts, but because they contain clues to the sources of the works' peculiar energy and to why they affect spectators' consciousnesses as they do. I elaborate by comparing different versions of *Eh Joe*.

Originally written in 1965 for Jack MacGowran, *Eh Joe* is not among the author's most acclaimed works. Some, such as Esslin, praise it highly, but others relegate it to "the bottom of Beckett's artistic heap" (S. E. Gontarski) or argue that it constitutes "a rare lapse of taste" (John Fletcher).[16] It has, in any case, the reputation of being one of Beckett's most accessible plays, which of course recommends or damns it depending on who is judging. *Eh Joe* is certainly Beckett's most bitter work, and there is no question that it has an obvious surface; it is also clear, however, that that obviousness is in the service of other aims.

The seven-page script begins by describing a man sitting on a bed, whom the camera sees from behind. The man looks out a window, locking it afterwards and drawing a curtain over it, does the same with a door and cupboard, looks underneath the bed, and then relaxes again in his original posture. The camera then dollies in to within a yard of his face and stops when a woman's voice begins speaking: "Joe . . . Joe." For approximately twenty minutes this Voice – which insists that it is not coming from his mind and identifies itself as one of his discarded lovers – verbally assaults Joe, and we watch the reactions of his face, which Beckett says is "impassive except insofar as it reflects mounting tension of *listening*." Voice reminds him of his past womanizing, ridicules his (apparently Catholic) faith, ridicules his habit of squeezing off the voices in his head, which have included his father and mother, by a process called "mental thuggee," and reports details of the suicide of another discarded lover. The words stop only for a few seconds at nine specified points, during which the camera pulls in closer to his face, so that by the final section we are no more than a few inches away as Voice finally fades out.

At first glance the play does seem straightforward: a middle-aged man is haunted by guilt over his past lechery, guilt in the form of a torturous voice from his past. Because Voice denies that she comes from Joe's mind, we immediately suspect that she does, and indeed Beckett has confirmed this suspicion on more than one occasion.

"Did you think of the voice as a concrete person?"
BECKETT: "It is a concrete person for Joe."
"But he invents himself what he thinks he hears?"
BECKETT: "She really whispers in him. He hears her. Only if she lives can he have the wish to kill her. She is dead, but in him she lives. That is his passion: to kill the voices, which he cannot kill."
(Dialogue with the German critic Siegfried Melchinger)[17]

These comments are problematic for several reasons, however, not least because they represent an unusual instance of the author making an interpretive choice. The text itself neither confirms nor denies for certain that Voice is part of Joe's consciousness, yet Beckett offers his opinion – which is, to understate matters, very convincing.

In fact, the most authoritative critical readings of *Eh Joe* have been based on unconditional acceptance of this opinion. And it seems so obvious to so many that Voice comes from Joe's mind that one is loathe to claim it is not true. It also seems obvious, however, that the text's interest extends beyond a display of melodramatic spleen only insofar as doubt about Voice's source remains active. Gontarski, for example, in his study of the *Eh Joe* manuscripts, says that Beckett's main compositional leap with the play was to jettison a draft in which Voice tells only her own story, which "would simply have been a maudlin account of guilt"; instead he had Voice offer "two versions of deserted women, Voice herself, who rebounded apparently successfully (although she doth protest a bit much), and the suicide victim."[18] For Gontarski, this change raised the conflict in the play to a level of complexity that was not possible before, because Voice was no longer merely an ill-tempered complainer but rather an extension of Joe's imagination, able to tell a detailed story about events he never witnessed (the suicide). In other words, for those who accept that Voice is a part of Joe, she need represent not only self-castigation but also interior struggle with one's creative powers. This is an ingenious interpretation and almost irrefutable if one looks only at the texts and manuscripts, but when actual productions are taken into account one can see that it is based on an assumption and offers an incomplete explanation.

At the opening of the 1966 BBC version, directed by Alan Gibson and supervised by Beckett, one notices first of all the bareness of the room: the uniform gray of the walls is interrupted only by three plain dark curtains and a small reading lamp next to the bed; aside from these items, the picture's emptiness is broken only by a single dark stripe on the bed blanket and the figure of MacGowran struggling, Estragon style, with a shoe. There is in fact so little self-explanatory information in the picture that we do not even learn that this is "his room," as Beckett specifies, until we see the proprietary air with which MacGowran performs the looking and locking business – which gives us much information at once, some of it humorous. The obvious question suggested by the business is: why is this man so ridiculously paranoid, even to the point of installing a curtain in front of his cupboard? And that quality of ridiculousness becomes an important contrast with the utter sobriety of what takes place afterwards.

Voice, played by Siân Phillips, does not exactly surprise us when she starts speaking, because the camera, by creeping toward Joe as soon as he sits down again, has already implied that he is not alone despite his careful checking. Thus, one's first impulse is to equate camera and Voice, though that equivalence is called into question as the play continues. The camera never moves while Voice speaks, and it sometimes seems like a separate, perhaps subordinate, entity. Zilliacus writes:

The camera is a registering device, as the voice is not; it also serves to intensify, by degrees, the effect exerted by the voice on the face which it registers. It is both objective and subjective, external and internal. At least in the BBC production Joe keeps this paradox within sight by trying the catch and focus, with his eyes, the voice which he thinks is coming from "that penny farthing hell he calls his mind."[19]

MacGowran does not react to Voice with the kind of shock one would expect from his discovering that he overlooked a "concrete person" in the room, but he does seem to search for it as if for a corporeal being, and in that way his performance builds on the text's ambiguity concerning Voice's source. Again Zilliacus writes, "there is a convention of the medium which tells us that if a camera comes to rest on a silent figure, then an offscreen voice stands for that figure's thoughts. But this time we hear a female voice accompanying the haggard face of a man: the convention is modified."[20] One could also say that the convention is used against itself, as if Beckett wanted to debunk its supposed universal validity.

We must remember that Voice is not necessarily telling the truth about Joe's past; as Gontarski says, she "is not a disinterested narrator" and seems to attack him with a (to her) clear purpose.[21] It's as if she has certain facial reactions in mind that she wants specifically to elicit, and Joe proves a recalcitrant subject. Certainly Voice is a creative agent, but she may or may not be one of Joe's. In performance, the picture on the screen, MacGowran's changing face seen larger and larger, communicates in more profound and compelling ways than any of her words, which, until the final section containing more concrete description than the others, seem important mostly for their music and the effect they have on that face. As Zilliacus reminds us, the play was written for MacGowran, not for Phillips. The picture is like a portrait that is worked by the artist before our eyes, using words as brushes.

Even if Voice is not a creative entity independent of Joe, it is impossible to deny the relevance of portraiture to this play. In focusing his action on a face, Beckett evokes the whole congeries of references and conventions associated with that genre, and they in turn reflect meaning back on his drama. What seems most germane is that, in representational painting, portraiture is said to be the genre closest to a Platonic Ideal because it carries the clearest set of expectations. To illustrate: a portrait can be painted without a nose, but the nose will be present, so to speak, through its obvious absence; whereas no one would ever remark that a given still life was missing, say, its banana, or a given landscape its lake. Thus there is an object-like quality to great portraits, which can reach a kind of Platonic perfection because the human face is such a knowable Form.

Eh Joe was conceived for a face Beckett knew well and loved, a face in which, we may guess, he saw a kind of perfection, an ideal defined exclusively by his art. Instead of merely freezing one or two of MacGowran's expressions to approximate that ideal, however, Beckett used the actual living face with all its vicissitudes in conjunction with the *idea* of facial perfection, and thereby clarified one of his own aesthetic definitions. The camera eventually

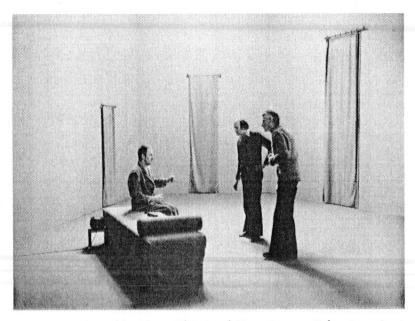

17 Rehearsal for *He Joe* (*Eh Joe*) with Heinz Bennent, Robert James Lewis (cameraman) and Samuel Beckett (director), SDR, Stuttgart, 1979, © Süddeutscher Rundfunk Jehle. (Photo: SDR/Hugo Jehle)

comes so close to MacGowran that we see only a partial view in the final picture – from brow to upper lip – and hence must accept a fragment as a culminating form. Beckett evokes the genre of portraiture only to turn directly around and question its very principle of sublime wholeness. His famous aesthetic of wholeness-in-fragmentariness (which has been associated with the rhetorical figure synechdoche), the way his works often reach completion through an act of withholding, functions in *Eh Joe* as a criticism of received assumptions about framing, not only in portraiture, but also in television drama and by inference all other genres.

To return to the image of Caravaggio's window, one could say that Beckett's window also turns inward, only its casing is even smaller than the painter's.

I don't think impotence has been exploited in the past. There seems to be a kind of esthetic axiom that expression is achievement – must be an achievement. My little exploration is that whole zone of being that has always been set aside by artists as something unusable – as something by definition incompatible with art.

(Beckett to Israel Shenker, 1956)

As many have observed before, however, Beckett achieves despite himself. *Eh Joe,* for instance, is an achievement of largeness in tininess, when one considers the hugeness of what such a long close-up can suggest about the unconscious. Like a miniature painting, the play is to a certain extent *about* the limitations of the viewer's perceptions and the use of instrumentation to augment them. The painter uses a magnifying glass to achieve a degree of detail not possible with the unaided eye, thus creating an impression of perfection, and Beckett uses the television camera to suggest the infinity of Joe's thoughts. And this is the point most often glossed over by those who dismiss the play on the basis of Voice's melodramatic monologue. Why would Beckett have used the camera so intensely, suggesting a portrait-like infinitude in Joe, if the monologue had said all there was to know about him?

The spectator watches MacGowran's every reaction like a voyeur at a keyhole in the hope that a coherent explanation of the nature of Joe's relationship to Voice will eventually arise, but he receives no more satisfaction on that score than one imagines Voice does from attempting to create her *portrait-vivant.* MacGowran listens intently from the beginning and, after searching for Voice with his eyes, briefly raises a finger next to his nose, and then clenches his fists on "penny farthing hell" instead of scowling as one would expect in response to such a direct insult. He continues to avoid immediate, straightforward facial reactions for the rest of the play, finding instead enigmatic gestures that frustrate, as if intentionally, any attempts to "see into" the interaction between him and Voice. His hand goes briefly to his forehead after "Throttling the dead in his head," his head bows down after "Not for the likes of us," and then he starts shaking perceptibly, his first sign of strain. The strain remains generalized, however, as if caused by the ongoing "mounting tension of listening" and not the acute impact of any specific words.

His most prominent shift comes after "If you ever are," when he gathers his coat lapels around his neck, as one does in the cold, and keeps his hand clenched in that position. From this point on he seems more contrite than before, his eyes start to fill, though they never tear, and his pitifulness indeed comes precariously close to sentimentality. Sentimentality is kept from dominating, though, by a number of interesting ambiguities: for instance, the way his clenched lapels provide an immediate visual correlative for "mental thuggee." When Voice says, "That's right, Joe, squeeze away," she seems to refer not only to his effort to strangle her with his mind, but also to his collar and to his eyes, which close tightly several times during the last two sections.

Finally, when Voice stops, his eyes widen and a smile gradually appears (the mouth is visible because his head has bent forward enough to bring it into the camera's eye), which conveys both relief, as if he is sure "voice has relented for the evening," and happiness, as if at some sort of victory. The idea that he has finally succeeded in stifling Voice creates a momentary feeling of disorientation because of the contrast it implies between activity and inactivity. The act of strangling, which was described as a physical one by the non-corporeal Voice, is achieved inside Joe's brain, yet we can see it, so to speak, through his physical act of smiling. Despite that contrast, though, the strangling does not really satisfy as an ending; one feels inclined to ask, what more has he won? Perhaps nothing more or less than we have, the chance to look even more deeply into him(self) than Voice's tirade permitted.

The 1966 SDR *He Joe*, although broadcast three months before the BBC version, was actually made shortly after it.[22] The German production holds the distinction of being the first theatrical event to credit Beckett alone as director, but that credit is somewhat misleading because he had considerable experience assisting other directors before, sometimes to the extent of taking over their rehearsals, and he obviously arrived in Stuttgart with firm ideas about what he wanted. Reinhart Müller-Freienfels, then head of television drama at SDR, had personally invited him (the start of a long and productive relationship between the two), and Beckett's friend, Deryk Mendel, a dancer/choreographer and occasional director, had agreed to play Joe. To be sure, Beckett still had much to learn about the technical practicalities of television, but he had already demonstrated, with radio, a remarkable ability to grasp such knowledge about new media very quickly, and now had the experience of working with Gibson and MacGowran.

Working conditions were indeed "singular." As described in Siegfried Melchinger's *Theater heute* article on the production, Beckett rehearsed the actors for days before the final taping, and was able to achieve a great deal of what he intended. Melchinger asked him afterwards if he had done things very differently from in London, and he answered, "No. But with different actors it will be different."[23] One has only to view both productions, however, to see that much more than acting was changed.

Immediately noticeable in the opening shot is that the room is darker than the BBC set. There is no lamp beside the bed, no contrasting stripe on the blanket, and the walls, dirty as if smudged with charcoal, are lit so dimly that the viewer's depth perception is restricted; even the outline of Mendel's torso on the bed is unclear at first. As Jim Lewis explains in an interview, Beckett uses this darkness habitually in all his Stuttgart productions.

JL: . . . The light is always faint. And I never succeed in making it faint enough for Beckett. We sit there, and we look at the control screen, and he says to me, "Jim, couldn't you reduce the light still a little more?" . . .

SS: *But why is the light always faint in Beckett?*

JL: In most cases, we evoke the past, memory, night and also dreams.[24]

One might add that the faint light also evokes the fact that the character onscreen is living and possesses a soul: "Not another soul to still," taunts Voice. Like the darkness surrounding Caravaggio's figures, Beckett's faint television backgrounds must be clearly distinguished from emptiness. Their darkness implies the inchoate comprehension of the nothingness in which Man (and man) exists, his projection of meaning onto the void, and the SDR environment for this drama achieves that effect better than the BBC's. Offscreen lighting accentuates the interplay of lights and darks, creating a sharp chiaroscuro that grows more and more intense and eventually makes the lighting seem like a volitional force in league with the camera and Voice; and Voice, played by Nancy Illig, whispers the entire text as if next to Joe's ear in a tone much more accusatory than Siân Phillips'.

But we do not learn all this at once. Beckett is very precise in this production about the manner in which the play reveals information. The opening business, for instance, is made into a visual joke: the door hanging stage center is of normal height, but the window and cupboard hangings to the right and left are, respectively, anomalously high and low. Thus the action begins with a drily comic atmosphere; the viewer laughs at Joe when the cupboard aperture is revealed to be far too tiny for a person to pass through. One of the reasons he is funny, however, is that we never see his face until well into Voice's first section, and then only dimly and partially, so we guess from his white hair and slow, careful movements that he is an old man. All the more surprising, then, when we see during Voice's second section a face even younger than MacGowran's, who was himself ten years younger than Joe when he played the part; Joe is in his "late fifties," writes Beckett.

Throughout, Illig speaks more slowly and precisely than Phillips, which is not to say that the latter actress ever gives the feeling of excess or imprecision, but that the former generates a driving, vicious, verbal music that works in counterpoint with the visual information about Joe that the viewer gradually acquires. The SDR version runs twenty-four minutes, compared with the BBC's nineteen, but that is also a result of translation. Beckett revised the play when he translated it into French during the summer of 1965 and incorporated some of those revisions into the BBC script, but Elmar Tophoven, his German translator, incorporated many more into his version, so the SDR script was closer to the French text than the English. The most significant changes in Beckett's French translation have to do with repetition: some nine or ten more of the digging title phrases, "Dis Joe . . . Dis Joe," and echoes of many key words during the final section.

BECKETT'S ENGLISH
Say "Joe" it parts the *lips* . . .
Imagine the hands . . .
The *solitaire* . . .
Against a *stone* . . .
Imagine the *eyes* . . .
Spiritlight . . . (p. 206)

BECKETT'S FRENCH
Dis "Joe", ça desserre les lèvres . . .
Les lèvres . . .
Imagine les mains . . .
Imagine . . .
Le solitaire . . .
Contre une pierre . . .
Une pierre . . .
Imagine les yeux . . .
Les yeux . . .
Clair d'âme . . . (p. 91)

TOPHOVEN'S GERMAN
Sag "Joe", das löst die Lippen . . .
Die Lippen . . .
Stell dir die Hände vor . . .
Stell dir vor . . .
Den Solitär . . .
An einem Stein . . .
Einem Stein . . .
Stell dir die Augen vor . . .
Die Augen . . .
Geisteslicht . . . (p. 63).

Illig's Voice comes to sound like a torturous interrogator, and Mendel comes to look like a cornered spy. He never searches for her with his eyes, as MacGowran did, but rather avoids the camera as long as possible, like O in *Film.* In the pause before "Das Beste kommt noch," his head sinks into his hands, as if in exasperation; this is a very large movement compared with MacGowran's finger next to his nose, but we cannot see enough of his face at this point to interpret the gesture with any certainty. The light has fallen full on him for the first time, but because he is sitting in quarter profile, and because the camera is much farther away than the fifty centimeters specified in the published German script, we still do not see him clearly.[25] As the camera comes closer he continues to use relatively large gestures but they do not take on specific psychological meaning; many of them seem like pure visual play, as when he moves his head in and out of the single light source, creating a dance of shadows.

After "Du kennst diese Drei-Groschenhölle," he leans his chin briefly on his fist, a much more acute reaction to the insult than MacGowran's, and we see approximately half his face for the first time. Only after "In deinem Kopf die Toten töten," however, during the third camera move, do we see his expression in detail: stony, determined, not at all contrite, and not about to become so. One also notices that he is a heavier, stronger man than

MacGowran, with a handsomer face, which adds immediacy to Voice's accusations of womanizing. Mendel plays a very hardened Joe. He closes his collar at one point but does not clench it tightly and even cracks a slight smile afterwards, as if to show Voice that it was not she who made him do it. After "Das ist das Schlimmste," his breathing grows noticeably deeper and he seems for a while to have become guilt-ridden; again, however, we cannot see for sure because during the next two sections he turns away from the camera, giving us only side views of his face. And here Beckett uses his prerogative as author to alter his camera directions and intensify the drama.

In violation of the regular movements in the script, the SDR camera surprises us by moving twenty or thirty centimeters during the pause after "Nicht wie die andere," thus framing the face in the screen from forehead to chin, and leaving the impression that the move is an attempt by the camera to trap the elusive Joe. (Recall the possibility that the camera and Voice are either equivalent or allied.) We now see Mendel's scowl in all its fierce fullness and recognize that he is not beaten but rather more headstrong than ever. There is an animalistic quality to the perfectly level mouth, the short stubble of beard and the beads of perspiration that seem to refuse to run down his cheeks; occasionally his eyes unfocus, and he seems not to be thinking at all in the human sense but rather preparing to pounce. The final two camera moves are barely perceivable, but they do ultimately bring the face close enough that the mouth is excluded from the screen. Thus, we recognize Mendel's final smile – which looks as sinister as it does happy – only from the slow rising of his eyes and the lines beside his nose, until at the last the corners of his mouth creep up past the picture's lower border.

Everything about this SDR production is controlled with a precision that makes the BBC version seem like a rehearsal. Which is not to say that Mendel acts the part any better than MacGowran, whose performance is excellent, but it does seem clear that Beckett used his first chance as sole director to fine-tune every moment with as much exactitude as he could command. During most of the action, the viewer is teased with comedy, sharp light contrasts, and fragmentary views of Joe, so that we are unable to judge the value of what Voice says despite the lapidary tone of her whispering. The camera is clearly in league with Voice, if not a part of her, and so we do not know what visual information to believe either. Like a good suspense writer, Beckett saves the telling information for last, and finds in Mendel a face that surprises still further by implying an evil even beyond what Voice describes. In the end we realize from his sinister smile that, regardless of whether Voice is a part of him, what she says is probably true and perhaps even understates the malevolence of which he is capable.

Ultimately, then, the English and German productions are similar in that, through hearing Voice out, we earn, so to speak, the chance to look deeper into Joe than is possible during her tirade. He shows his cards only after he thinks she's gone, and the dramatic impact of that revelation depends on maintaining the ambiguity of Voice's source; if the viewer is sure from the outset that she comes from Joe's mind, then no verification of her words is necessary, and the play does become "a maudlin account" of self-deprecation. Furthermore, accentuation of this mystery-story quality in production is a matter less of apologizing for an imperfect monologue than of coloring it with an irony which, judging from the author's direction, was probably intended, and which is similar to that found in many other Beckett passages about memory and sexual relationships.

Memories are killing. So you must not think of certain things, of those that are dear to you, or rather you must think of them, for if you don't there is the danger of finding them, in your mind, little by little. That is to say, you must think of them for a while, a good while, every day several times a day, until they sink forever in the mud. That's an order.   ("The Expelled")

Or I might be able to catch one, a little girl for example, and half strangle her, three quarters, until she promises to give me my stick, give me soup, empty my pots, kiss me, fondle me, smile to me, give me my hat, stay with me, follow the hearse weeping into her handkerchief, that would be nice. I am such a good man, at bottom, such a good man, how is it nobody ever noticed it?   (*Malone Dies*)[26]

That this irony is indispensable to the play's effectiveness can be demonstrated by comparing the BBC and SDR versions with the French premiere, in which Beckett was not an active participant.[27]

The French translation, *Dis Joe*, was published even before the English original, but it was not produced in France until two years later, when Michel Mitrani directed it with Jean-Louis Barrault and Madeleine Renaud. It is possible that this 1968 production was influenced by the earlier two, since it seems to borrow some cosmetic details from them: for instance, the dirty walls and the relative sizes of the curtains, which are exaggerated even more than in the SDR set. The production's essence, however, is wholly different. The room is considerably lighter than either the BBC or SDR rooms, and with a general illumination instead of a coherent source near the bed, which contributes to the viewer being immediately distracted by visual minutiae: an empty space between the bed and wall, rumples and folds in the blanket, a gratuitous footstool and long rows of variously shaded parallel planks in a parquet floor. The initial picture is cluttered, not at all focused on Barrault, and it starts the play off with a quality of diffuseness and overfamiliarity.

We see Barrault clearly, face included, during the entire opening business, which he performs quickly and with obvious, exaggerated attitudes. He rushes all at once to the window, leans out as far as he can on tiptoe, then rushes all at once to the door, where he leans out similarly and then closes the hanging with a flourish, pausing a moment afterwards to pose. One wonders briefly whether this style is some sort of Expressionist abstraction of paranoia, but that interpretation is not borne out by the rest of the action, which ultimately reads as an overdone attempt to portray realistic paranoia. In any case, the exaggeration defuses much of the humor in the opening, which is most effectively handled through understatement such as the SDR's tiny cupboard aperture unaccompanied by comment, and it sets a rushed pace for the play in general: the French version runs only fifteen minutes.

When Voice begins, the tone of diffuseness disappears for a while, mostly because Renaud delivers the monologue with a driving, ruthless whisper similar to Illig's, tempering it with tiny rhetorical sashays that seem expertly calculated to disturb Joe with maximum efficiency. Barrault's reactions grow more and more demonstrative, however, until by the end he has undone all the value of Renaud's subtlety. During the first and second sections he communicates a gruff but measured indignation at being disturbed, readjusting his coat and clenching his fists in his lap, but after "Tu sais cet enfer de quatre sous" he releases his grip on his coat with a graceless air of disgust, a larger reaction to the insult than either MacGowran or Mendel made, and the start of a sally of overacting. Teeth clenched, he glares into the distance as if locating Voice in a specific spot, then with wrinkled brow darts his eyes off in another direction. Shortly, Voice seems to penetrate his defenses and he becomes extremely emotional. During the section that begins "L'autre," his eyes visibly water and his expression is utterly contrite (then why hear the rest of the monologue?). And after "Jamais su ce qui s'est passé?" he wraps his arms around his shoulders in self-embrace, lays his head in his arms, and raises it again to reveal a tear in one eye. By the middle of the suicide story, tears are running freely down both sides of his face.

Moreover, Barrault's demonstrativeness is not the only distraction. Perhaps taking his cue from Beckett's SDR production, Mitrani departs severely from the script's camera instructions, adding wide side-to-side arc movements during the nine approaches. In the third section, for example, it is stage left, showing only Barrault's profile, and by the fifth it has traveled to extreme stage right, showing the other profile. Superficially, the effect is comparable to Mendel's side-to-side head movements, but it is far less mysterious because it diminishes the purity of the camera pushing relentlessly inward. This camera is terribly clever, as if it wants to be something of an *artiste*, like Voice, and not merely an interrogator/torturer that may be subordinate to her. It even makes several atextual movements: an extra push closer, to frame only eyes and nose, on "Voilà l'histoire," and a pull back at the very end to reinclude the mouth, which smiles slightly but not nearly as long as in the other two versions. None of Beckett's atextual camera movements at SDR distracts spectators the way Mitrani's do because they serve a purpose within the action and do not call attention to themselves as technical embellishments.

The only real irony in this production is that the play is made to seem undramatic because of a director and actor's efforts to amplify its "drama" (read: sentimentalism). We know who this Joe is, so to speak, almost from the beginning, having seen his room in detail (despite the fact that there was "no need to record [it] as whole"), his well-lit face from various angles before Voice even starts, and his inner attitudes writ large on his external movements from the first walk toward the door curtain. The truth of Voice's words and the fact that they come from inside Joe are taken for granted, and the result is that the monologue becomes the play's center. As even Beckett seems to have noticed, however, the monologue alone is too static to sustain the action; it requires contrast and challenge from the visual image, not immediate corroboration. In the SDR production, the camera is used to make Joe appear inscrutable, thereby creating a worthy adversary for Voice and a dramatic action more complex than her unquestioned words provide.

But Beckett's directing decisions in Eh Joe are not only important for what they teach about focusing that play's action; they also prefigure his creative decisions while refining all the subsequent television works. In an essay comparing the 1976 BBC production of Ghost Trio with the SDR Geistertrio made shortly afterwards, James Knowlson discusses a large number of production changes that, along with the ones I have been describing, establish a clear pattern. To mention only a few of his points: in Geistertrio the actors' costumes were altered to accentuate a visual parallel between F and the Boy, their movements were slower and more puppet-like and, in Knowlson's words, "everything had much more precise lines and angles than in the earlier version, the corridor in particular being narrower and more sharply geometrical."[28] Keeping He Joe in mind, one might add: the scene in general was darker; the German voice was gentler and more whispered than the English one; much care was taken to hide F's face from the camera except for the two views designated in the script, and his final smile was happier and thus more surprising than the one in the BBC production.

All of which is to say that Beckett refined Ghost Trio along similar lines not only to Eh Joe but also to all his other SDR productions. Generally speaking, his last minute adjustments result in increased focus on the central figure or figures (through point sources of light and dim surroundings), and in a more precisely controlled action, conducted as if it were music, which maximizes the dramatic impact of the increasing detail. In . . . nur noch Gewölk . . ., for instance, the 1977 German version of . . . but the clouds . . ., the basic shot of M bent over the table, which was already hard to recognize as a human figure in the BBC version, is enlarged even further so that it appears only as an obscure shape; one sees it initially as an abstract composition and only

18 Helfrid Foron, Jürg Hummel, Claudia Knupfer and Susanne Rehe in *Quadrat (Quad)*, directed by Samuel Beckett, SDR, Stuttgart, 1981, © Süddeutscher Rundfunk Jehle. (Photo: SDR/Hugo Jehle)

gradually comes to read it as a partial view of a man after the camera returns to it fifteen times. Similarly, during the 1981 filming of *Quadrat* (the German title for *Quad*), a routine check of the performance on a black-and-white monitor sparked the idea for *Quad II*, which consists of one cycle of the *Quad I* action done much slower, without color, and with footsteps as the only sound. The effect is to magnify the action already seen and make us "look again," as we must at Joe's face, at the rectangular parts of F's chamber, and at the distorted close-up of M.

In each case we are shown a fragment and eventually led to consider it as a whole, which then leads us to reconsider all that has come before in light of the new idea of wholeness. This pattern of action is both a basic formal structure for all the television works and also, somehow, a partial explanation of their extraordinary power. Esslin writes:

The impact of *Eh Joe* essentially depends on the fact that television is an intimate medium, which, with its small screen, puts the spectator into intimate contact with a face that is on the same scale (close-up) as other faces in the room . . . It is almost impossible to find, in the vast literature of television drama, another play which is as totally conceived in terms of the small television screen and its intimate psychology as *Eh Joe*.[29]

What he says about close-ups was also said long ago about portraits, though; it is true – really another example of Beckett applying old artistic theory in modern circumstances – but does not satisfy as an explanation. The impact of the television plays (as Esslin acknowledges in a later article, "A Poetry of Moving Images") is a result not just of the size of the images but also of the fact that they are much more carefully constructed than those we have come to expect in this medium, a comment intended not to pay Beckett a niggardly compliment but to point up a truth about audiences.

The works startle for the same reason Robert Wilson's stage productions do: because the author/director makes every framed moment answer to impeccable standards of precision like those we expect in painting – which is even more surprising in television than in theater because TV studio time is so expensive. Beckett differs from Wilson, though, in the same way Caravaggio did from most of his sixteenth-century contemporaries: the window, or camera lens, turns inward on particular psychologies rather than outward on epic panoramas. Beckett's interiority provides all the spectacle necessary to hold audience interest, especially when he accentuates it in his directing through specificity, repetition and enlarging. Unlike Wilson, and like Caravaggio, he has both remarkable insight into the psychology of his characters and a visual artist's skill at communicating that understanding in graphic terms.

I once heard John Calder say that Beckett could have been a great painter had he chosen that discipline, and I thought the comment somewhat blithe until I saw these Stuttgart productions. It is self-evident that they are the work of a gifted visual artist, displaying with pictures the same punctilious craftsmanship and idiosyncratic accents Beckett always used with words. Having all but revolutionalized the drama, in his seventh decade Beckett found in television a medium that perhaps suits his temperament and talents best of all.[30] The pinnacle of linguistic economy is to tell a story through pictures, and the ultimate directorial control is to freeze the perfect performance forever, like an icon.

7   The gamble of staging prose fiction

Beckett never set out to be a dramatist, he tells us. He says he originally turned to the theater because he needed a break from the novels, which he still considers his most significant writing. Regardless of what one may think of that judgment, it does seem clear that his prose fiction comprises a body of work that would distinguish him as a master even without his plays. The point is of course moot because his prose fiction is no longer perceivable entirely apart from his drama, which has had much greater circulation and has directed attention back to the novels and stories. Georg Hensel writes:

Without the theater Samuel Beckett would be a rather unknown writer. Before 1953, before the worldwide success of *Waiting for Godot*, his novels were barely read, and today they are still an esoteric matter for a small circle. Beckett's step onto the stage was also a step into popularity: one doesn't read him; one sees him in the theater.[1]

There is a kind of frustrating irony, then, in the fact that Beckett's theatrical success has caused scores of theater practitioners to seek out his non-dramatic work only to read it *in terms of* his dramas. Despite the author's repeated statements exhorting faithfulness to genre, almost every one of his published fictional texts has at some point been adapted for the stage.

The causes of this trend are various, but surely one of the weightier ones is that Beckett – through no choice of his own a spiritual patriarch of the contemporary avant-garde – has not written a "full-length" play since 1961. Thus, avant-gardists looking to him to feed their insatiable hunger for the New have had either to wait for the appearance of the short, late works (which, as already discussed, contain highly restrictive stage directions and must be grouped together in sets of two or three to make economically viable evenings) or to construct new scripts themselves out of whatever else he publishes. These new scripts often seem to be manufactured from a standpoint of petulant defensiveness about Beckett's greatness as a playwright, as if their purpose were to convert some hypothetical group of unbelievers by saying, "Look, even his prose fiction is theatrical!" As we shall see, though, this statement is not necessarily wrong just because it is made petulantly, nor are the productions always ineffective even when they are done without Beckett's endorsement.

As he stated explicitly in a 1957 letter to Barney Rosset, Beckett does not like the idea of cross-genre performance: "If we can't keep our genres more or less distinct, or extricate them from the confusion that has them where they are, we might as well go home and lie down."[2] He has very specific visions, while writing, about how his works are to function as imaginative stimuli – recall his comment to me, mentioned in chapter 5, about visualizing dramas on his "mental stage" – and those visions are necessarily genre-specific. In contrast to his unflagging condemnation of concept productions of his plays, however, he has become more and more tolerant of prose adaptation over the years. Indeed, in 1962 he himself helped direct the one-man Jack MacGowran production, *End of Day*, and later assisted in revising that show into *Beginning to End*, which became the impetus for the trend of cross-genre works.[3] In 1965, he assisted Shivaun O'Casey with her production of *From an Abandoned Work*, and in 1985 he approved a request from the Gate Theatre of Dublin to develop a one-man show based on *Molloy*, *Malone Dies* and *The Unnamable*; that production was eventually titled *I'll Go On* and performed by the actor Barry McGovern to great acclaim on several continents. In subsequent years Beckett has remained open to other suggestions as long as they are brought to him before a production is mounted. Ruby Cohn quotes this 1978 letter to an Irish actor:

Had you asked me in the first place – as you should have done – for permission to do this "hodge-podge," I would have refused, as you no doubt surmised at the time. Now you ask me to bow before the "fait accompli"! Ah well, go ahead. Yours, Sam Beckett.[4]

Beckett's practice of granting permissions personally on a case-by-case basis has had some unfortunate consequences, however: e.g. the refusal of rights to directors who do not have access to him or who want to develop their work in the course of rehearsals, and a resultant abundance of unauthorized productions. Of course, one cannot but respect Beckett's right to administer his works as he sees fit, but the truth is that no consistent correspondence exists between authorial permission and quality or effectiveness of performance, at least in the dozen-odd cross-genre adaptations I have seen. Like concept productions of the plays, these adaptations exist, for better or worse. And much more interesting than the question of permission is the question of why this author's prose fiction should have inspired so many original and provocative theater events.

It is important to remember that these adaptations are not Beckett plays. The texts were not originally conceived as theater, and any dramatic life they come to have is given them by the adapters. They do not necessarily even aim at achieving effects similar to those of Beckett's dramas, though they sometimes do, and in that sense consideration of them is peripheral to a discussion of his theater. It would nevertheless be naive to overlook the fact that any director or actor inspired by the prose fiction has almost surely been inspired by the drama, too, which was certainly true of MacGowran. MacGowran had already seen numerous Beckett productions and played in five by the time he prepared *End of Day*, and he stated later that one of his purposes was to "correct the seriousness with which [Beckett was] taken" in most play productions.[5]

In other ways, though, *End of Day* and *Beginning to End* were atypical of the tradition they inaugurated. Instead of focusing on a single work, MacGowran developed what he called "a composite character of the intellectual tramp" who spoke selected texts from plays, poems, novels and stories, slipping seamlessly from one to another as if delivering a single soliloquy. It did not disturb spectators, even those familiar with the prose works, when a section from, say, *Malone Dies* was performed standing up and not from Malone's bed, because no text was used that mentioned the character's location. Nor did it disturb them when a passage from, say, *Embers* was recited under full stage light, since nothing in the words revealed that their source was a radio play. MacGowran created a strong, singular personality and used *it* as his production's through-line, adapting all passages to it without worrying overmuch about attitudes and physical circumstances in the original fictions – which provided him with a very sturdy, effective structure that Beckett subsequently helped refine.

That structure, however, could not possibly be of any help to directors such as E. T. Kirby, who staged *Molloy* in 1969, or Joseph Dunn, who mounted *The Unnamable* in 1972.[6] In choosing to stage a single work of prose fiction, a director saddles himself with the problem of how to dramatize events in that work, which may often take place in the mind and not be easily articulable in other terms. The action, to borrow a word from drama, in Beckett's novels is only occasionally organized into linear plots with consistent, identifiable characters, and even then it is often hypothetical, i.e. the product of a narrator's musings. Frequently, the narrators themselves lack conventionally fixed identities, because the plots consist in their imagining themselves into diverse identities through the exercise of storytelling. Thus, the director's task becomes doubly difficult, involving the risk both of illustration, which is invariably disappointing compared with what the reader's imagination could provide, and of simplification, the choice to put some things onstage in lieu of others itself constituting a decision about priority of events, which is exactly the kind of choice Beckett's narrators are reluctant to make.

One might generalize about the task as follows. For the faithful, the main question in adaptation is: how much of an anecdote can be suggested through mimesis of selected events before the performance begins seriously to distort Beckett's aesthetic by explaining his text's ambiguities? And for the unfaithful, who take mimesis for granted, it is: how can those events which do make good logical sense be extracted and tied together into a story the audience can follow? That is at least how the situation appears theoretically. In reality, however, very few adapters fit neatly into either camp. Most of them enter rehearsals with something of both attitudes, an ambivalent blend of faith and faithlessness born perhaps of uncertainty about whether it is feelings of love or competition in regard to Beckett's work that drive them.

Frederick Neumann, who has staged *Mercier and Camier* (1978), *Company* (1983), *Worstward Ho* (1986), and has plans for other stage adaptations, has known Beckett for almost forty years, which means that their acquaintance predates Neumann's working relationships with Lee Breuer, Warrilow, Akalaitis and the others who eventually formed Mabou Mines. Partly because of this old friendship, Neumann has several times received permission to adapt where others had been repeatedly denied. Though he too has been turned down on at least one occasion – after a request to stage *More Pricks Than Kicks*, Beckett wrote, "Dear Fred, Please leave the poor little thing alone" – in general he seems able to count on a receptive ear.[7] Neumann is a particularly respectful adapter from a textual viewpoint because he tries to avoid cuts and changes whenever possible. The price of that respect is sometimes theatricality, however, as the example of *Company* demonstrates.

Company, the entire eighty-nine pages of which Neumann memorized, is about and/or by a character "on his back in the dark" whose solitude is disturbed by a "voice." This "voice" discusses the relative merits of different types of "company" and tells anecdotes about boyhood, manhood and old age – "company" meaning anything that interrupts nothingness, even an itch, a hand movement or a memory. But whose is this voice, and does it even belong to anyone in the various anecdotes? Such questions, as might be expected, are never answered for certain. One reads of a character on his back in the dark, alone, and at first assumes that the "voice" is his, as the Unnamable says about his "voice that is not mine, but can only be mine, since there is no one but me."[8] After a short time, however, the pronoun used for this character switches person, and then switches again, for reasons the text makes a fleeting effort to explain. "Use of the second person marks the voice. That of the third that cankerous other. Could he speak to and of whom the voice speaks there would be a first. But he cannot. He shall not. You cannot. You shall not" (p. 8).[9]

This designation for the second person seems perfectly clear – the appearance of the word "You" means that the "voice" is speaking to the character, "He," who for some reason cannot be called "I" – but we never entirely believe it. We are told nothing definite about the "voice's" source, and continue to suspect that it comes from the character himself, who is presumably singular and using the language-play to keep himself company. The narrative technique is similar to that in *The Unnamable*, with important differences. In *The Unnamable* the narrator periodically professes indifference to point of view, giving the numerous pronoun switches an appearance of arbitrariness.

> But enough of this cursed first person, it is really too red a herring, I'll get out of my depth if I'm not careful. But what then is the subject? Mahood? No, not yet. Worm? Even less. Bah, any old pronoun will do, provided one sees through it. Matter of habit. To be adjusted later. Where was I?

> Who, we? Don't all speak at once, there's no sense in that either. All will come right, later on in the evening, everyone gone and silence restored. In the meantime no sense in bickering about pronouns and other parts of blather. The subject doesn't matter, there is none.[10]

In *Company*, however, the pronoun switches always seem connected to specific secondary intentions. While reading, one never entirely rids oneself of the impression that the singular character/voice is Beckett, at least in his narrative persona, and that "You" refers to the reader as much as to the character. It's as if a major portion of the book were written imperatively in order to intensify the reader's imaginative entry into the narrated world, an effect all but destroyed when one represents the narrator onstage and suggests that the "You" is him. In the prose, the narrator remains obscure, his singularity undecided.

In his interview with me, included in part three, Neumann quoted a brief exchange from his pre-production discussions with Beckett, and I interpret the exchange as an indication of the author's concern about just this issue.

> "I don't know, Fred, what you could do with it. It all takes place in the dark."
> "Like the theater, in the dark."
> "Touché."

Beckett concedes the point in this conversation as reported by Neumann, but one senses behind his initial objection an acute sensitivity to the fact that imagined darkness can be filled with a plurality of indeterminate visions, whereas actual theatrical darkness is broken only by one perspicuous vision at a time. This is exactly the problem most adapters fail to solve, and though Neumann's performance is manifestly intelligent, at times demonstrating a sophisticated understanding of the Beckett text, he too ultimately fails to solve it. In fact, he seems to proceed on the assumption that it is a given limitation, necessarily insoluble, and in that sense his *Company* is typical of the large subset of adaptations that have fallen victim to their creator's respectfulness, their attempts to meet Beckett halfway by keeping theatrical ingenuity to a minimum.

The stage is furnished with two dilapidated rocking chairs that face each other with a small table and lamp in between.[11] At the rear of the stage are three white, ten-foot parabolic disks, which look like radar transmitters, facing right and slightly upward. As the piece begins the disks turn to face the stage, creating a section of a dome, which is described later as the character's location: "Suggesting one lying on the floor of a hemispherical chamber of generous diameter with ear dead centre" (p. 32). The disks are illuminated in a putrid green color that is broken by blotches of darkness recalling trees (the hemisphere as "dark cope of sky"); in the performance's more contemplative moments they recall a human brain (the hemisphere as platelets of a skull). The lights dim, Neumann enters, dressed only in an old gray greatcoat and heavy boots (this costume almost identical to the one MacGowran used in *Beginning to End*), and sits in one of the chairs.

When the light rises he is reclining with legs stretched out toward the audience. He starts his monologue, but instead of addressing the empty chair across from him, as one expects, he speaks in no particular direction. Suddenly he says, "Quick leave him," the stage blackens, and he switches chairs. He speaks again to the air from that side, reclining as before, only this time the rising light casts his huge shadow onto one of the disks, as if that shadow could be an "other," another creature capable of keeping him company. The switch makes the audience wonder, for a time, if the actor is now another person, and thus begins the performance's amalgamation of the text's diverse indeterminacies into a series of hints that the character is not really alone.

These hints are organized into a three-part structure, moving from a total pretense of separateness, to a whimsical participation in anecdote, to a final resignation about being the narrative's object: from total disregard, to selective regard, to total regard for the narrative's directions. In other words, Neumann adopts three different attitudes toward the anecdotes he speaks, which could be seen to correspond to the three viewpoints in the written narrative, childhood, adulthood and old age – the same tripartite view found in *That Time*.

At first, he is somewhat abstracted, speaking in a strange, detached mode which one assumes is related to the pretense of separateness maintained by his tableau of shadow, man and empty chair, and to Beckett's "voice's" pretense of having a source apart from the character. Shortly, he changes his tone of voice to one of clarified purpose, speaking animatedly as if trying hard to entertain himself, which seems to correspond to the end of the pretense, all but declared by Beckett about halfway through.

Deviser of the voice and of its hearer and of himself. Deviser of himself for company. Leave it at that. He speaks of himself as of another. He says speaking of himself, He speaks of himself as of another. Himself he devises too for company. Leave it at that.

(p. 26)

During this section, the table and chairs are removed and Neumann's character entertains himself by *not* acting out his anecdotes event by event. Like Speaker in *A Piece of Monologue*, he acts out what he is saying partially or incorrectly, or acts in complete contradiction to his words: for instance during the line, "A dead rat. What an addition to company that would be! A rat long dead," he chases an imaginary rodent across the floor, swatting at it with a cane. Finally his actions begin to follow the words more precisely. He kneels on all fours during a description of crawling, moves his cane around in circles during a description of the second hand on a watch, and ultimately, resolving the obvious contradiction that has existed all along, lies down, on his back in the dark.

The only trouble with this tripartite structure is that it never grows prominent enough in performance to become a significant experience for spectators. The most forceful element remains Neumann's character's personality, which binds all three attitudes together. Unfortunately, spectators do not tend to ask general questions about truth and falsehood in the text, as do readers, but rather topical questions about the nature of the flesh-and-blood character in front of them. What kind of person could have had experiences like those described in the anecdotes? What kind of person spends time speaking to himself of events in his past as if he were telling stories to someone who had never heard them before? These questions are not so much irrelevant as insufficient. Neumann succeeds in creating a clear impression of a reflective old man who finds as much joy in the complexities of his own mind as in his experiences of the external world, but he fails to convey that that identity is somehow precarious.

Ironically, despite his careful avoidance of mimicry in the anecdotes, his performance ends up consisting almost entirely of mimesis; for his approach is to posit a singular persona and then reproduce it onstage. His only attempt to mitigate that conventionality is occasionally to bark out the slightly pugnacious phrase, "Quick leave him," whenever it recurs, but this turns out to have the opposite effect in the theater to the book. Instead of jolting us into a reality, or a present action, outside the story of the narrator/character's musings, the phrase causes us to reflect on whether we want to be bossed around by the man Neumann is playing. (A problem that almost never occurs in reading Beckett's novels or stories; for one invariably comes to feel affection for his wilful narrators, not as men in the world, but as collections of attitudes understandable only in terms of their provisional, metaphorical circumstances.) Neumann would doubtless have had more success emphasizing some other short phrase that took attention away from his person and focused it on the imagination – for instance, "From nought anew," which is also repeated plangently, as if to remind readers of their and the narrator's continual attempts to make something from nothing.

When *Company* first opened in 1982, many critics, including myself,

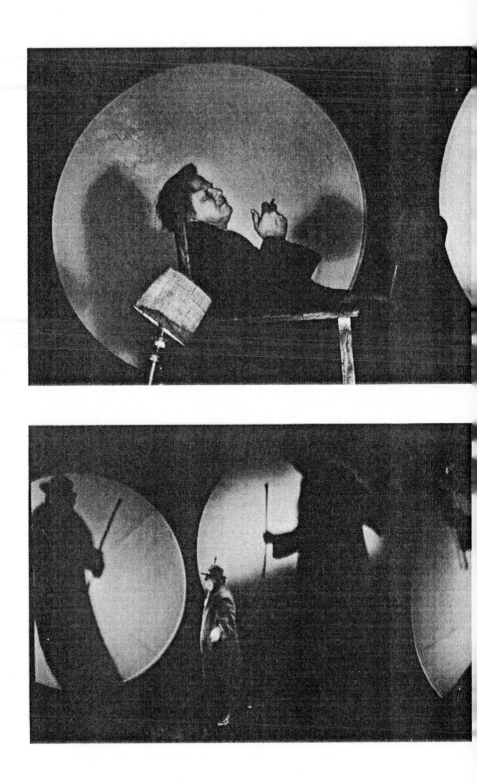

attributed its problems mostly to the complicated syntax in Beckett's prose fiction. And it has become standard practice among reviewers of adaptations to point out the difficulty of understanding any of Beckett's narratives quickly and completely enough when they are recited in performance. Discerning the sense of a sentence like this one, for example – "What with what feeling remains does he feel about now as compared to then?" (p. 22) – depends on perceiving the need for pauses, or imaginary commas, after "What" and "remains," and on recognizing "feel about" as the verb. Such recognition might take readers one or two rereadings, but theater spectators don't have that chance; even if they remembered the line, they might miss three or four others while stopping to mull it over.

This is an important objection, but the fact is, Beckett hasn't always made such clear distinctions between the way language functions in his dramatic and non-dramatic works. His oeuvre is replete with examples of what Gontarski calls "generic androgyny," texts that became dramas extremely late in composition and "could easily have become [works] of prose fiction."[12] One could say that, in general, Beckett tries to use complete, easily speakable sentences in the dramas, so that spectators may contemplate the stage activity as well as the language, but in some plays, such as *That Time* and *A Piece of Monologue*, stage activity is almost non-existent, language is clearly the "star," and its syntax is just as complicated as in most of the novels and stories. It is too simple, in other words, to claim that the dramas are built on a principle of ready accessibility lacking in the prose fiction. The only reliable difference I perceive is that Beckett often compensates for the complicated syntax in his drama through various kinds of repetition. He seems to do this sometimes for musical purposes (the repetitions often become incantatory), sometimes to emphasize key meanings (recall the recurring phrase, "There are no more" in *Endgame*), and sometimes to give audiences another chance to understand his plot (e.g. the da capo in *Play*).

A director aware of the need, however, can supply some of these effects himself, and after seeing other adaptations, including Neumann's *Worst-word Ho*, whose weaknesses were similar to *Company*'s, I have become convinced that the problems of language-accessibility thought to be associated with the prose fiction can be solved, or at least reduced to secondary importance. *Company*'s tediousness was a result of its conceptualization as theater: by making the narrator into a singular, identifiable man, Neumann gambled that the audience would like him enough to listen to his thoughts for an hour and three-quarters.[13] As others have shown, the text invariably

19 and 20 Frederick Neumann in the Mabou Mines production of *Company*, directed by Frederick Neumann and Honora Fergusson, Public Theater, NYC, 1983. (Photo: Susan Schwartzenberg)

becomes easier to listen to when a one-man performance is not dominated only by personality. Gerald Thomas' 1984 production of *All Strange Away* provides a good example of how audience attention can be distributed between a character and his environment when the director allows himself more latitude in the staging concept.

Thomas is a Brazilian/Englishman whose work is not widely known in the United States; he is reportedly fairly prominent in Brazil and has also worked in the United Kingdom. Like Neumann, Thomas has met Beckett and claims to have adapted with his permission.[14] Especially with the dramas, he is not one of Beckett's most textually faithful directors – he told me in an interview that one must take a "casual" attitude regarding stage directions ("The director has to be given authority even by Beckett") – but he is a well-educated man who does not make alterations lightly. And, in fact, *All Strange Away* was ultimately performed intact as published, except for one two-page cut in the "grey punctured rubber ball" section.[15]

To anyone who knows the text, the very idea of adapting *All Strange Away* for the stage must seem quixotic. Even among Beckett's late prose fiction, it would be difficult to find another work more inaccessible and forbidding than this twenty-six page monologue by a speaker whose habit is to imagine things, then retract them with little self-admonitory phrases: "Light out, long dark, candle and matches, imagine them . . . No candle, no matches, no need, never were" (p. 41).[16] As with many of the later texts where Beckett does his best to avoid punctuation, just reading *All Strange Away* for its sense can be hard work, and there are some passages, especially toward the end, that defy such effort altogether. Inasmuch as its story can be summarized, though, it goes as follows.

The narrator begins with the self-canceling statement, "Imagination dead imagine," whose gallows humor is typical of Beckett in that it communicates a measure of hopefulness merely by mentioning a human faculty, but after several pages it becomes clear that this narrator may not value such hopefulness and may in fact desire the ultimate nothingness of "imagination dead." Failing that blissful void, however, which may or may not arrive in the end, he contents himself with describing a specific person in a specific place, a character who talks to himself "in the last person," often with "no sound," whose location and physical characteristics change at the speaker's whim, and for whom "Fancy is his only hope."[17] The reader of course suspects that the character is the speaker but, as in *Company*, is never told for sure. To begin with, at least, the character is a man described in one sentence as dressed in a black shroud which, two sentences later, "hangs off of him in black flitters," and the place is a plain cube, "Five foot square, six high, no way in, none out," with a stool in it (pp. 41, 39).

At one point, the intermittent light in this cube, which has "no visible source," is said to make "all six planes hot when shining" (p. 43). And at another point, erotic images of a woman ("Emma"), or rather parts of her, appear on the four walls: "First face alone, lovely beyond words, leave it at that, then deasil breasts alone, then thighs and cunt alone, then arse and hole alone" (p. 43). The narrator never remains satisfied with any of these descriptions, however, and repeatedly changes them. As if driven by some demon, he decreases the dimensions of the cube, decreases them again, changes the place into a hemispherical chamber, and then alters the dimensions of that, following each change with a detailed description of the physical consequences of it for the figure within.

And, further, about a third of the way through the character changes to a woman, Emma herself, and all personal pronouns switch to "she." Emma is described lying on one side, then the other, murmuring audibly and then inaudibly in this mutable rotunda, with "Fancy" as "her only hope," unless "Fancy dead." In the end we read of the "slip of [her] left hand down slope of right upper arm" (p. 64) and suspect that she has died, except that the text has several times suggested that the entire action may be post-death anyway (e.g. "murmurs sometimes as great a space apart as from on earth a winter to a summer day", p. 50, or "lashes burning down . . . like say without hesitation hell", p. 56). And far from clarifying this point, the final words are as self-canceling as the opening ones: "fancy murmured dead."

As John Pilling explains, *All Strange Away* is unusually scattered because it is the text in which Beckett first worked out the style and range of subjects for much of his later prose fiction. Though not published until 1976, it was actually written in 1963/64 and, in Pilling's words, "contains in embryo almost all the elements from which Beckett was to construct" *Imagination Dead Imagine, Lessness, Ping* and *The Lost Ones*.[18] Thus, it is a mark of Thomas' acuity as a reader that he was even able to recognize one thematic movement in *All Strange Away* that could sustain amplification and thereby become useful as a primary present action in performance. Obviously uninterested in approximating the multiform nature of the reader's experience, he concentrates on a few facets of it that serve him in his intention to make a self-consistent performance with its own *theatrical* integrity.

The production begins with a live voice speaking in darkness, and the lights remain off even through the words "when the light comes on." Only on "Now he is here" do we see the set: a glass cube about ten feet to a side, with a silver-gray floor and no top, situated diagonally so that one corner is upstage center; to begin with, the front two walls are transparent, the back two black. Inside, sitting on a child-size stool, is the actor, Robert Langdon-Lloyd, dressed in a tattered, beige pajama-like outfit, and gesticulating like an ingenuous child trying to imagine each word into physical existence as he speaks it. The way the character is obviously trapped by the cube, making febrile attempts to stimulate his brain through descriptive monologue, recalls the phrase "art of incarceration" that Beckett once used in relation to Bram Van Velde's painting.[19] Needless to say, his space never does transform into a hemisphere, and he never does change into a woman. The illusion of his aloneness is soon broken, though, by a low, throaty voice from overhead, which sounds like a technically distorted version of Langdon-Lloyd's, and which continues to interrupt him throughout the performance.

Questions about this Voice-over immediately assert themselves: who is it and what is its relationship to the onstage character? Why does it speak only at some points and not at others? At first one expects a dialogue to develop because Langdon-Lloyd reacts to it, sometimes even obeying its directions. His reactions, however, never build a sense of conversational exchange, no relationship is ever established between two distinct characters, and sometimes he even addresses his words to the floor, in the opposite direction to the Voice-over, as if trying to communicate with some third party down there. Thus, the interchanges ultimately make sense only as communications between a man and some submerged aspect of himself (conscience, unconscious, etc.), or between that man and his personal God: two different possibilities that the performance suggests may be rough equivalents.

In succeeding sections, separated by blackouts, first one and then the other rear wall of the cube are revealed to be mirrors, so that the scene is eventually dominated by a *mise en abîme*, regressing virtual images of the set and actor continuing upstage to infinity – the implication being that the character can see only himself and thus can probably imagine only himself as an "other." And another blackout near the end ushers in a still more startling change: blue light rises to reveal an old man in demoniacal Kabuki make-up, bent over a tiny glass cube (about one foot to a side), speaking in the same deep tone as the Voice-over. It is a bird's-eye view of the previous action, suggesting similarity between two levels of being. As Beckett writes in *Watt*, we may sometimes observe the unknowable by comparing it with the knowable:

For the only way one can speak of nothing is to speak of it as though it were something, just as the only way one can speak of God is to speak of him as though he were a man, which to be sure he was, in a sense, for a time, and as the only way one can speak of man, even our anthropologists have realised that, is to speak of him as though he were a termite.[20]

One had to experience this production in the theater in order to comprehend fully how the changes in the set affected spectators' perceptions of the character inside, how one came eventually to see the environment as part of the character, a metaphor for his consciousness, and so looked to *it* for information about his inner state. The spectator can be both outside and

21 Setting for *All Strange Away*, directed by Gerald Thomas, Samuel Beckett Theatre, NYC, 1984. (Photo: Andrzej Dudzinski)

inside the character simultaneously, a dramatic approximation of the story's shifting points of view, and that double perspective is what most distinguishes this performance from Neumann's. For it is true, up to a point, that both productions make use of a conventional mimetic structure; each posits a singular personality and then creates a live psychological portrait of it.

In *All Strange Away* this portrait is of a man who derives inordinate comfort from the act of description: the more completely he can describe an imaginary scene, the more he knows it and the less "strange" it is. (Langdon-Lloyd delivers the title phrase like an incantation intended to spirit away everything unfamiliar: "All strange away-y-y!") But every time he approaches this ideal state, either he or the Voice-over disturbs it by altering the configuration of his imagined world and forcing him to scramble to revise his description. Thus he himself repeatedly undermines his professed goal of "Fancy dead"; though initially annoyed by the changes, he shortly comes to enjoy each new descriptive task. This aspect of Langdon-Lloyd's performance is not much different from Neumann's reflective old man. The originality of *All Strange Away* rather consists in the degree to which it succeeds in subordinating this personality to questions about point of view, so that spectators are discouraged from conventional ways of experiencing the action.

The only means of understanding this personality is in terms of its environment. The frustrations, pleasures, physical sensations, etc., which the environment causes turn out to be markedly similar to the ones the character visits upon himself, and before long the audience realizes the equivalence of the two forces and becomes as interested in the cube, the mirrors and the lighting as in Langdon-Lloyd. It is a kind of *Verfremdungseffekt* that leads us to think about why the character has this particular personality, this obsession with description, while we contemplate the descriptions themselves. Attention is lifted off the actor's mimesis – which exists on two levels: his exemplification of a certain personality and his occasional efforts to act out what he says – and shifted onto a more engaging present action that explores why such an impulse toward mimesis ought to exist at all.

As the mirrors are revealed one by one and the images of the cube multiply, Thomas seems to be saying that imitation is less a conscious choice than an ontological condition, it being impossible to identify some actions as authentic and all others as imitations. And the final scene suggests that this may also be a metaphysical condition. To use Esslin's phrase for the television dramas, the *mise en abîme* functions as "visual poetry," constituting a simple, economical expression of a highly complex irony: the character's attempt to escape confinement through the infinity invented by his imagination produces endless images of himself. Infinitude and incarceration amount to the same thing. And yet, in the final Beckettian twist, his mind nevertheless insists that some thoughts can be "strange," unfamiliar, and preserves its sanity through those invented variations, all the while, of course, claiming to wish "all strange away-y-y." Thus the creative impulse itself, "the obligation to express," suffices as a reason to "go on."

All this may sound a bit complicated for a theatrical performance to communicate, but it is actually very clear until near the end. There are a few places where Thomas' devices are too clever and escape the audience – such as dimming the stage lights whenever the character blinks – but his main, deceptively simple idea with the mirrors is easily correlated in the spectator's imagination with the narrator's plural identity, which the text constantly reiterates.[21] Only in the last section does some confusion arise, because the two levels of being presented are similar but not equivalent. One is disturbed not so much by their age difference as by the fact that the old man is a demon, which implies, with very un-Beckettian buoyancy, that Langdon-Lloyd's character (read "Man") is superior to his deity for being more compassionate and humane.

Nevertheless, one hastens to add that a certain general, underlying buoyancy may be partly responsible for the popular success of *All Strange Away*. Literary critics remind us frequently that Beckett's entire oeuvre is characterized by duality – his negativity always stands tongue-in-cheek alongside a certain celebration of isolation – but that duality is not just a matter of themes and motifs. Directors such as Thomas have long recognized it as the key to the accessibility of Beckett in the theater. If "art is the apotheosis of solitude" (*Proust*), then it is not sufficient simply to stage the solitude, as did Neumann in both *Company* and *Worstward Ho*, Liz Diamond in her 1985 *Fizzles* at P.S. 122 in New York City, and many other directors. Apotheosis depends on what one does with the given fact of isolation. As Stanley Kauffmann wrote in his review of *Beginning to End*, "both Beckett and MacGowran know that there is only so much nothingness that the human mind can face in two hours – two hours of the theater, at any rate."[22] And one could see the author's comments about Van Velde in this context; in an "art of incarceration" the creative object is the mimesis of itself and of the mimetic impulse:

An unveiling without end, veil behind veil, level upon level of imperfect transparencies, an unveiling toward the un-unveilable, the nothing, the thing again. And the entombment in the unique, in a place of impenetrable proximities, cell painted on the stone of the cell . . .[23]

This could almost be a literal description of the vision Thomas presents. Despite the fact that his directorial decisions give priority to certain events and viewpoints, the performance is not disappointing, even for those already familiar with the text; for the theatrical experience itself feels complete and thoroughly in sympathy with Beckett's aesthetic.

If I say, then, that it is possible to go still further than this, to create an adaptation that shows more than sympathy with the author's aesthetic but that actually approximates the audience/stage transaction in his plays, I intend no dispraise of *All Strange Away*. There was one stage adaptation, however, which involved spectators in the depicted metaphor so strongly that in retrospect it makes Thomas' mirrored cell seem like an altered box-set. *The Lost Ones*, originally staged by Lee Breuer in 1974 and undoubtedly the most famous cross-genre performance, succeeded both in depicting a type of artistic "incarceration" and in generating an experience of such incarceration in spectators.[24]

The Lost Ones was not even originally intended as an adaptation. Unlike the other directors discussed in this chapter, Breuer did not know Beckett when he began his work (although David Warrilow, the main actor, did), and no discussions about permission were thought necessary at the time. As Warrilow explains in his interview in part three, they had "intended to do a staged reading, but in three weeks of rehearsal it turned into a performance." The story of Beckett's subsequent reaction is told differently by different people, but most agree that he eventually arrived at a toleration of the production, which he says he did not see.[25] In any case, no one challenges the fact that *The Lost Ones* was an enormous and utterly unforeseen international success, both critical and popular, and has since become a kind of avant-garde legend.

By far the most accessible of the three texts discussed in this chapter, *The Lost Ones* is a relatively straightforward tale told by a third-person omniscient narrator whose identity is not subject to whimsical shifts. The fifty-six page story takes place in a cylinder, "fifty metres round and sixteen high for the sake of harmony" and constructed "of solid rubber or suchlike," where some two hundred "lost bodies roam each searching for its lost one" (pp. 7, 8).[26] The general atmosphere in this cylinder is agitated, not only because of the constant emotional tension of searching but also because the light and temperature fluctuate every few seconds between extremes of high and low, accompanied by a shrill sound described as "a faint stridulence as of insects" (p. 38). Brief respites from this environmental throbbing come in irregular intervals, but these "momentary lull[s]" are so infrequent that the inhabitants forget them and are stunned whenever the next one arrives.

The effect of this climate on the soul is not to be underestimated. But it suffers certainly less than the skin whose entire defensive system from sweat to goose bumps is under constant stress. It continues none the less feebly to resist and indeed honourably compared to the eye which with the best will in the world it is difficult not to consign at the close of all its efforts to nothing short of blindness.   (pp. 52–53)

Life in this purgatory consists almost entirely of the seemingly involuntary activity of searching, which is made especially difficult by the endless movement of the naked inhabitants, and of course no one is ever said to have found his or her lost one. The people, or "bodies," search either in the throng of the central arena or in a series of niches, leading to tunnels, in the top half of the cylinder wall, reachable by any of fifteen ladders around the perimeter. Use of these ladders is governed by complicated and strictly enforced rules, but much more interesting than those rules is the apparent reason for the general impulse to climb.

From time immemorial rumour has it or better still the notion is abroad that there exists a way out . . . Regarding the nature of this way out and its location two opinions divide . . . One school swears by a secret passage branching from one of the tunnels and leading in the words of the poet to nature's sanctuaries. The other dreams of a trapdoor hidden in the hub of the ceiling giving access to a flue at the end of which the sun and other stars would still be shining. Conversion is frequent either way . . .

(pp. 17–18)

Throughout the story, the desire to find the "way out" exists alongside the wish to find the "lost ones," and in the end the irreconcilability of these two goals seems to be one of Beckett's points. We learn, for instance, that with mimimal communal cooperation the tallest ladder could easily be propped up in the center of the arena to test the trapdoor theory, but no such "instant of fraternity" is possible, this sentiment being "as foreign to them as to butterflies" (p. 21).

Thus, incapable of fulfilling themselves in any way, the people use themselves up, running down after a while like battery-powered machines in a regressive process Beckett does not describe but rather implies by classifying the present population in four groups.

Firstly those perpetually in motion. Secondly those who sometimes pause. Thirdly those who short of being driven off never stir from the coign they have won and when driven off pounce on the first free one that offers and freeze again. That is not quite accurate. For if among these sedentary the need to climb is dead it is none the less subject to strange resurrections . . . Fourthly those who do not search or non-searchers [later called "vanquished"] sitting for the most part against the wall in the attitude which wrung from Dante one of his rare wan smiles.   (pp. 13–14)

With typical wryness, Beckett suggests that the "vanquished" are the luckiest of all and writes about them with guarded reverence. The story's closing section, separated in time from the preceding action, tells of the final conversion of the last remaining "sedentary" searcher to the "vanquished" state, and how in that exact moment utter silence descends in the cylinder and "the temperature comes to rest not far from freezing point" (p. 62). The equation of the environment with the lives within it is obvious, as is the slightly platitudinous moral that the "bodies" have exhausted themselves searching externally for what they might have sought internally: "For in the cylinder alone are certitudes to be found and without nothing but mystery" (p. 42).

So much for plot summary. Really to do justice to the experience of reading *The Lost Ones*, however, means stressing the strange, disquieting nature of the work and the tenacious quality of its prose, which holds the reader fast with the feeling that stopping mid-way would be unbearable. The text, which commands too much allegorical resonance to be labeled a fable, reads immediately like something extremely old and might more properly be called a myth, at least in the colloquial sense of an ahistorical fiction with a persuasive weight similar to that of ancestral utterance. This persuasiveness is partly an inexplicable by-product of the specifics of the allegory, but it is also partly traceable to subtle editorializing by Beckett's deceptively plain-spoken narrator.

One of the author's most masterful creations, the narrator in *The Lost Ones* is like a voice transplanted from satire into unsatirical discourse. Its studied, detached manner, as if utterly indifferent to the emotional implications of what it is saying, causes the emotion behind its words to build up like water behind a flood wall. Imagine the dogged pedantry of Swift's projector in *A Modest Proposal* combined with the perplexed benevolence of Melville's solicitor in *Bartleby* and the biblical prophets' tendency to inject ethical comments *passim* among plot events, and you have some idea of the attitude this speaker brings to his job. Especially on rereadings, one is fascinated as much by his identity as by the details of the story itself. How does he know, for example, that outside the cylinder is "nothing but mystery" or that "All has not been told and never shall be" (p. 51), and from what position of involvement does he make implicit judgments like these?:

It is as though at a certain stage discouragement had prevailed. To be noted in support of this *wild surmise* the existence of a long tunnel abandoned blind.

If then the vanquished have still some way to go what can be said of the others and what better name be given them than the *fair name* of searchers? [My italics]
(pp. 12, 32)

He is clearly much more knowledgeable, and possessed of much more leisure, than the people in the cylinder, but it is nonsense to think he is as unconcerned as his tone implies. As usual in Beckett, the possibilities arise and multiply but never solidify into certainties: a god?, a prophet?, the nameless poet, who is not Dante, who spoke of "nature's sanctuaries"?

Perhaps Breuer's most brilliant decision during what Warrilow describes as three weeks of brilliant decisions was to concentrate on developing this narrator and his relationship to the story events, and *not* to concentrate

22 David Warrilow in the Mabou Mines production of *The Lost Ones*, directed by Lee Breuer, Theater For The New City, NYC, 1975. (Photo: Richard Landry)

primarily on depicting those events – which was probably especially tempt-
ing with the straightforward plot of *The Lost Ones*. In the sizable critical
literature on this production, greatest attention has been invariably concentrated on the designer Thom Cathcart's admittedly excellent idea to seat
spectators amphitheater-fashion around the edges of a vertical, dark-rubber
cylinder, thus drawing an explicit parallel between the audience and the
story's characters from the first moment. The conceptualization and
portrayal of the narrator, however, ought to be recognized as equally
responsible for the work's uniqueness.

Warrilow enters in darkness and, in a thick Irish accent, begins speaking
like an institutional lecturer. The lights rise after three sentences, on "The
light." This straightforwardness is in keeping with the text's relatively
conventional structure, which throughout makes it easier for spectators to
follow logically than was possible in the other two performances already
discussed. We see him leaning against the cylinder wall, head bowed, a small
box under his arm, dressed in dirty sneakers and a plain jacket and trousers.
For the rest of the performance the light continues to illustrate, although not
precisely, the environmental fluctuations described in the text: e.g. flicker-
ing strobes under spectators' seats and occasional blackouts. Electronic music
by Philip Glass approximates the "faint stridulence."[27]

Warrilow approaches the audience and proceeds to speak with a slightly
tired air, as if employed to give a demonstration he has given many times
before. He takes a tiny ladder out of his pocket and places it against the wall,
where it looks ridiculously small, then opens the box to reveal an assortment
of other ladders and dozens of plastic doll figures. These he dumps on the
floor in a circle of light and then he produces a cutaway section of a model
cylinder, complete with niches, beside which he kneels in order to arrange
the figures in the queues and other comportments Beckett describes.
Spectators may examine this scene more closely through opera glasses found
beside their seats.

As Warrilow explains in his interview, he and Breuer concentrated from
the beginning on molding a dispassionate personality that would generate an
atmosphere of calmness:

We started out with a character: the kind of man who was a guide at Versailles, who
probably was something in his life, then fell on hard times and found himself doing
this rather menial task, but bringing to it a great deal of knowledge and grace. On top
of that, Lee then said, "Let's see what it sounds like with a bit of an Irish accent." . . .
So the Irish accent came in . . . and what it did was to provide a sort of distancing and
a strange intimacy at the same time; it gave a quality to the storytelling which was
deceptively comfortable.[28]

Had they stopped conceptualizing at this stage, however, and tried to sustain the production only with this personality, they would have encountered exactly the same problem Neumann did when he based his performance in *Company* simply on mimesis of a single, posited set of character traits. Thankfully, this simplicity ends almost as soon as it begins, as Warrilow's behavior grows more and more irregular, sometimes appearing to comment on itself, sometimes seeming wholly anomalous. He handles the figures at first with tweezers, implying god-like control over them, but then a short while later claws at the set's cylindrical walls as if trying to climb out, implying equivalence between himself and the characters. Still later – on "his chances of rapid redescent will be increased though far from doubled if thanks to a tunnel he disposes of two niches from which to watch" (p. 24) – he places a figure in his ear and, with sleight of hand, extracts it from his other ear, implying equivalence between himself and the cylinder. (Recall my comment above about the environment coming to rest as the last searcher is "vanquished.")

Thus, spectators are given an array of different messages about his connection to the story, and then left to make up their own minds about which, if any, to accept. Not surprisingly, the possibilities are contradictory, yet they are presented with an equanimity implying that a single coherent idea integrating them should be obvious. Each suggestion – god, searcher, environment – is made with equal candidness through wholly unambiguous actions, yet that very candidness serves to divert attention from the fact that the suggestions refuse to resolve with one another. Moreover, Warrilow's demeanor provides no reliable "truth content" against which their veracity can be measured, because it too alters as the performance progresses; the opening composure alternates with hints of extreme vulnerability such as shivering and chattering teeth. It's as if Breuer went out of his way to create ambiguities that would remain ambiguous even under pressure, and to make audiences accept his adaptation more as a complex set of alternative readings than as a unique interpretation.

Here again, though, this complexity does not distinguish the piece from others such as *All Strange Away* in which directors have managed to preserve Beckett's ambiguities through depicted metaphors spatially separated from spectators. In order to account for the ultimate emotional coherence of *The Lost Ones*, the quality that, night after night, left the majority of spectators too stunned to applaud, one must consider the theater environment. As the performance goes on, emphasis gradually shifts from one level of mimesis to another – Warrilow behaves less and less like a lecturer and more and more like a character in his story – making the space where the audience actually sits into the literal and metaphoric context for the most immediate action.

This shift is in fact hinted at quite early in the piece through the device of

actors planted in the audience. Someone laughs loudly when Warrilow
speaks of the possible "ways out," and someone else screams during the
description of a searcher being accidentally stepped on – both of which
incidents could be understood within the lecture context, i.e. as heckling.
That interpretation, however, soon comes to seem unwarranted as Warrilow
grows less interested in his "job" of demonstration. Abandoning the model
cylinder, he walks about the space, sitting among the spectators, lying on the
floor, and eventually removes his clothes to act the last quarter of the piece as
naked as the "bodies" in Beckett's story. For a time, this appears to be a clear
transformation, from narrator into searcher, but the clarity doesn't last long.

His metamorphosis remains incomplete, as if he wanted to keep the
audience slightly unsure about who he really is. Despite his nudity – which
really intensifies the action in a general sense as much as providing a visual
correlative for a searcher – his behavior is oddly unspecific. During the
description of the vanquished woman called "the north," for instance, a nude
actress appears crouched down against the cylinder wall, but he ignores her
instead of playing out the moving final episode of the last searcher's contact
with her: "On his knees he parts the heavy hair and raises the unresisting
head" (p. 62). He remains aloof, associable only in a general sense with the
fictional population and never with any single identifiable person or position
within it.

What happens is this: the performance *seems* to replace mimesis of
demonstration (toy figures as searchers, Warrilow as narrator) with traditional mimesis of theatrical action (Warrilow and spectators as searchers,
theater and world as cylinder), but actually makes no such definite transition. Both levels of action continue to coexist – the former merely down-
played and the latter accentuated – and something about that uncertainty,
that refusal to dictate one point of view, combined with the nudity, actually
breaks down emotional defenses in the audience. The difference between
Warrilow clothed and Warrilow nude is the difference between spectators
feeling that someone is in control and them feeling abandoned to the hell in
the story.

As discussed further below, the performance gives an impression of brutal
honesty that, I think, causes spectators to agree unconsciously to accept their
experiences of it in a more actual sense than is usual with a play. I hasten to
add, though, that this emotional impression should not be confused with the
work's evident structure, which ultimately casts doubt even on the honesty.
As the nude Warrilow speaks his final anecdote to a toy figure balanced on his
knee, illuminating it with a penlight, apparently dispensing with distinctions
among contexts, some questions arise that threaten to throw all mimetic
readings into confusion: could all foregoing vacillations of identities and
contexts have been nothing more than this man's games? Is it possible that

the true subject from the outset was really him and only him, the actor/storyteller?

For the sake of argument, let me compare the perceptual process called for in *The Lost Ones* with those described in chapter 2 for *Rockaby* and chapter 3 for *Waiting for Godot*. As with *Rockaby*, spectators respond first not to the intellectual puzzles in *The Lost Ones* but to the verbal music of the soothing Irish accent and the rich simplicity of the spare, dark stage picture. Then, despite this reassuring tone, as information gradually accrues about the fictional world, discrepancies become apparent between the story and Warrilow's activities, as they do between the recorded tale about a woman rocking and the actual rocking activity of the actress. And in the end, both performances leave spectators pondering enigmatic tales of unreliable veracity, which stick fast in memory partly because the startling, *live* "passions" that accompany them have ultimately occupied attention as much as, if not more than, the tales.

Stated another way, like Beckett's production of *Godot*, *The Lost Ones* never makes a full commitment to illusionism, instead requiring its audience to perceive external and internal action simultaneously. One soon recognizes that Wigger/Didi and Bollmann/Gogo's world *is* a staged performance and ceases to expect any normative action such as realism or Brechtian commentary, just as one soon recognizes that Warrilow's action of narrating *is* the essential anecdote and ceases to expect much from the pretense of demonstration. In the end, spectators at *Godot* are led to reflect on their own circumstances – e.g. sitting in a theater waiting for a character to arrive, for a plot to resolve – and eventually compare themselves with the characters. Similarly, spectators at *The Lost Ones* are led to focus on their circumstances – e.g. sitting in a rubber cylinder where a nude man tells a story about people in a rubber cylinder – and eventually compare themselves with him.

Bert States writes about *Godot*:

In fact, it is precisely its success in inducing a certain degree of boredom in its audience that makes the play interesting. I would not explain this seeming paradox by saying, as some have, that the play puts *us* in its own state of ontological estrangement, but rather along more basic lines: whether you are waiting for God or for a bus you are reduced to much the same state of suspension in any empty or unproductive interval, and this brings into play a special kind of attentiveness – on one hand, a scaling down of interim expectations and, on the other, a heightening of one's availability to interim reality.[29]

Boredom is not a major theme in *The Lost Ones*, but that work's performance circumstances also cause spectators to compare themselves with the story's "state of ontological estrangement," without putting them in it, which in turn scales down, or defines, their "interim expectations" and heightens their "availability to interim reality." In both cases, the mixture of authentic and theatrical action in a metaphorical space the audience cannot escape produces the powerful effect, that sense of almost unbearable ontological honesty Robbe-Grillet described as being "irremediably present."

One can of course draw out such comparisons to the point of distorting both terms, but the most important point here should already be clear. With no previous planning, and with only his own experience and theories of stagecraft to guide him, Breuer ultimately succeeded where countless Beckett imitators had and have failed miserably in creating an audience/stage transaction approximating that of Beckett's plays. Which is not to say that he was religiously faithful to any general ideal of Beckettian construction. He did not set out to make a Beckett play, he set out to make a Breuer play, yet the final result reveals that he had already internalized many of Beckett's dramatic discoveries to the extent that they became his own convictions.[30] And, indeed, it is difficult to imagine his conceptualizing *The Lost Ones* as he did without previous experience with Beckett's theater, a statement not intended to deny other major influences on his work, such as Brecht and Oriental theater.

And in light of similar comments made above about MacGowran and Thomas, we might return to the question raised at the beginning of this chapter: why has Beckett's prose fiction inspired such effective theater events? Part of the answer is obviously, "because of his dramas"; for the theatrical effectiveness of the stagings often comes from dramatic qualities that find their source in Beckett's theater, projected onto the texts by the directors. This observation is not meant pejoratively; indeed, I imagine most directors would appreciate their work being seen as derivative of Beckett's. But it is, in any case, an insufficient answer, because it does not explain why the same directing techniques would not be equally effective with any other randomly chosen texts. One must consider qualities inherent in Beckett's prose itself.

I have asked many directors their opinion on this issue and received, strangely, few coherent answers. One of the clearer formulations was Neumann's in the interview in part three.

I understand his texts as not just written words but as something almost three dimensional, and meant to be experienced in space if only with the ear. There are always voices and always something representing the stage, also darkness and something like day, an announcement of the beginning of things, as in Genesis – the void, the emptiness and some kind of spark of something there that takes place, to be seen and heard, and perhaps even ignored.

His point about the vocality of the texts is well taken; as Kauffmann writes in the review quoted above, "Beckett shares with Shaw and Joyce the Irish

23 David Warrilow's hand and tiny figures in *The Lost Ones*, directed by Lee Breuer, Theater For The New City, NYC, 1975. (Photo: Richard Landry)

inability to write a line that cannot be spoken well, that cannot be *improved* by being spoken aloud." Neumann's other point about darkness and light, however, does not satisfy as an explanation of anything but his own purposes; for it constitutes a somewhat conventional view of some very unconventional texts. He isolates certain events and prioritizes them as in a linear plot with the intention of representing them onstage – precisely the process directors such as Thomas, Breuer, and numerous others in the contemporary avant-garde, work consciously to avoid in their productions.

The aspect of the prose fiction that seems to interest these directors is its very strategy of uncertainty. Beckett's readers may never completely lose themselves in a comfortable imaginary world because that world undergoes eccentric shifts that periodically transfer interest to the tellers of the tales, and hence the act of reading is often called into play as an unspoken subject – which is of course equally true of many other twentieth-century writers. What particularly distinguishes Beckett's books, though, is the unnerving precision of the process; you are out-maneuvered, second-guessed, so often in your attempts to gain some overview of the narrator, or the situations he relates, that it sometimes begins to feel as if you are reading about the structure of your own thoughts. And this experience of the functioning of your mind can be so actual, so present, that you end up asking whether it should even be called "reading."

In other words, there *is* a certain theatricality to the act of reading Beckett's prose fiction despite the fact that it is a solitary act. It is this quality of demonstrative reflexivity, which Knowlson and Pilling compare with painting in their wonderful phrase, "frescoes of the skull," but if the theater was originally a "seeing place," as etymologists tell us, then that skull may be just as easily likened to a stage. It should not be surprising that such texts appeal to directors with the historical avant-gardist ambition to question age-old mimetic models of theater, such as Aristotle's, and the perceptual habits that accompany them. What is surprising is when those directors assume that the solitary theatricality of reading is directly transferable to the public circumstances of the stage.

Almost without exception, the dullest and least inspired adaptations I have seen are those in which the director has declined to use significant settings or physical activity, instead choosing to "let the text speak for itself," either because of his or her own preferences or out of respect for Beckett's standing injunction against anything but "straight readings." When the performance space offers no visual metaphor to occupy spectators' imaginations in some way similar to the filmic scene shifts in the narratives, when the actor or actors make no distinctions among the narrator's various personas, or between the narrator and the characters he invents, when no thought is given to finding a theatrical equivalent for the reflexive perceptions that occur in readers' minds, then the performance becomes simply a barrage of words, opaque, unprocessable, unbearable. As stated above, the novels and stories are not dramas, they cannot stand alone as theater, and any attempt to stage them is at least as much of a gamble as staging a new play or performance-art work, requiring the independent and fully engaged creative consciousness of the director.

This recommendation of greater directorial involvement is, of course, not a criticism of Beckett but rather a general objection to half-realized productions of any kind and a recognition that all works of the imagination are, to some extent, genre-bound. If directors are going to stage prose fiction – and indeed Beckett's is not the only oeuvre that has been rifled for material during the dearth of good new playwriting in recent years – then they might as well do it well.

It is unfortunate that much of this work goes on against the author's wishes but, as I discuss presently in my conclusion, Beckett has the misfortune of being a great writer in an age of mediocre writing that cannot answer to the standards of precision that his can; thus, his strictness on matters such as stage directions and genre becomes harder and harder for theater practitioners to understand. Some of his most prominent aesthetic and spiritual heirs have very different artistic temperaments from his – not predominantly writers per se but rather directors or auteurs for whom sanctities such as classic genre divisions are old-fashioned – and they are, quite frankly, starved for texts.

8 Conclusion: the question of context

When critics speak of Beckett's cultural context they usually mean his place in literary history, the great museum of classic authors T. S. Eliot called "tradition." In the mountain of commentary discussing Beckett's indebtedness to Descartes, Proust, Joyce, his affinities with Sartre, Kafka, Camus, and his stylistic influence on Pinter, Albee, Handke and countless other younger authors, we find little that clearly distinguishes theater from drama, or drama from literature in general, and still less that situates him specifically in *theatrical* history.[1]

After all, one of the main preoccupations of theater in this century has been the gradual displacement of the Author, so how can we insure his canonical position without considering him as a purely literary figure? The fact is, though, that Beckett's playwriting distinguishes itself from most other dramatic literature to a large extent because of its effects in production, its demands on those acting, directing and watching it. Though the author's directing has had almost no influence, his drama, far from subsisting chiefly on library shelves, has continued to influence new ideas about performance and has in fact insinuated itself into the best work of the contemporary avant-garde – a process sufficiently advanced for Herbert Blau to suggest that Beckett is the logical starting point for historical discussion of any significant new work, "the *locus classicus* of the problematic of the future."[2]

But the question of Beckett's context is complicated for other reasons than this literary/theatrical question. First, his presence has created no end of confusion on both sides of the profit/non-profit dividing line. On the one hand, many commercial producers have stayed away from him, terrified of what is not immediately assimilable in familiar terms (though this situation shows signs of changing in American regional theaters, particularly with the early plays), and on the other hand many avant-gardists, with important exceptions such as Mabou Mines, also distrust him because of his ties to conventional drama and his reputation as one of the great moderns. Beckett is avant-garde to the conventional and conventional to the avant-garde; he straddles two milieus in a way that would seem like equivocation if he had consciously sought the position.

Second, his longevity presents a related problem, for we must recognize progress in his career. Beckett is Artaud's junior by little more than a decade, Brecht's by only eight years, which means that he can be both precursor and contemporary to Handke and Müller. Thematically, temperamentally, his work has remained fairly uniform over time, but stylistically it has undergone considerable change, which is only to be expected in any author; but what is unusual is that his oeuvre encompasses what some critics claim to be a revolutionary cultural shift. After earning a reputation as the only significant heir to the Joycean tradition, the brand of aesthetic Faustianism that manifests itself in a will to style, Beckett seems to have broken faith with spoken language toward the end of his life, and he thus figures frequently in the popular debate of modernism versus postmodernism. I shall have more to say presently about this specious debate and its relevance to Beckett.

Beckett and the actor

When we speak of Beckett pejoratively as an old-style German *Regisseur* in the tradition of Saxe-Meiningen, we do well to remember that the most prominent avatar of that tradition, Max Reinhardt, was also often confronted with the criticism that he treated actors like puppets and denied them any significant creative influence on productions. Reinhardt's actors, however – such as Max Pallenberg, Werner Krauss and Emil Jannings – were eventually extolled as among the greatest of their era, which to an extent retroactively vindicated the director's methods, one of which was preparation of detailed *Regiebücher* for all productions. In a sense, Billie Whitelaw serves a similar function with Beckett, for in her the author finds a performer who will not question his restrictions but who can nevertheless bring about a kind of transcendence of his texts in performance. Thus she stands as a vindication of those restrictions as a basis for acting, and in effect challenges those who would accuse Beckett of wanting only "disembodied puppets of his will."

As discussed in chapter 2, *Rockaby* in fact leaves a great deal of responsibility in the actress' hands. Whitelaw helps keep the play from melodrama by recognizing the primacy of its steady verbal music, and she also manages to deliver her four one-word lines in a way that both manifests and builds on the text's central uncertainties regarding active or passive consciousness and the narrator's identity. She does not make her choices on the basis of articulated ideas about ambiguity, or from any conscious analysis whatsoever, but many comments of hers demonstrate that she knows such ideas exist in the work and has a profound understanding of them. Thus the play in the end, instead of limiting her, actually becomes a kind of showcase in which she can reveal her sophisticated grasp of Beckett's aesthetic and of the human experience dealt with in his play.

In this sense *Rockaby* is paradigmatic of all Beckett's dramas: because the script functions as a kind of test not only of the actress' craft but also of her human depth, the stakes, so to speak, are higher than in most other plays. We use the old-fashioned word "wisdom" to describe what performers supposedly gain with maturity that readies them to play great classic roles such as Hamlet, Lear and Medea, and there is a widespread misconception that such wisdom has to do with powers of mimesis. What makes such roles daunting, however, is not the depictive problem of the characters' opaque surfaces – the fictional personas are really not so difficult to embody – but rather the deeper problem of transparency, the quality in them that denudes the actor and reveals the degree of sophistication in his or her experience. The dignity in great performances is always to some extent nonrepresentational, and in this sense all of Beckett's plays are possible actor's "vehicles." His theater always involves that same fear of, or opportunity for, exposure, though the effect is subtler in the late works than in the early ones. To use a formulation of Whitelaw's, actors inevitably "grin through" their roles "like wallpaper [patterns] through distemper."[3]

Unlike in classic roles, however, actors in Beckett are barely even given opaque surfaces to hide behind if necessary; for the author's habit is to make the actor's denuding a part of his subject matter. Performers in the early works have found that they can progress only so far by imagining and imitating specific personalities; even after developing strong characterizations, they find themselves facing an emptiness onstage that is unbearable for them *as actors*. That emptiness is the essence of what Robbe-Grillet called their "irremediable presence," also a primary experience for spectators, a condition of acting qua acting that makes it impossible for audiences to believe completely in either the action's lifelikeness or its illusionism. Many productions have attempted to swing the audience's belief toward one or the other of these biases – e.g. Schneider's 1961 and 1971 *Godots* – but rarest are those that demonstrate how action can be suspended between them – e.g. Serban's 1979 *Happy Days* and Beckett's 1975 Schiller Theater *Godot*, in which movement was minutely choreographed and the musical motifs in the dialogue were accentuated. The general dilemma of the Beckett actor is subsumed in this problem of suspension: he need not convince anyone of particular truths (that his character or situation are real, for instance, or that we should accept this or that ideology), he need only keep on going, keep on acting, but with conviction and clown-like charisma if he is not to lose his audience and with it his *raison d'être*.

Gratuitousness is at the center of Beckett's theater, which is why, when we look to situate it historically, the tradition of Brecht is so ill-fitting. To be entirely fair to Beckett, which means honoring his express distaste for tendentiousness, involves seeing that his work really follows in the tradition of Artaud, for whom the theater was "an immediate gratuitousness provoking acts without use or profit" – a strange irony indeed when one considers Beckett's stand on fidelity to texts.[4] But the point need not be pushed too far: inasmuch as theater since World War II has in fact manifested the Artaud/ Brecht split – internally focused performance acting on and through the psyche versus externally focused performance concerned with social forces and acting for social change – Beckett fits squarely into the former camp. Moreover, Artaud's call for religious intensity in performance also points to Beckett, his idea of an "affective athleticism" whereby actors could be trained to tap into primitive impulses that, when activated, would then evoke sympathetic responses in spectators. The ecstatic overtones and the ethic of painful, enforced purgation are foreign to Beckett's world view, but thoroughly Beckettian is the underlying idea of a religious theater that searches nostalgically for a mode of existence more authentic than what is usually witnessed on the conventional stage.

Anyone who balks at this comparison should take another look, in the interviews following and elsewhere, at some of the actors' comments about the physical agony they have endured while performing, such as these by Whitelaw and Worth.

I have actually twisted my spine by doing *Footfalls*, because in fact something happens whereby my spine starts to spiral down as though I am disappearing. And it's physically very painful to do. Each play I do, I'm left with a legacy or scar. Now, perhaps I'm being silly, perhaps I shouldn't do that, but I feel that the shape my body makes is just as important as the sound that comes out of my mouth. And that's the shape my body wants to take, of somebody who's spiraling inward.   (Whitelaw)

I had to go to a special doctor, because I'd got into a kind of terrible muscular spasm through tension [during *Happy Days*]. And so I've had to learn to get just the right sense of relaxation in my body and my shoulders and my neck and yet give the sense of being trapped.   (Worth)[5]

Beckett requires a "holy" actor no less than Artaud and Grotowski, a fact obscured by the considerable attention given to his work's supposedly "Brechtian" aspects; critics are fond of pointing out that "existence onstage" (Guicharnaud's phrase), for Beckett, necessarily involves consciousness of the theater's artificiality, both for the spectator and for the actor. Awareness of ambiguities between life and theater, between life and art in general, however, has pervaded twentieth-century culture and is hardly the sole province of Brecht. For Beckett, as for Artaud, artificiality is a natural state, and part of the theater's job is to demonstrate that: the theater is not mendacious when it avoids explicit contact with social issues; it is rather mendacious and manipulative when it fails to proclaim its duplicity, the essential collusion of its natural and artificial natures. And that collusion is most effectively shown through the actor's body, his physical presence, and not through words.

Part of what drives Artaud is specifically the "identity crisis" in theater caused by the burgeoning of film. He is searching for theater's "difference," in Derrida's terms, as is Grotowski, his most famous spiritual heir, and in that search he fixates on images of decomposition: cruelty, the plague. But this fixation is far more than an idiosyncratic outgrowth of his own illness. It provides the essential, "archetypal" thematic focus for a theater-of-the-body, and it anticipates what Joseph Chaikin was to formulate explicitly several decades later: that theater's difference consists not in the living actor but in the dying actor; that it finds its most stable identity, its most powerful platform for expression, in the fact that the performer could die at any moment, is in fact dying as surely as we spectators are, in the same room. Beckett, who is also sometimes called morbid, is the natural culmination of this difference, the playwright *par excellence* of theater in the age of film and television.

His topic was "existence onstage" even in *Godot*, but he focused on it more and more closely as his career progressed, eventually depriving his figures of names and entirely abandoning the pretense that they were fictional characters in the usual sense. The actor of a late role inhabits a given space, adopts a specific physical attitude, as a self-sufficient activity because, for Beckett, that physical predicament *is* the figure's complete ontological condition. Any psychological condition develops *from* the physical one – e.g. kneeling but not sitting behind a cutaway urn and waiting for a spotlight to prompt you to speech, or sitting on a high stool with your head strapped to a backrest and completely masked except for your mouth – and speech emanates from these bodily conditions, is a vocalized aspect of them.

If, so the theory goes, the actor sufficiently refines his physical comportment, the resulting purity and specificity of form will generate corresponding mental states not only in him but also in spectators, as in Biomechanics. It is a process of acting "backwards," so to speak, from the outside in, whose historical roots reach back even before Meyerhold to Delsarte and Dalcroze; the consequence, however, the spectacle of the actor *in extremis*, is entirely original with Beckett.

The problem for the actor in these plays is even more acute than Ben Barnes implies in his phrase, "forfeit the notion of character"; for the theater in fact has a long history of requiring actors to perform for reasons other than impersonation of a given fictional figure. As the comparison of Epstein, Warrilow and Schmahl demonstrates, the problem in late Beckett is rather that the actor is asked to forego all intellectual volition to begin with. What Goldman calls the search for a "privileged subtext," the province of the actor from time immemorial, turns out to be counterproductive because there is no

encoded information, no authentic source of truth that the actor is responsible for making available to spectators, except whatever is contained in his or
her corporeal state itself. Thus, acting effectively involves a kind of quest for
an indescribable grail inside the author's stage directions and the music of his
words, a process, long and torturous to some, of learning to trust the text.

Beckett's theater has proved itself to be fundamentally text-centered, not
because of any predetermined authorial dogma – i.e. his definition of "text"
to mean an exact guide to *mise en scène* in addition to speech – but because of
the post-production testimony of actors who have actually played in his
works. With a unanimity of spirit rarely found outside ensembles such as
Grotowski's or Brecht's, Beckett's actors come away from productions with
enormous trust in the author's theatrical sense, even when he is not present
as director, and even when the directors who are present do not, as frequently
happens, share in the performers' acclaim for him.

Beckett and the director

The autocratic tradition of the director has been with us for over a hundred
years and is more firmly entrenched than even some directors perceive. Like
the bourgeoisie in the eighteenth century, producing ecstatic republican
tragedies as if unaware that its dominant social position was already long
secured, directors in the late twentieth century still rail against the tyranny
of the author as if more than a handful of contemporary playwrights actually
posed as much as a passing threat to them. The sloganizing one hears about
"servitude to the text" (Herbert Blau), "the stranglehold of the writer"
(Charles Marowitz) and "textual imperialism" (Patrice Pavis) has a pallid,
unconvincing air to it, especially the latter phrase, which sounds like fanatic
shouting outside some beleaguered foreign embassy. In fact, the slogans are
a form of projection, since those who shout them are really asserting the
imperialism of the director, simply a differently ordered aristocracy.

The truth about directing in the contemporary theater is that it is not
really a discrete art; it is a locus of power, an administrative job, not even
particularly pleasant but nevertheless coveted because it is at the top.
Directing has far more to do with petty ego battles, questions of practical
convenience and monetary exigencies than with high-minded ideals, and
when directors are being completely honest, as happens occasionally, even
they admit this. Breuer writes:

Have you ever met a director with anything to say? I doubt it. Have you met a typist
with something to write about? There is no such thing as a director because directing,
like typing, is a skill. Who you probably have met, in the theatre or on the set, is some
creative individual, say, a poet (Brecht) or an actor (Stanislavsky) or a painter
(Wilson) with a tangential skill.[6]

We must be careful not to make a mystique of the director, the primacy of whose position is not a moral principle but rather a fact of power politics in an era of fealty to administrations large and small. Nor should we take too seriously the frequent forecasts that this age of autocracy is ending. In the 1960s, avant-gardists introduced a new rhetoric of egalitarianism, soon appropriated by the theatrical community at large, professing an ideal of "collaborationism" and implying that directors would relinquish significant authority to performers. Only a very few avant-garde ensembles, however, really work toward this ideal anymore. And if such a major transition were ever truly to approach the mainstream, then as surely as Cronus swallowed his children we would have the early warning signal of a smear campaign against the performer resembling the one that has long persisted against the writer.

It might be argued that directors do have one solid justification for their present dominance: that in the 1970s and 1980s their work has been, on the average, far more interesting and original than that of playwrights. As the empirical philosophers once discovered, however, it is very difficult to derive an "ought" from an "is." Thus, when we are asked to believe that a text-centered theater is necessarily wrong or immoral because directors in general are more talented than writers, we must see that attitude for what it is: the proscriptive credo of a status quo, a calcified habit of thought that will not suffer contradiction. Beckett is confusing, even infuriating, to the average director precisely because he constitutes the most convincing and disturbing of contradictions: proof that theater events can be envisioned in the mind, at the desk, so completely, and those visions notated so faithfully, that the resulting notations are blueprints for visual poems as profound and theatrically effective as anything most directors could create even after years of workshop rehearsals.

The operative word here is "blueprints," which directors want nothing to do with, not because they doubt the genius in them, but simply because they are someone else's. Beckett's theoretical importance is recognized almost universally, but directors nevertheless perceive him as limiting their creative freedom. When he asks to be treated as an exception to the notion of the playwright as, in Richard Schechner's words, "an absentee landlord: someone whose turf ought to be seized," he makes himself exceedingly undesirable, controverting the most cherished received notions about authority in the production process.[7] From the standpoint of contemporary performance theory, he is the embodiment of the director's nightmare, the Ghost of Banquo in the person of the Author, who was supposed to have been mortally wounded at the end of the last century and dead since Artaud. No one like Beckett is *supposed* to exist in our era, and yet there he stands, the indomitable *écrivain*, to borrow Barthes' terminology, laboring to produce a spatio-temporal *écriture* for the stage. Directors such as Charles Marowitz, of course, have decided that this effort is futile, a priori.

There are a handful of playwrights one might cite as touching the border of this "other theatre" (Beckett, Ionesco, Genet, Bernhardt [sic], Handke, Straus [sic!]) but the overriding fact is that it does not exist in the work of writers, nor can it.[8]

Beckett does not demand authority on principle, though, as do directors; he demands it on the basis of demonstrated merit, in order to call attention to the fact that his spatio-temporal *écriture* answers to a standard of justifiability as strict as Joyce's. ("Monsieur! Can you justify every word in this text? Because I can justify every word and every *syllable* in everything that I write!" – Joyce to René Crevel when presented with the Second Surrealist Manifesto.)[9] Beckett does not ask that the theatrical value of his works be taken on faith; he asks only that the texts – which, as already mentioned, include stage directions – not be dismissed out of hand. He understands the "intentional fallacy" as well as his critics – did ever an author live with a more acute sense that he would not always be around to say what he meant? He asks only that the issue of intention not be summarily discarded in production. Even this degree of humility, though, fails to move many directors to compromise.

Part of Beckett's problem with directors, of course, stems from the fact that critics and reviewers have proclaimed his works "classic" during his lifetime (almost immediately in Germany, and after slight delay in England, France and America) – in any era but ours a boon to be welcomed unconditionally. In the late twentieth century, however, this boon is a kind of curse because any play labeled "classic" automatically makes directors want to alter it. Jan Kott became the spiritual father of this directorial trend with his book *Shakespeare Our Contemporary*, which argued that we cannot help but see texts nearly four hundred years old through the filter of events in our own time. Essentially equating themselves with this formidable scholar, directors have gone on to interpret his argument to mean that their own perceptions and impressions, however subjective or uneducated, can suffice as text analysis in productions. Even Kott does not approve of that kind of Know-Nothingism, however, much less support its extension to the work of living authors, against their will.

The trouble is that what Martin Esslin calls a play's "autonomous existence" now seems to begin the instant it leaves the author's hands.[10] I have in fact heard several directors – let them remain nameless – call Alan Schneider "uninspired" because of his textual fidelity while rehearsing Beckett's premieres; the playwright, it would appear, is not even entitled to a first production of a play done according to his original vision. And any objections he might subsequently make to perceived mistreatments of it will

be answered with essays denouncing "ownership of texts . . . a role reflect-
ing the values of capitalist individualism."[11]

In the case of JoAnne Akalaitis' *Endgame* at ART, such denunciations
were given credence by an actual legal threat to shut the production down,
which is unfortunate because, as I found out when I spoke with him, textual
ownership was not the main issue in the author's mind. (I strongly suspect
that scholars will eventually make important distinctions between Beckett's
role in this affair, and others like it, and that of those representing his
interests.) The issue was really his feelings, easy to ignore from a legalistic
standpoint, but we are concerned here with people who consider themselves
artists.

"Why is it less important to respect an author's text after he's dead?"

"Well, just because then you can't hurt his feelings."

Imagine creating an artwork that conspicuously breaks out of a certain
established mold, and then seeing it reduced back to that mold, to communicating with the public according to the rules from which it originally
departed, because the person presenting it failed to understand the source of
its innovativeness. That would sadden even an avant-gardist with a prin-
cipled aversion to "masterpieces," yet it is what happened at ART.

In her interview with me, Akalaitis maintained that "there was no fuss to
be made about" her production, and when we consider it only in the context
of the production history reviewed in chapter 5, she is right. Her *Endgame*
was more textually faithful and theatrically effective than many others seen
in the decade previous to it. When we judge it wholly apart from the scandal,
however, comparing her theatrical notions with Beckett's, we can see that
her choices were in fact quite conservative. In trying to contemporize and
Americanize the setting as a subway tunnel, she revealed that she understood the play mainly as a historical allegory. Her few presentational
gestures, such as unusual lighting and occasional mechanistic speech patterns, were easily overpowered by the representational lure of the background, which anchored the actors as characters embedded within a certain
history. Thus, the production participated in exactly the tradition of ideological dramatic communication against which Beckett has spent his entire
career reacting.

One would think Akalaitis' experience with Mabou Mines would have
equipped her to see that an ahistorical setting such as the bare room Beckett
specified is essential to focusing audience attention on questions of presentationalism. As demonstrated in much of her independent work thus far,
however – e.g. *The Balcony, Dead End Kids, Green Card, Leonce and Lena* –
her deeper intentions are really ideological. She pays lip service to the avant-
garde by borrowing certain stage techniques but creates performances whose

essence is really that of agit-prop. Ironically, then, in certain ways Beckett is closer in spirit to the New York avant-garde than she is.

Far from being unique, in overlooking the significance of ambiguous time and place Akalaitis was in fact typical of contemporary directors, the vast majority of whom, along with many literary critics, still see Beckett's significance in his having replaced the exciting events of conventional drama with mundane events. It is the rare director who understands that the plays reach beyond representations of banality and that they involve a presentational concern (i.e. in the present time of the performance) with the impossibility of making believable, event-filled plots at all. Tabori's *Godot* is the only "concept" production I know of that has clearly displayed such understanding. All others have been elaborate attempts, in the name of directorial subjectivity, to impose specific histories on the situations and characters by means of this or that added metaphor: a chicken-wire cage, a junk-strewn attic, an old-folk's home, a skull, a womb – literally whatever pops into mind.

To state the obvious, then, the problem is not so much directorial freedom as directorial mediocrity, a cast of mind unwilling or unable to recognize that a writer could have anything to teach us about concrete stage action. (To be fair, let me concede that very few contemporary playwrights do, but we must be willing to recognize exceptions.) In their rush to reinvent the world every day, nervously dogging the New in order to earn themselves a place in theater history, directors, particularly in America, effectively devalue that history by ignoring the accomplishments of others that form their historical context. Hence, the seemingly inexorable redundancy in the mainstream, whose conventions are like the muck in the Augean stables, irremovable save by a Herculean hero. We do not so much lack heroes, however, as the wherewithal to welcome or recognize them when they arrive, and I sometimes wonder whether Beckett's obdurate insistence that his works be performed as written might not really constitute a gesture of historical self-preservation, his quixotic attempt to insure that they will appear before audiences at least no more retrogressive than directors and actors can imply by employing his actual words and settings.

If directors still plead their paranoiac case against "King Text," perhaps it is partly out of an unconscious sense that their emancipation has come to an impasse or crisis in which it is actually a major cause of the theater's enslavement to old values. I have no more proof for that irresponsibly optimistic statement, however, than I do for suggesting that the recent renascence of Beckett performance in the United States is symptomatic of a general breakdown of enthusiasm for unlimited directorial license. Both ideas may be mere wishes. In any event, the American mainstream could benefit immeasurably from taking a much closer look not only at Beckett but also at its own avant-garde, which has understood and moved forward from the way Beckett perceives stage time and space.

Because that avant-garde seems to me the arena where Beckett's theatrical ideas have been most consistently appreciated with a minimum of anti-intellectual prejudice and historical naiveté, I end with a discussion of it, specifically of his connection with the performance tradition known as postmodernism. Before proceeding, however, let me digress briefly on the subject of this tradition's name, which I feel obscures far more than it clarifies about Beckett's influence and the purposes of the avant-garde.

Terminological digression

George Orwell once wrote that "from time to time one can . . . if one jeers loudly enough, send some worn-out and useless phrase . . . into the dustbin where it belongs." And nothing could deserve vituperation in that spirit more than postmodernism, possibly the most meaningless critical term since neo-Dada but one whose recent vogue has led to much abbreviated thinking and even a kind of moral terrorism reminiscent of the French post-structuralists' use of jargon. There is no point in denying that the characteristics of recent performance which the term is usually employed to classify are real and important, but the word itself is hopelessly vague and euphemizes a more or less desperate underlying impulse simply to toss out language along with outdated forms of theater.

The modern, which was an unfortunate term to begin with, has been widely defined and has had its own history; most American critics now understand it as an undeclared, unconsolidated period or movement beginning with Flaubert in the novel and Ibsen in drama, characterized by questioning and violation of expected, mostly nineteenth-century, structural norms and skepticism about the responsibility and ability of artistic language to represent those norms critically. The word is also sometimes used more broadly to describe those changes in the artist's attitude toward his task that accompanied the social transformations of the late Renaissance and persist today, one common characteristic of which is the general romantic tendency to kill the father and remake him in one's own image. The original reason for the name, however, and the only definition that ties the movement to the word's meaning, is quite colloquial and can be traced etymologically to the French phrase *la mode*: modern as something that seems contemporary.

For Adorno, the most oft-quoted authority, modern means literature since Baudelaire. But a critic such as Gilman can extend the category as far back as Büchner (in *The Making of Modern Drama*) by pointing out not only that his plays violate many of the same formal expectations as the usual modern dramas, but also that audiences still feel them to be contemporary, i.e. consonant with their experience and not "old-fashioned" or seemingly consonant with the experience of past audiences. Thus "post-" modern would seem to refer to works that are ahead of their time, or "beyond" audiences – hardly a promising feature for theater that hopes to be effective. The subtitle of one of Richard Schechner's essays, "The Crash of Performative Circumstances: A Modernist Discourse on Postmodernism," contains the essential irony in its tacit admission that all effective theater, *especially* that which the essay defines as postmodern, is modern.[12]

One might suggest finding a new name for the movement Schechner describes, if the clustering of works of the imagination as movements were not such a questionable practice in the first place, but that is a different diatribe. In any event, the self-canceling name it now has means, precisely, nothing – and not in the sense of Dada, a playful appellation for a clear path of negation, but rather in the sense of inadvertent contradiction. The very word is self-cannibalistic, its use symptomatic of the penchant for despair that every intellectual claims to see running through this century but none seems to know how to stop. Critics seem able to offer only substitute names, such as pluralism which, though it describes a very real set of circumstances in the avant-garde (a sharing of power structures), has a similar connotation of desperation.

What has all this to do with Beckett? Well, since use of the term postmodern involves the arrogance of suggesting that we have decisively left "all that" in the modern, which for most critics and practitioners includes Beckett, then in relating Beckett to the avant-garde one must defend against the potential charge of comparing apples with oranges. Many commentators and artists would have us believe that the latest avant-garde work is *sui generis*, or at least that its sources, such as traditional and oral theater like Kabuki and street entertainment, exclude modernism.

We need only glance with a historical eye at a few examples, however, to disprove this. Richard Foreman's sets are carefully chosen collections of objects and images, often arranged around a particular theme, which the spectator uses as a basis to organize impressions, collage style, into a unity, despite the author/director's intention to work against unity by compartmentalizing experience through various framing devices. Elizabeth LeCompte opens productions to audiences long before they are finished and acknowledges her debt to Joyce by calling them "Works in Progress." Wilson's slowly moving stage images would be unthinkable without the precedent of surrealist performance and the decades of experience we have reading the illusionism in surrealist painting. Spalding Grey sits at a table and tells fascinating stories from his life, and is extolled by Breuer for offering the century's third new idea in acting after Stanislavsky and Brecht, as if Mayakovsky had not demanded of audiences a similar suspension of *belief* in fictional character in 1913 when he wrote, directed and performed in *Vladimir Mayakovsky: A Tragedy.*

The possible observations are unlimited, and I provide this list not to denigrate the artists, nor to suggest that their work is devoid of innovation, but rather to point out that the habits of modernism are far more tenacious and long-lived than we have been led to believe. They form the very fabric of the historical continuum in which these artists exist; even rejection of them is reference to them by way of negation. Of course, one cannot expect all artists to recognize this: every avant-garde adopts one or another apocalyptic vision that serves to pump it full of energy; indeed, part of the avant-garde's identity is to believe that what it is doing represents a revolutionary departure from the past. Critics and theorists ought to know better, though, especially after nearly a century of experience with similar phenomena.

Most likely, Schechner would respond to all this by pointing out that, in my comments above about individual practitioners, I isolate effects and values from their performance context, which supposedly does differ from that found in modernism. All postmodern stage communication, he says, occurs within a system of "multiplex signaling" which stands in opposition to the notion of "spine" in conventional plays and to the more general idea of unity in any performance.[13] This signaling system presents a new perceptual framework to reflect a new age in which humanism is thought not to be the prevailing ethos: man has abused his position as the measure of all things, so the theory goes, so he now faces institutional and socio-cultural models that accept "limits to human action – limits that are not the outermost boundaries of knowledge or ability but a frame consciously set around what is 'accept-able' defining anything outside that frame as 'undo-able.'"[14] Thus, instead of capitalism and Marxism, our culture is or is soon to be dominated by much more limited and stable structures such as sociobiology, computer languages and multinational corporations.

All of these share a rejection of experience – ordinary happenings along a linear plane, a story in the simple sense of "this is what happened," or "once upon a time." Instead, these apparently different systems view experience as what the Hindus call *maya* and *lila* – illusion and play – a construction of consciousness. The "ultimate reality" lies somewhere else – in the genes say the sociobiologists; in the flow of goods say the economists; in the exchange of information say the multinationals . . . Postmodern means . . . the organizing of experience in a period when experience is *maya-lila.* Finding ways to organize bits of information so that these bits exist both as experience – what performing art is always dealing with – and as what underlies, is the foundation of, experience. A very difficult job of doubling.[15]

His comments are unusually lucid for discussions of this topic, but they also make possible formulation of a general objection not only to this but also to most other definitions of postmodernism: if we do not accept this world view, then all the apocalyptic claims of the aesthetic system associated with it collapse. At best Schechner identifies an "extra-" or "anti-modern" tendency that struggles against certain established traditions, but such struggling would be utterly pointless if the prefix "post" were understood literally and the battle were already won. Indeed, doesn't it seem a bit premature to declare the end of all humanist ideologies and their mytho-histories? If we are not prepared to reject everday experience as a basis for judgment in art, and I suspect most people are not, then it is inevitable that "multiplex signaling" be viewed either as experience or as a conveyor of metaphors about experience, no matter how it is intended. In the reality of the theater, it becomes a modernist tool like Brecht's *Verfremdung* or Beckett's ambiguity of place, diverting spectators' thoughts toward their own watching processes. And what Schechner calls "doubling" becomes an intensified version of an age-old theatrical experience: perceiving the dupli-citous nature of the performance event, which I have already discussed in connection with Artaud.

Hence, my preference for the term avant-garde which, though it has its own drawbacks, not the least of which is overuse, is at least explicitly definable. By avant-garde I mean the series of artistic movements that have continued unbroken throughout this century, each of whose "inexorable destiny," in Renato Poggioli's words, is "to rise up against the newly outstripped fashion of an old avant-garde and to die when a new fashion, movement, or avant-garde appears."[16] And I mean the complex of sensibil-ities distinguishing these movements, which Poggioli divides into four categories: activism ("acting for the sake of acting"); antagonism ("acting by negative reaction"); nihilism ("attaining nonaction by acting"), and agonism ("sacrifice and consecration: hyperbolic passion, a bow bent toward the impossible, a paradoxical and positive form of spiritual defeatism").[17] Though most of them would deny it violently, almost all innovators in contemporary performance really represent new waves of the avant-garde in this sense, an established tradition of the modern. The term is vastly preferable to "postmodernism."

Less is more – Beckett and the avant-garde

Part of Beckett's importance as a cultural figure is that he blurs ordinary distinctions between mainstream and avant-garde. Because he was embraced so readily as a classic he was able, in effect, to smuggle certain progressive ideas across the border of mainstream culture, and that achievement is, rightfully, his most celebrated: he has actually changed many people's expectations about what can happen, what is supposed to happen, when they enter a theater. Not surprisingly, then, many avant-gardists, true to the bohemian habit of mind that considers any work compromised as soon as it attracts a wide audience, perceive this achievement as already ancient history and assume that their own work represents a radical departure from Beckett's. Actually, though, his work, particularly the media and late plays, remains in certain ways just as radical, as unassimilable into traditional structures of theatrical production, as theirs.

In light of the paucity of direct contacts between Beckett and members of the American avant-garde, let me posit a few obvious concessions. His temperament is clearly opposed to the extroversion of recent performance in general. He is not interested in deconstructing texts, as is LeCompte, except insofar as his own texts are naturally deconstructed by the public in the course of being perceived. He is not interested in the time-honored "cult of technique," one reliable indicator of which has always been composite names such as "ego-futurism," "cubo-futurism," "neue Sachlichkeit" – or "Onto-logical-Hysteria."[18] He is not interested in the kind of pluralism that manifests itself in selective excursions into the past, perpetrated like mid-night raids by LeCompte, the late Charles Ludlam and others, whose peculiar mixture of reverence and irreverence for sources recalls the hybrid structures of recent architecture. And his work does not flaunt a historical conscious-ness, except sometimes by negation, which distinguishes it from much performance on which Brecht is a major influence. Where Beckett does connect is in the more basic philosophical interest that binds all these tendencies together: what Schechner calls the "natural/artificial contro-versy," which has always existed implicitly in theater but which the avant-garde has brought explicitly to the foreground – using the theater's unique duplicity to convey that the nature of truth is contextual.

One reason Beckett is often considered irrelevant in this regard is that some of the most influential generalizations about him date from the 1960s and are thus based only on his first few plays. In 1969, no less astute an observer than Peter Handke wrote that he saw in Beckett nothing more than a variation on the Elizabethan *theatrum mundi*, stage as world as stage, posing no challenge to representation as such: "the fatal signifying structure (stage means world) remained unreflected upon and led, for me, to the ridiculous straightforward [*eindeutigen*] symbolism of the Beckettian pan-tomimes . . . That was no novelty for me, but rather a falling for the old meaning of the stage."[19] As I discussed in chapter 3, I do not agree with this assessment – the early plays can be produced in ways that stress the presentational – but it is important to accept the fact that Handke, and others like him, experienced only performances that led to that belief.[20] In general, productions of the late plays do not have the same effect; for the actors' physical predicaments in them are so severe that they become prominent as content, like the antics of Handke's Kaspar, and any symbolism generated by the precisely delineated stage action is reflected back onto the live actor in a way that reifies it and makes it far more immediate than what can be caused by processes of mental transference, as in *theatrum mundi*.

Immediacy in this sense, leading the spectator to become conscious of spectating, is the main shared purpose of nearly all avant-garde performance today, and it is pursued through a variety of means, many of which are also used by Beckett, e.g. replacing linear narrative with "information bits," maintaining indeterminacy of time and place, avoiding all readily iden- tifiable political and ideological orientations, and maintaining obvious separations between roles and performers. In other words, Beckett is too much aligned with the avant-garde to be designated unconditionally as its enemy. Still, he is not exactly a faithful ally either, having acted essentially as a maverick his entire creative life.

Perhaps the most significant assumption he does not share with the avant- garde is that artistic goals must be pursued in a spirit of aggression and panic, which is really part of Artaud's legacy: the conviction that the world and the theater have deteriorated to such a state that the only appropriate response is to scream. Beckett's inner calm, his unceasing effort to pare down, to weed out every inessential syllable, discarding all technical "gimmicks," stands diametrically opposed to the ethic of eclecticism and entropy in what is sometimes called "pluralistic" performance (Wilson, Squat Theater). The avant-garde has in fact ceased to search for the icon, as does Beckett in his late works, since that search represents a quest for unity, and unity is antithetical to the model of a "radiating" action that explodes *from* a center (Foreman). Like Caravaggio, Beckett dares to focus his gaze inward on particular psychologies at a time when nearly all the best artists in his field focus outward on behavioral *manieri* and the most respected theorizing supports that latter outlook.

What is more, his inwardness turns out to be just as effective as the outward techniques at calling attention to contextuality, if not more so, because Beckett's habit in all media is to tell a story about the ultimate failure of some attempt to perceive clearly. In the avant-garde's terms, his aesthetic of wholeness-in-fragmentariness *is* a critique of unity. And that critique is the unspoken "content" behind his use of a medium known for its coarse- ness, television, or his invention of narrators who lose the threads of their narrations or forget their characters' names. And it is also the theatrical significance of the mathematical specificity with which he describes certain objects (in *Watt*, say, or *The Lost Ones*) until the reader is quite sure he is thoroughly unfamiliar with them. In other words, in place of the avant-garde's refusal even to try to depict, he offers the spectacle of depiction failing, in effect using representation against itself by literally presenting its impossibility.

"Look again," says Beckett, not only at the image before you but at the way you looked the first time, at why that may have been inadequate. And if people willingly obey him, if even sophisticated audiences accustomed to avant-garde values trust him to use representation provisionally, then it is because he handles this model of the double-take, so to speak, with extraordinary specificity. As many critics have observed, the avant-garde, due to its historic distrust of all forms of established language, has often run into the cul-de-sac of unspecificity and vagueness. Patrice Pavis writes:

Avant-garde theatre has brought about a crisis in the semiotic and referential relationship of the sign with the world. It has lost all confidence in a mimetic reproduction of reality by the theatre, without having invented a semiological system and an autonomous theatrical language capable of taking its place.[21]

Thus, when Beckett transfers his Joycean control over written language to visual language in works such as *Quad, Nacht und Träume* and the various versions of *What Where*, he touches a nerve in the avant-garde's public, who suddenly recognize what has been missing elsewhere. And when he turns round yet again and produces language structures of unprecedented beauty, such as *Ohio Impromptu* and *Rockaby*, he does not appear hypocritical because he has long since convinced us that he understands the limitations of language articulated by Artaud and compendiously prophesied by Hamlet ("Words, words, words").

One might say that Beckett's relationship to language has always been quasi-Duchampian, if one accepts the idea that Duchamp's greatness lies not so much in the fact that he stopped painting as in his managing to have that act recognized as significant. You have to be quite a writer before your refusal to write can be received as a statement in itself. Beckett's works have grown shorter and shorter – displaying complete disregard for the commercial notion of a theater "evening" – and yet they have not ceased to appear. His language has grown sparser and sparser, yet it continues, the voice practically whispering, "careful on." (*Quad* and the *Acts Without Words* remain the only works completely devoid of spoken language.) Thus, as avant-gardists return to an interest in language after their long disaffection from it (since the rediscovery of Artaud in the 1960s), they again confront Beckett, who seems to stand both behind and in front of them.

Today there is taking place among artists a slow recognition of the cul-de-sac described by Pavis: that language cannot be merely one equipotent element among many in a composite stage language, as Artaud insisted, for it inevitably becomes more important than that in performance, constituting the very structure of the viewer's thoughts (Wittgenstein) and the object of our natural impulse to name experiences. Hence, Breuer and Akalaitis begin to publish their performance texts, which are often developed in rehearsal. Foreman asserts the value of his performances as literature, saying, "I have confidence . . . that in time people are going to be able to relate to my texts and see that they have the same coherence and density as a lot of twentieth-century poetry."[22] Ludlam earns a long overdue reputation as a playwright, adding to the praise he always won as a director and comedian. And Wilson pursues an ongoing collaboration with Müller, whose texts have constituted critically needed infusions of life-blood into this auteur's productions.

This last point was made poignantly clear to me by a coincidence that occurred in West Berlin in 1987: I saw, within one week of one another, Wilson's production of Müller's *Hamletmachine* and Wilson's *Death, Destruction & Detroit II*, an older work for which Müller tried to write a new text, but then abandoned his effort. In an open letter to Wilson included in the program, Müller wrote that the structure of *DD & D II*, "more than your previous works, consists in its own explosion . . . Perhaps the explosion had already grown too much . . . for a text, which necessarily means something, to be able to write itself in the whirlwind of the eruption."[23] The textless *DD & D II* turned out to be an unbearable, four-and-a-half-hour barrage of technical marvels, embellishing a series of trite and overstated tableaux, while the staging of *Hamletmachine* was a simple, elegant and unforgettable correlative to certain discernible meanings within a text that many have found incomprehensible.[24]

Theoretically, this obviously widespread attitude change on the part of the avant-garde's directors/auteurs ought to present an exciting new opportunity for writers. In reality, however, only a handful of contemporary writers seem up to the task of fulfilling the auteurs' very particular requirements. Most commonly, the latter seek texts describing non-linear action that does not prioritize events as in a conventional story. Consequently, their attention turns to authors such as Müller, William Burroughs, Lilian Atlan, Kathy Acker and Jim Strahs, who consciously avoid the "coercive" patterns of conventional storytelling and thus offer a unique degree of creative freedom in rehearsal, in addition to suggesting new viewing perspectives for stage action. And their attention also naturally turns back to Beckett, specifically to the highly fluid narrative patterning in his prose fiction which, for all the reasons just mentioned, they sometimes consider better dramatic material than his drama.

In short, inasmuch as the avant-garde has abandoned total sacrifice of language at the eleventh hour, it has encountered Beckett like an ambivalent Angel of God. It's as if he hovers over their work as a spectral oracle that no one can interpret but the skeptical nevertheless dismiss as relating only to the past. Blau, to his credit, at least attempts a kind of oracle-reading in his book *Blooded Thought*:

There is a pulsation of something like this, a progressive vanishing? or a vanishing progress?, in the *"fixed gaze"* of Beckett's Clov (who wants to be a solo performer, outside of history), resembling the Angelus Novus, something taking its course that he can't quite keep out, the long trail of repeatable catastrophe, two thousand years of western history like a propagating stalemate in his voice: "Finished, it's finished, nearly finished, it must be nearly finished. (*Pause.*) Grain upon grain, one by one, and one day, there's a heap, a little heap." We might very well have been discouraged, but the heap is fabulous.[25]

Risking interpretation myself of this characteristically "blooded" passage, I venture to guess that Blau's fabulous heap is the humanist tradition, which the avant-garde gradually, reluctantly, realizes it cannot simply turn its back on. Doubtless we will see more comments like this one in years to come, as more and more avant-gardists cease chasing Artaudian windmills, cease fearing the bugbear of "logocentricity," and recognize that one of their guiding spirits actually turns out to be a classic author. Not just any author, but the last best hope of the Author in the theater.

PART THREE

Conversations

When I began conducting interviews for *Beckett in performance*, I had no intention of publishing the transcripts as a collection. I intended only to compile primary material for a critical study, asking the same or similar questions of many actors and directors in order to collect a broad range of opinion on a number of controversial topics. In the course of conducting them, however, I discovered that many of the interviews were interesting in their own right, constituting conversations of publishable quality that augmented as well as supported the critical work. The following selected excerpts overlap at a few points with passages already quoted, but all of these bear repeating in their original, conversational contexts, both out of fairness to the artists and because these contexts reveal other meanings than the ones already pointed out.

All the transcripts have been edited and approved by the interviewees, and I have limited their brief introductions to lists of Beckett productions, the dates beside the titles being those of the premieres. In the case of Mabou Mines it is misleading to assign definite dates to productions, because that company's pieces evolve in performance over a span of time that often extends before and after the official premieres. Rather than giving no date at all for these productions, however, I have used in most cases the dates listed as premieres in a "Performance History" kindly provided me by the Mabou Mines Development Foundation, Inc.

JOANNE AKALAITIS, one of the original members of Mabou Mines, has directed two Beckett works: *Cascando* (1976), a stage adaptation of a radio play, and *Endgame* (1984). She has also performed in several Mabou Mines Beckett productions, including *Play* (originally 1967, revised 1971), *Come and Go* (1971), and briefly as a screamer in *The Lost Ones* (1975). This interview took place in New York City on March 7, 1986.

Jonathan Kalb: Are there particular skills you look for in actors when directing Beckett?

JoAnne Akalaitis: Well, I wouldn't say particularly Beckett. For certain kinds of theater you need actors who have some kind of vocal technique but also an inner force that enables them to wrap their tongue around the language, the words. And I would say that applies to Genet, too, and Büchner and Shakespeare.

K: When you adapted the radio play, *Cascando*, for the stage, how did you come up with the concept of seven actors at a table?[1]

A: It just came to me. It really comes from a vision of Nova Scotia, people in houses in the winter around tables. People sit around tables a lot. They're sort of trapped in their own world, because the outside world is so formidable and so uninviting. And they create their own world, and the world, the center of that universe, is the table.

K: How does that relate to the action of the original play, in which one character, Opener, speaks to two others, Voice and Music?

A: Well, it just was some way I wanted to do the play. I wanted to do it with a particular group of people, so I divided the dialogue, and in that case really quite a lot of liberties were taken with it. Some of it was on the radio. There was a live cellist.

K: When producing the play for radio, directors face the problem of characterizing the music, making it work as dialogue. Did you work with the cellist [Arthur Russell] as another player, as if he were someone speaking?

A: Well, he *was* a voice. He was a voice and also an actor, in that he was on the stage and he did things; he acted. He didn't just pick up his cello and play. He was as much a performer in the play as all the people sitting around the table, as was Fred Neumann [Opener]. So he was used as a voice, and also in a very classical and conventional way as an accompanist, in that Ellen [McElduff] sang and Phil [Glass] wrote the cello part under that vocal.

K: How did you decide when or how the emotion should change in relation
to the music – whether the music should be petulant here, angry here, benign
here?

A: I think, the way directors usually do. It's very intuitive. You have a
sense of what the text gives you. It's also in the logistics of doing a play: you
want something happy here, something sad here, in a very simple-minded
way. And I think it's interesting the way one works with musicians; you
don't necessarily talk a lot about the play, especially with very good
musicians. You say, "I want 15 seconds of happy music here, and then I want
20 seconds of slow romantic," something like that. What amazes me about
working with musicians is how general you can be but at the same time how
specific you have to be, like it's got to be 20 seconds or 15 seconds.

K: What are your thoughts about the scandal that blew up around
Endgame?

A: I feel it was sort of made up in a way. There have been plenty of
productions of *Endgame* which interpreted the design widely. And I think
our production was no wilder than any other production, among the more
unusual productions that have happened. So it was almost an accident that
someone decided to make a fuss about it. Because if you saw it, you'd see
there's no fuss to be made about it.

K: You've met Beckett, haven't you?

A: I met Beckett once in Berlin. And in fact he saw the set for *Cascando*,
which was this junkheap corner room. And I think he did not like it, but I also
think at that moment he did not want to make a stink. He's a very polite
person. He asked to hear some of the music, and Arthur played some of it,
and he didn't say anything about it. Then we had this nice visit, the company
and Beckett, and I asked him then if he'd write down the permission on a
paper napkin for us to do it in Switzerland, because his agent said we didn't
have it. I still have the napkin.

I think in the case of *Endgame* Beckett was away from it, he didn't know
me or he didn't remember me. And, frankly, it never occurred to me to write
to Beckett and say, "I'm going to set this in a subway." I mean, one does
what one does when you direct. You take the script as a guide, and in the case
of Beckett even more of a guide. In rehearsal every pause was, for me, almost
sacred. Some pauses meant one thing, some meant another. In other words,
when Beckett said, "Pause," in the script, the Assistant Director yelled,
"Pause," so that the actors had a way to know that there was an objective
structure that I wanted and that they had to internalize it. They had to sing
the same song, and it was very rigorous, very, very rigorous. Very
mechanical. Like: "Okay, you take five steps to the left, and then you

breathe, then you pause, one, two, then you go." It was not free wheeling, wild and crazy, let's play around with Beckett. It was athletic, strict, and followed Beckett's structure.

K: What was your reason for choosing the subway setting?

A: When people say, "Why did you choose that setting?," it seems so obvious to me. We had another kind of set before; we had a kind of underground tunnel. It was vaguer; it was a vague place, very primitive. But then I thought it looked like a set for *King Lear* or *Macbeth*, and Doug [Stein] did too; it was a muddy cave that didn't seem urban. And I wanted something that *was* urban, that could touch us, refer to our lives. Something that was not European, not arid, that had a kind of energy and funkiness. I was interested in all those values. We started with the idea of tunnel, and slightly

24 *Cascando*, directed by JoAnne Akalaitis, Public Theater, NYC, 1976. Opener: Frederick Neumann (sitting alone). Voices: Thom Cathcart (right of table), David Hardy (back to camera), Ellen McElduff (standing), William Raymond (next to Ellen) David Warrilow (left of table). Cello: Arthur Russell (back corner, not in view). (Photo: Tony Mascatello)

behind that the idea of post-nuclear, but that was never a major considera-tion. Then from tunnel to under the ground, to a kind of pure tunnel, a white tunnel, to a tile tunnel like the Holland Tunnel or something like that. Then to an underground vaguer space, and then to the subway itself, which in design terms (the way the stage is very wide) could flatten it out, open it up. All of those were very interesting things that Doug and I were playing around with. And we rode the subway a lot.

K: I'm sure by now you've heard the argument against specificity – that it was setting it in a specific, recognizable place that annoyed people, not just the subway. What do you think about that argument?

A: I think it's idiotic. I mean, everything onstage is in a specific place. At least it's in the theater. At least it's in Cambridge at the American Repertory Theatre. If you have it in a black box and put a chair onstage, the audience does not walk in and say, "We are in no-man's-land, we are in a vague, abstract, Platonic space." I mean that's the thing about theater; it doesn't happen in your mind, it doesn't happen on the page, it happens in a place. And frankly I find that so irritating. It's very academic, that whole idea that directors can't be specific. Everything is specific. I mean if you put a chair onstage it is chosen by someone and it means something.

K: You described your work with the actors as "very mechanical." Can you talk a little more about that?

A: Well, the structure that we had, the technique, was mechanical, but not the work itself. *Endgame* is probably the greatest contemporary play, I think, and it calls on a lot for an actor to perform. It calls for an actor to go very, very deep, go to the bottom, and then come up, with whatever he comes up with from his own history, his own life – which informs that mechanism, informs that kind of mechanical structure that we were working with. A book that influenced me a lot was Oliver Sacks' *Awakenings*. I read from *Awakenings* to the actors, because I thought that something about it applied to *Endgame*, something about being stuck, being trapped, about the two characters being trapped in different ways in their bodies. And especially for Clov – the story about the woman who gets stuck, and then once she starts going she just goes through the house, up and down, opens doors, slams doors, and then manages to get somewhere. John [Bottoms] really got that; he really went for that.

   And we also dealt with naturalistic things. Like: do they have diseases? What diseases do they have? Are they father and son? What were the relations of the people in the play? Do they have sex? Did they have sex? Those are hard questions to answer in Beckett, and I don't think we ever really answered them, but some information on that level was part of the work process. A lot of talk about physicality, talk about *Awakenings*, talk about being stuck, talk about being paralyzed, talk about being in pain, talk about relationships, talk about being trapped. We never talked about post-nuclear anything. I mean, that just wasn't relevant in the actors' work, although it was behind everything. And we talked about how men are together, you know, a society of men, a man's community. It was really deep work, it was very, very hard work, and exhilarating.

K: You had an opening that I had never seen before where Clov starts talking like a machine, very frontal, mechanical. Later on he switches and speaks in a human tone. What was your intention there?

A: I didn't think it was mechanical; I thought it was formal. I thought it was a song, a formal song. But it was really hard to do. You know, he really had to prepare it because I wanted it in a certain high range: "Finished, it's finished, nearly finished, ba dum, ba dum, ba dum." And that's how Ellen started *Cascando* – I thought about that later – "dum, ba dum, ba dum, ba dum." And I think it came a little bit fom the way we did *Play*. Lee [Breuer] had this idea we called "equal weight." Every syllable had equal weight, and only the punctuation and the pauses were observed, they structured the piece. It could seem very arid, but it's not; it's quite wonderful, that "dum, ba dum, ba dum." It's a kind of chanting from the beyond.

K: Does Hamm "break into song" in this way, too?

A: Yes. Hamm sings different songs. He sings more operatic songs. I see his songs as melodramatic arias.

K: Why were the lines, "Go and get the oilcan," etc., repeated several times?

A: Well, that was about being stuck; that impulse, that rhythm, that structure, was in the show, and in this case it was accented. And the repetition of those lines was, for me, the only liberty I took that I felt a little uneasy about, the only thing I did that I felt could be challenged.

K: Why?

A: Because maybe the playwright wouldn't want his lines repeated, because he didn't write them repeated.

K: You said before that you talked about whether they had sex, whether they were father and son, etc., that you asked those questions but didn't necessarily answer them. The play's full of that kind of ambiguity, and one could say that if anything constitutes its meaning it's that collection of ambiguities. How much do actors who play in *Endgame* or in any Beckett play, have to understand the meaning in order to do it?

A: I don't think I understand the meaning of the play, frankly. There are lines in *Endgame*: I have no idea what they mean. And I can call on all kinds of dramaturgs to find out. But for me working in theater, working on plays, is very intuitive, so I tend not to try to understand, except in a way that comes at it from strange vectors. I never sit down and say, "This is what this play is about, this is what *Endgame* is about." And I'm sure I don't understand *Endgame*, or any Beckett play, or maybe any play at all. For an actor to be intellectual tends to work against his work. Because then you get stuck. And I'm not anti-intellectual, I like intelligent actors, but I think a good handle on Beckett is the rhythm of it and also the way these lines just explode. You know the way Beckett has these completely perfect, wonderful lines. And you kind of coast until you get one of those lines, and then you have an explosion of universes and universes and universes that is for me very Jungian, very unconscious. Really opening up all kinds of worlds. This must be understood by performers in a physical, intuitive, subconscious way.

K: What about the four actors you worked with? How much do you think they in particular carried with them ideas about the meanings in *Endgame*?

A: They're very different kinds of actors in their working on *Endgame* or any play, so there's no way that I could characterize them as a group. John works on *Endgame* the way he works on everything, which is very intuitively, very physically, and worried about the language. Somebody like Rodney [Hudson] also works on *Endgame* the way he works on everything, which is: he tries to find, what does this mean? What do these lines mean? I don't think actors at a certain stage in their career apply themselves differently to different plays. They might say, "Oh Beckett is harder than William Inge." Beckett is very hard, he is very very hard. But after that is agreed upon no more is done; there is no more change in an actor. And with these actors there was no resistance to it. They were really thrilled to do it.

K: You were also criticized for the interracial casting. Do you have any comments about that?

A: I think in 1984 or 1985 you just can't even ask those questions. It really doesn't deserve a comment.

K: What was your intention with the music, which was yet another area of criticism?

A: I like, when people come into the theater, for something to be happening. I like it in Beckett just as I like it in everything else, music is playing, people are doing things. I use it a lot in my work. The use of music inside the play was pretty minimal, pretty sparse, so the music was used in a very conventional way, i.e. to get people in the mood. What I wanted was something threatening, slightly off-putting, intense, repetitive, and Phil did all of those things with that piece.

K: I asked you once before what you thought about politics in directing, and you answered that you can't always put things in political terms but that you had a social responsibility at least to try and see if you can put it in a political context. Were you thinking about that in *Endgame*?

A: Well, of course in the sense that I wanted to make it real. Real, applying to all of our lives, seeing it in the United States. But that was not the agenda, I had no agenda, that's not what the play was about. The play is not about homeless men, or people who sleep in the subways. It is a setting, and perhaps it leads you to think about that, but that is not what the play was about. And I think it trivializes Beckett to say that, and people attempted to do that, which I thought was a little silly. We were never asking ourselves, "Is this politically and socially relevant?" when we were working on it; we were saying, "Does this work?" And the energy of the men, the way they were dressed, seemed contemporary to me, very urban, and exciting. Kurt [Wilhelm] and I sat at a Mexican restaurant in New York City and looked out the window, and we said, "My god, look at how all these people are dressed! This is how we want the people in *Endgame* to look." So we decided that Rodney would wear a woman's hat and a blanket as his costume, and Ben [Halley] would wear the dreadlocks. It just seemed quite wonderful to me that Hamm and Clov are real people, and not European, French actors from 1955. They belong in 1985.

K: Did you ever consider changing the credits from "*Endgame* by Samuel Beckett" to "*Endgame*, from a play by Samuel Beckett" or "adapted from *Endgame*," as was mentioned as a compromise before the opening?

A: But it's not. I mean, then you would say that anyone who does not take the Samuel French specifications on a play would have to have the same kind of billing. My example is that you get a Noel Coward play and he says that "a short, blonde woman walks into a room, lights a cigarette, and sits down on such and such a kind of chair." If you cast a tall brunette and have her not light the cigarette, and sit down on another chair, do you then say, "*Private Lives* taken from Noel Coward"? I mean, what we did with *Endgame* was what directors and designers do. Never was that even considered for one second. I mean, this *is* the play; it's a production of *Endgame*. Like with Sam Shepard and *True West*. He gave the rights to Joe [Papp] to do it; later he hated the production – which is a very legitimate thing to do, say, "This director has ruined my work." But once you give the rights, you've taken that chance. You don't give the rights and then say, "I'm going to stop the play." A significant factor was that Beckett never saw it.

WALTER ASMUS has been Beckett's Assistant Director for the majority of the author's directing projects in Germany: *Waiting for Godot* (1975), *That Time* (1976), *Play* (1978), *Ghost Trio* (1977), . . . *but the clouds* . . . (1977) and *What Where* (1985). He has also directed all of Beckett's plays himself in various European cities, beginning with *Happy Days* and *Endgame* in Copenhagen (1978). He has directed Beckett once in the United States – *Waiting for Godot* (1978) at the Brooklyn Academy of Music, which was an attempt to recreate the author's 1975 Schiller Theater production with American actors. This interview took place in Hannover, West Germany, on January 7, 1987.

Jonathan Kalb: What were your responsibilities as Assistant Director during rehearsals? In general, what did Beckett expect from you?

Walter Asmus: With *Godot* he didn't expect very much. But when he was really in the full, emotional power of the working process, he would turn round every now and again and shout toward the audience, "What do you think?" And it was very embarrassing not to be present at that point. So that could happen. When he was really engaged in a situation with blocking, say, and I had a bird's-eye view whereas he was onstage, he'd turn and say, "Is it okay like this?," and so on. As you know, he writes all his *Regiebücher* beforehand and has very precise ideas and concepts, yet of course all that has to be proved in practice. And he listened to suggestions; one *could* say, "Oh, I think it's better this way than the other way," and so on. But mainly, I must say, especially in the beginning, there was a feeling of being overawed and sitting there just being invisible and making no noise. By and by it became a normal working relationship, which is to say we developed a mutual respect for one another and got to know one another better and better. And there developed a sort of truthfulness between us where he knows that he can rely on me, and I know that I can rely on him. Perhaps you know yourself, or from other people who know him, that you can absolutely rely on him. Of course, you don't know exactly in the beginning what it is that makes you go on with Beckett. Every now and again you find out little things. Even today, even now, if I have a problem, or think about a poem, it sometimes strikes me: "Oh, I've had this experience with Beckett."

K: Can you talk about some of the productions you've done without Beckett? What about the *Endgame* you did in Poland?

A: I did that without knowing one word of Polish. I worked through a

Polish interpreter who had done the translation, an academic who has a good feeling for theater.

K: How did that work?

A: Oh, it's difficult, of course. It takes up much time. He didn't know German, so I had to speak English with him, and that eats up a lot of time – apart from the moments when you really get angry and start to shout in German, and the Polish actors understand your German. Funny thing. That was right before the Marshall Law came in, in 1981, and it was really a political situation. *Endgame* has these repeated phrases, "there are no more bicycles," "there are no more biscuits." Well, "there are no more" in Polish comes out *nie ma* [he pronounces the words very clipped and biting], and that was very real for the audience. They were hanging on every word, because they could recognize the truth of their situation of simply running out of things in Poland. The stage situation could be seen as referring to the shops; you couldn't buy anything, in the same way things run out onstage.

K: I've seen that kind of thing happen several times in Europe, a spontaneous political reaction to just a phrase, but I've almost never seen it in America. It seems as though American audiences will react in that way only to something bigger, a whole scene perhaps. Do you think it's a peculiarly European phenomenon?

A: Yes, and even more in Eastern Europe, in the East Berlin theater, for example. I think it's wonderful there, the contact between the stage and the audience about the play. They are much more aware even than people here about political evolution. They are full of it, which we as West Germans often don't understand. It can be very subtle there, and the theater really has a social and political function. I think that's something we really miss here in West Germany because everything's so *beliebig*. You can do whatever you like, you are free to do everything, and that's not really a challenge and a fight. In East Germany if you do theater you do it with another consciousness. I like that . . . And actually, I still find myself digging in Beckett's plays for political and social relevance. That has nothing to do with putting it onstage as actual political stuff, but with being truthful to what he does, to find out where it really concerns me as a political and social being.

K: Beckett obviously never talks about politics when he directs. And in another interview you once commented that there was no discussion of psychology in his *Godot* rehearsals either. How then did the actors resolve their need for motivation?

A: He gave them images for understanding their relationships. For example, Gogo and Didi belong one to the stone, the other to the tree. That means they are connected, and at the same time there is always the tendency to go apart. He used this image of the rubber band: they pull together by means of a rubber band and tear apart again, and so on – which makes sense if you have to make crossings onstage. Beckett says, "every word, one step," and that tells the actor that there is not only an outer approach of moving this way, but also an inner approach of becoming more and more, say, tender or subtle in talking to one another. Things like that which tell something about the characters' relationship.

K: These images, and the others you mention in your rehearsal diary for *Godot*, are almost all about movement, but not all movement is human. A rubber band, a rock and a tree, for instance, aren't human. Many an actor will hear directions like that and say, "But I can't act that. Give me something I can act." How did these actors develop what they needed in terms of a human relationship? Did they perhaps make use of a friendship that existed beforehand?

A: Yes, in the Schiller Theater *Godot* at least, Gogo and Didi had their own friendship. And they played these games in private, too, to a certain extent. You know, all the ping-pong, ball-throwing, and teasing between them – they did that. Being colleagues for decades, they had this personal relationship, and also a feeling for irony and sarcasm. They knew exactly when they were hurting one another while pinching, torturing, and teasing in private, too. It was more difficult with the actor who played Pozzo, which I think is the most difficult part. Is it a psychological explanation, for example, if you tell the actor he overcompensates? Pozzo is a character who has to overcompensate. That's why he overdoes things, has a tendency to describe the sky and so on as very big, why he tries to impress people, and this overcompensation has to do with a deep insecurity within him. Those were things Beckett said, psychological terms that he used: that Pozzo was a weak character who has to overcompensate.

K: That's exactly the kind of thing actors are always asking for. What is Beckett's attitude toward that kind of comment?

A: Yes, he'll do it every now and again. But if I say that there were no discussions of psychology . . . You know, when I direct, I need to work with actors whom I know. We talk about our lives, fantasies, things that don't really belong to the play, just to have an atmosphere of understanding among us. Beckett never did that. He used precise terms, such as over-compensation, to explain a situation to an actor, but he was, I must say, reluctant about it. He didn't want a flood of these things, though he knows precisely everything about the psychology. Of course, he could explain it if he wanted to. I think he knows exactly why his characters behave as they do.

K: Do you think his reluctance was because these actors were giving it to him anyway?

A: No, I think it was a kind of self-defense. He tries to go the direct way, to take the direct line. And I think he expects actors – and there he is not a director, one must say, and he knows that – he expects actors to read his plays as he reads them. As a director, I become angry myself every now and again either because I don't have an explanation at hand or because I am too lazy thinking. I get furious at actors because apparently they don't read the play the way I do. If they read it as I do they couldn't ask. During rehearsal I think, "Well, they mustn't be able to play this. What are they all asking about? What do they want?" And that's a fallacy, of course, that the job of director is to help them see it your way. But Beckett really has, I would say, a naive way of approaching a part. He has written it this way, and his mind goes this way precisely, and he wants them to do it. And that's why he gives a lot of line-readings. That's his way.

K: I know he gives a lot of line-readings when he directs his late works. He even gave Billie Whitelaw a tape of the whole text of *Rockaby*. But were there a lot of line-readings in *Godot*, too?

A: Yes. But there was such a good working atmosphere that the actors listened, and knew how to transfer it into abstract terms, and then transfer it back into acting. You see what I mean? As a director I know you are always tempted to give line-readings, because it *is* the direct way. But when I give a line-reading, I cannot be sure – I know that by experience – that the way I speak the line is exactly what I mean, because I am not talented enough, or not good enough to give the exact reading. Beckett . . . I haven't experienced one play with him where, at some point in the work, somebody (an actor, or whoever) wouldn't say, "Why don't you play this part?" – because his line-readings are so fabulous, so inspiring, so true. It's a matter of truthfulness that you sense is there; he is at that moment what any actor should be, simple and true at the same time. So as an actor, you try to get the spirit, and then you have to think about it, make your own thing out of it, and not try simply to reproduce it.

K: Would the actors have been so accepting with another director?

A: No.

K: Then why with Beckett?

A: I'd say they loved him as a person. That has a great deal to do with it.

And that even happens to me, too. There are actors who like me and work hard, and people whom I don't get along with and who don't get along with me. And in the theater you can't solve this problem really. If I have the feeling an actor doesn't like me, it's very difficult to gain his love, or vice-versa. You have to use tricks. You have to kill him and then build him up again. But it's a fight, you have to fight, it's never a direct, normal human relationship – you know that loving relationship. And that was the case with Beckett. But of course it also has to do with Bollmann having worked with Beckett before on *Endgame*, and both he and Wigger knowing *Godot* very well, having done it ten years before. And it is no secret that Beckett has had greater difficulties with other actors. In *Footfalls*, for example, the actress had a very difficult time.

K: Did Beckett ever discuss issues of metatheater, questions about who they are playing for? For instance, are they playing for each other or the audience?

A: He more and more built up the fourth wall. I think in *Endgame* he cut out all the stuff where they look into the audience. There are some moments in *Godot* also where, for instance, Didi pushes Gogo toward the audience and he is flabbergasted and draws back in horror.

K: But he didn't cut that out in *Godot*.

A: No he didn't, and that's because he thinks *Endgame* is a more perfect play so he could do without it. It was not necessary to use theatrical conventions in this sense. *Endgame* is really a claustrophobic society which has nothing to do with the audience in the least. You only watch them as if they were behind a glass door. He did put in a kind of fooling – Clov fools Hamm – in the latest production he did with the San Quentin Drama Workshop. In the script Clov climbs up the ladder, looks out, and makes a report about the weather outside; Beckett reduced that to Clov jumping on the floor, and not climbing up the ladder. Hamm asks him what's it like outside, and he answers rain and so on. He cheats him as a blind man, which is a play thing Beckett invented as a director.

K: Were you involved in the discussions about costumes for *Godot*?

A: Not in the discussions with Matias before rehearsals started. That was all worked out. But he started with describing the costumes the first day he came.

K: Can you speak about what he wanted to achieve with these particular costumes: Didi wore striped trousers and a black jacket too small for him, and Gogo wore black trousers and striped jacket too large for him, then they switched during intermission. These outfits were clown-like but also gave an impression of informality unlike, say, the French premiere where they wore ties.

A: That has to do with the close connection between the two characters: being the same and not the same. It doesn't fit and at the same time it does. And there it's really dialectical. It is the same, and at the same time it's not the same. But there was no discussion about ties and so on; they were supposed to be tramps. Nothing very specific. I think sometimes Didi has a tie because he's considered more academic or whatever, and Gogo is thought to be more careless about his outer appearance. But it was a stylized thing.

K: What was the genesis of your production at the Brooklyn Academy of Music? How did the idea of transferring Beckett's Schiller production to an American stage with American actors first arise?

A: Well, I was very lucky. It was a wonderful opportunity to do it there. At first Frank Dunlop asked Beckett if he would do it. Dunlop had started to form a permanent repertory company at the Brooklyn Academy at that time. They had done *Julius Caesar* before, and they wanted to do three or four productions during the next season. Dunlop asked Beckett to direct *Godot*, but he said he would never come to America and recommended me. Then Dunlop asked me if I'd like to do it.

K: Can you talk about the difference between working with the German and American actors?[2]

A: Yes, I had a very hard time – because I wasn't Beckett, you know. They wouldn't eat out of my hand. I had to find things to give them motivation, and it was very difficult for me. Also, it was the first time I directed it sticking so close to another concept. I had it all somehow in my mind and feelings, the whole production, and I had to be very, very careful not to overrun them – and I did, I know that. Not to expect too much, not to anticipate things they couldn't fulfill because they didn't know about them.

K: Did you tell them explicitly that the plan was to transfer Beckett's concept?

A: Oh yes, there was no secret about that. I didn't sell it as my own thing. I wouldn't have done that. We agreed on that. And I started very fast with blocking; we were blocking within a couple of days – the same way as Beckett did it, by the way – but that proved to be very difficult because they couldn't fill the gaps. So we had to find a conventional,

25 *Waiting for Godot*, directed by Walter Asmus, Brooklyn Academy of Music, Brooklyn, NY, 1978. Sam Waterston as Vladimir, Austin Pendleton as Estragon, Michael Egan as Pozzo, Milo O'Shea as Lucky. (Photo: Martha Swope)

psychological way of explaining things, and I found it very difficult as a director. When you plan the play yourself, you have your ideas, but you do this work as you go along, occupying yourself with the play, how to put it across to the actors, and so on. But here it was all pre-formed in my head and that was the other way round – to find explanations for something which is already very clearly in your mind, very fixed – but you haven't *really* created it.

K: What do you think of the frequently drawn parallel between Brecht and Beckett, which some critics mentioned in connection with your BAM production? Is it something you think about in your work?

A: I think it's worth investigating. I always recommend that to hopeful young academics, try to encourage them to pursue that. I think that in terms of aesthetics and dramatic theory, and even in staging, there *is* a connection. The Brechtian *Verfremdungseffekt* is a form of what you called metatheater, only in Beckett it becomes natural. It is not linked with theory. The form of reduction in Beckett has to do with that; a reduction of some process onstage tells you something about life which is not life. It opens your eyes to reality, to life, without being naturalistic. And to a certain extent, that's what Beckett and Brecht tried to do – to get away from naturalism, to see things anew and start to think about them anew. And there's a link, too, with abstract painting, where Beckett comes closest in literature. If you look at a Picasso, he doesn't tell you about real life, in that sense, but he tells you about reality, different forms of reality. He's more real than life. Or he's more true, because the painter captures a very true moment which you can never see with your own eyes. Every now and again you do, perhaps you overhear people in a conversation and say, "that's terrible," because you don't hear what they say in context. It's unbearable in the same way these two people living together in *Endgame* becomes unbearable, or grotesque.

K: It seems very significant that there's never been a "Berliner Ensemble for Beckett," so to speak. There's a very developed technique for Brecht's plays, but where is the Beckett technique? Obviously some people play Beckett very well, but if you try to play it like Brecht it doesn't work.

A: Yes, there's a link with the *Verfremdungseffekt* but it's not a thing of practice, of practical theater; it's more a thing of theory, or thinking of art, of how to put life onstage, or see life onstage. There is always some sort of life onstage, but it has to do with aesthetics. What I said earlier about always trying to find the political/social implications, I think that's exactly the wrong way, of course; I would never try to explain Beckett in this aesthetic form. You see what I mean? Beckett becomes more and more abstract, he refines his art, he cuts out, he's like a sculptor – less and less and less – but the behavior of his characters gains in truthfulness by this process, I believe. In significance. And that's so challenging, to see it, and to know all about that thing he does away with.

K: In your article on Beckett's Berlin production of *Footfalls*, you wrote about difficulties the actress, Hildegard Schmahl, had in approaching the character psychologically. I know of some things Beckett said to try to help her; for instance, telling her the story he'd heard from Carl Jung about a girl who was "never properly born." But could you elaborate on the problem in those rehearsals?

A: It's difficult to explain. I can't remember any real motivation which Beckett gave for *Footfalls*, about why she should speak her lines in a certain way. The position of the body, for example. Beckett used to stand with his arms crossed like this [he assumes the posture of May], looking forward, pacing, and seeing things with his mind. And what he said was very forceful, very sharp then. And that has to do with the position of the body. If you grip your arms and you have a fixed, physical point here where you hold yourself together more or less, you can speak rather easily and sharp at the same time without pushing it with the body. You see what I mean? It's a technical thing, which of course doesn't give the actress any inner motivation. [He reads a bit from the text, imitating the way Beckett spoke it: voice very low like a loud whisper, punched out almost conspiratorially in short phrases.] I can only indicate it. How do you explain to an actress why to speak it in this way, which he gives as a line-reading? He didn't really give reasons for that. Later on when I directed the play it struck me that there is a real hate relationship with the mother, which is very realistic and which you can really discuss with an actress, who has her own mother experiences and so on. You can invent situations where a girl fights her mother, or tries to stand up against her mother, things like that, which are all in the play. I think it's a play about an inner revolution of a girl against her mother.

K: You found that those kinds of discussions helped?

A: Yes. It helps to discuss with an actress, in a mutual way, fantasies of how somebody invents their stories. Inventing stories is a way to feel yourself in existence, to be alive. It's a normal process of writing; the piece you have written is part of your life and you are proud of it, and it gives you the feeling of being, of being somebody. Inventing the story of Mrs. Winter, of course, is May's revolution against her mother, and at the same time she invents, projects herself into life, into somebody. And that's what Beckett means when he speaks of a girl who was never born; she starts to invent and create her own life without being alive in our social sense. And yet there is a real social story behind it, which we can find if we talk about our lives and our relationships to our parents and so on.

K: So he was not willing to have this kind of discussion with the actress.

A: No. He would never have this private discussion as we have. We have intimate, really to the point of intimate, exchanges where an actress has to open herself, has to talk about her own experience. And I give an example, a first one just to encourage her to do it.

K: And yet you said at the end of your article that in the end Schmahl was good in the part.

A: Yes I did. I worked with her a couple of times when Beckett had just left the rehearsal and said, "Oh, you can go on for a bit." And we tried to talk about it, and that helped her, I think, because there was a strange relationship between the two. She adored him as a man, I would say, as a woman adores a man – of course, I don't know any woman who doesn't. So it was really a love thing, and it was all the more frustrating for her not to fulfill his obvious demands, which he had as a director. She wanted to fulfill all the things that she sensed he wanted, but up to the very last rehearsal she used to break down, to give up. And in the end, she found, yes, a bit more and more and more, in layers.

K: Yet her problem isn't all that uncommon, especially in the later plays. Actors say, "How can I play this if I don't know what it means?" Some directors and actors say that they must come at it from a different angle. David Warrilow, for example, says that he must first find the "right tone" for his voice, and use that as the ground for character. These seem to be opposite approaches. Do you think both can work?

A: Yes. There are actors who need real detailed information about the background of the character they are supposed to achieve. And there are actors who can do a lot of things from the point of language, let us say, and musicality, without being less truthful. There are different approaches toward creating a character from the point of view of the actor, definitely.

K: Did Schmahl have similar difficulties when she worked on *Play* with Beckett?

A: Yes, there were similar difficulties. But in *Play* there were more difficulties with the other actress. Hildegard Schmahl, she finds her way, she succeeds somehow, she is a great actress; the other one was plainer and tried to make it by means of musicality and so on. And in *Play* you can do a lot if you have a sense of the central situation; you are carried away by the speed of the whole thing and the spirit of the play.

K: At one point in rehearsals Beckett asked for a piano to be brought in, so it does seem as if he was trying to make the actors work musically.

A: Yes.

K: But then later he changed his mind? You quote him as saying, "Perhaps I overemphasized the problem of the note."

A: I think that is about the gap between ideal and reality. You have the ideal vision of having a piano and giving a note for each of the three actors – one this, one this, and one this – as precise as music on the piano. And somehow you come to a point of resignation where you see that there are three different human beings involved, and you can't bring it to that perfection. It's not just music. So he gave up and said, "Oh try it your way." And that's the struggle. That's, for example, why I'm asked so often whether it's boring to do *Godot* again and again, or Beckett again and again. You come to a point where you have this longing for perfection. I was touring with the San Quentin Drama Workshop in Europe last Spring, and I saw almost every performance every night, and they were always different. It started to become music. And you go home so happy when you have the feeling, "Oh, it's eighty-five percent now." You see what I mean? You get a longing to experience it as mere music, not in terms of tones but in terms of feelings, or relationships between people. That's ultimately what Beckett wants, I think.

K: He speaks often about gray, a gray color that he wants to dominate when he directs. Does that relate to what you've said?

A: Yes, but he's very happy if color creeps in, you know, if it's the right color, the true color. I remember with Klaus Herm in *That Time*; where the text was supposed to be very flat and one tone, he started to create a painting out of it, with all the colors. But the colors must be true within the soul of the situation, and that's so tricky. With *Godot*, for example, it's a matter of timing: to be faster than real life but not become cold and mechanical. You start to understand certain sequences not from the meaning of the words but from the music – or they go together, the meaning of the words and the music of the exchanges. And that's a perfection one starts to strive for.

K: It seems that Beckett comes closest to the perfection he seeks when he directs for television at Süddeutscher Rundfunk.

A: He has a very personal relationship to Stuttgart. He knows and likes Jim Lewis, the cameraman for all his TV plays, very much, and knows he can rely on him and his taste and feeling for his work. It may be that he can get a better result there than elsewhere. And I think that the working conditions in Stuttgart are absolutely singular in the world. I doubt very much whether he ever had conditions like that at the BBC. You can get everything in Stuttgart, any time you want it.

K: In your article on the 1986 television version of *What Where*, you say that Beckett made a comparison between *The Lost Ones* and *What Where*. Can you elaborate on that?

A: From the point of view of image they are similar. In *The Lost Ones* there is this *auswegslose* situation. There is an exit which can't be reached, so there is no exit, and the number of survivors becomes less and less. And in *What Where* it is a situation where they try to find a way out, but there is no way out. He mentioned it as an allusion to repetition of themes within his work.

K: What about the colors that were planned for the characters in that play, colors taken from a Rimbaud poem? Why were they discarded and the production recorded in black and white?

A: I think, again, that the problem with Beckett is explaining Beckett. If, in directing a Beckett play, you start to explain things onstage, it becomes very wrong; it becomes terrible. The play itself doesn't convey the meaning – the pure play – if you start to provide extra explanations. And I think he had the feeling that color was a gimmick; it was explaining the inner situation by means of decorative things.

K: You also quote a funny short poem about Stuttgart from Beckett's collection, *Mirlitonnades* [still untranslated into English].

A: Yes. He read parts of these poems to me once when I went to see him off at the Stuttgart airport. He had written some of them in his hotel room. We were sitting in the airport restaurant, waiting because we were early, and I said, "What did you do all this time in Stuttgart?" And he said, "I can read you something I've written about it," and brought out his little book. And we're sitting in this place, hundreds of people around us, and he leans forward and starts to read. It was so absurd. All these loudspeakers, you know, plane announcements, "754 to Tokyo taking off now!" And Beckett's sitting there reading. It was so touching.

ALVIN EPSTEIN has acted in numerous American Beckett productions, including the New York premiere of *Waiting for Godot* (1956), the American premiere of *Endgame* (1958), Alan Schneider's TV film of *Godot* (1961), the triple-bill *Ohio Impromptu, Catastrophe, What Where* (1984), and the radio productions *All That Fall* (1986) and *Words and Music* (1987). In a recent production of *Endgame* (1984), he both directed and played Hamm. This interview took place in New Haven, CT, on March 4, 1986.

Jonathan Kalb: Can you tell me whatever you remember about creating the role of Lucky in 1956, how you came to it, how you produced what you did onstage?

Alvin Epstein: Well, I've never approached any of the roles in Beckett differently from the way I approach any other role. I never considered them special in that sense – that there was *a way* to do Beckett differently from the way you do anything. In that sense, every role is different from every other role, and you find a way to do every role. You can then begin to find similarities between various roles by the same dramatist, because in one way or another the concerns may be the same, the style may be the same, something comes through. It's like a family – even though the roles are different and the people are different, you see the family resemblance. But I certainly did not see that at the beginning when I worked on *Godot*, because that was my first part in a Beckett play. And I didn't know anything about Beckett at the time or about anything special except the difficulty of it.

K: So what did you do? How did you come up with the personality that was Lucky? There would seem to be nothing of value, for instance, in a Method approach to the work, research into the background of the character.

E: But there is. I mean, you sit down and try to figure out: who is this character? Why is he behaving this way? Why is he saying what he's saying? I did do that. Now, I might not describe that as the Method approach, but it has to do with it. I had to figure out what his relationship was to Pozzo, why was he on the end of a rope, what did Pozzo mean in his description of Lucky when he said, "So I took a knook"? What is a "knook"? Pozzo doesn't explain it; he doesn't explain it to Gogo and Didi. And why does Lucky carry the baggage, and the stool, and why does he obey orders? Those questions are easy to answer. What was really hard to figure out was the significance of his abject slavery, and what I discovered gave color to the simplistic and obvious explanation that he's a servant. He obeys everything, every order, and is rather cruelly treated but doesn't protest. That's clear, but what kind of slave, and how long has this been going on? Then you begin to extrapolate.

K: What were your answers to those questions?

E: I got them from the speech, when Lucky does begin to speak. He's ordered to think, not to speak, but clearly from Lucky's utter compliance to Pozzo's every order, he understands that his "thoughts" are to be spoken; he's identified as a "thinker" who must communicate *his* thoughts (not someone else's) through speech. And then some place in the play Pozzo speaks about the way he used to think. His thinking now consists of these broken and apparently unrelated phrases, phrases that come back over and over again repeated ad infinitum. Well, how did he think previously when he thought well? It seemed to me that then the phrases were sensible, coherent, not repeated ad infinitum, that there was a thesis he developed, and that he really was saying something. And what was he saying? He was presenting a thoroughly coherent philosophy which presumably dealt with the problems of life on a philosophical and elevated plane, and which Pozzo looked up to. He was like a guide and a teacher. He might have been a tutor to Pozzo – I mean in the old aristocratic European sense; he was a servant. Aside from that he was also an artist, because Pozzo makes him dance, and it's clear from other things Pozzo says that he was once a dancer. I think that in a way Lucky is a representative of that whole class of servants who were artists, musicians, philosophers, teachers. They were the Mozarts and the Haydns and the Moses Mendelssohns of this world, who hired themselves out to wealthy protectors whom they entertained and educated and created works of art for. There's an element of the King's Fool as well, the court jester; they were entertainers in that sense. That's what he was to Pozzo, and in that sense he was very valuable. He was a mark of distinction.

K: What did Lucky, I mean your Lucky, understand about being taken to market?

E: He's lost his value completely by having sold out – by being bought and sold to begin with – and little by little through the years he's been destroyed. He can't think anymore, he can't dance anymore, he can't do anything anymore, so it's perfectly natural that he should be sold like an old horse that's been used up. He's used up; all he can do now is carry the luggage and obey the orders and think badly and dance badly.

K: To me, your performance as Lucky, especially your delivery of the speech, is particularly memorable for its clarity of purpose. Can you talk about how you came up with that delivery?

E: Well, I tried to do exactly what I've just told you. To Lucky, these thoughts were not meaningless at all. They were the remnants of creative thinking. It wasn't received knowledge; he was a philosopher, he wrote this, created it, and his mind is full of the remnants. His head is a trash heap of broken shards of everything that he invented, and everything that he understood. So every single phrase, every little bit of it, is meaningful to him. His desperate effort is to try to create order out of it, but he can't. The work I did on my own, outside of rehearsals with Herbert Berghof, was really to try, first of all, to punctuate the speech, so that I could break it down into memorizable, understandable phrases. Because the speech is written without any punctuation at all, which means something obviously – it means it's a steady flow – but within it is obviously meaning. So I broke it down and tried to understand each bit, what part each bit might have played in the whole when it was whole. It's like a smashed stained glass window, a broken statue, and you have to find out where the pieces belong.

K: What does Lucky want to get across to Vladimir and Estragon? How does he see them, and why does he care about them as listeners?

E: I'm not sure that he does. I think the command "Think, pig!" is an opportunity he doesn't get very often anymore from Pozzo to try to put his life back together again.

K: Did you think your performance changed noticeably between Berghof's Broadway production and Alan Schneider's 1961 television film with Zero Mostel and Burgess Meredith?

E: Yes. It wasn't a difference I liked very much, because I didn't really like what Alan was asking me to do on camera. Onstage, when Herbert directed, I stood still – that is to say in one spot. I was in constant motion – trembling, gesticulating, collapsing, recovering – but I stood in one spot for the whole speech. Pozzo was seated and Gogo and Didi were standing there watching me, and I had my little area to do my thinking in. So I did it all in that one little spot, and I was able really to concentrate on what I was doing; there wasn't anything else to deal with. On camera, Alan insisted that I move. He had plotted the whole thing with me moving, and that just seemed absolutely wrong to me. And nothing I could do could persuade him against it. I didn't want to do it, but that was the way I had to. And you know in a movie you're more or less the slave of the director; you do whatever he tells you, because that's the way the camera shots have been set up.

K: How did you approach the character of Clov? Was there any significant change from the way you did Lucky?

E: Well, certainly there was a big difference. It was a wholly different role, situation, and character. The similarities are simply that Clov is the servant and also obeys orders – that's not much of a similarity though, because Clov is really not a thinker. He's not an entertainer; he's the oppressed son of Hamm.

K: What about Clov's relationship to Hamm? What does he believe about why Hamm is telling him to do things?

E: Hamm is helpless, Clov has never known anything except subservience to this man, and so that's what life is. He dreams about something else, but his experience is all that. Remember, he's grown up doing this. I think there's some hint that in the old days it was better, that there was enjoyment, that they enjoyed each other, but I don't think Clov has a memory of that. I don't think he has any nostalgia for the past because the past is a blank to him.

K: If Clov listens to Hamm because Hamm is helpless, does that mean he has compassion for him?

E: Yes. You see I can't really separate anymore what ideas I might have had in the original production from the ideas I had thirty years later when I was directing my own production and playing Hamm. I believe that Hamm is definitely blind, he really *is* blind, and it's Clov who might be lying when he answers Hamm's questions about the outside world – because you *can* lie to a blind man. I directed Peter Evans, who played Clov, to be telling the absolute truth, but Hamm is never sure that he's telling the truth, because he has no way of checking up on him. Hamm feels victimized.

K: So you played Hamm to be blind.

E: Yes.

K: Yet I noticed that at one point you waved to Nagg in his ashbin.

E: Because I know he's there, and also because I want him to think I can see him. One way of dealing with him, controlling him, is to make him think, "Maybe he can really see me." There were times, maybe just in rehearsal, when I wanted to lift my glasses and look at him with my blind eyes to make him think I could really see him.

K: One of Beckett's stage directions at the end is that he wipes his glasses, which is sort of odd for a blind man.

26 Peter Evans as Clov and Alvin Epstein as Hamm in *Endgame*, directed by Alvin Epstein, Samuel Beckett Theatre, NYC, 1984. (Photo: Martha Swope)

E: Yes, but it makes him laugh. I think he laughs at the absurdity of what he's doing.

K: Did you ever see Beckett's production of *Endgame* or any other productions he directed?

E: No.

K: Beckett's Nagg remains almost completely still and doesn't even lean over toward Nell on the kiss. Nagg in your production twists completely around toward Hamm, and is generally very animated. How did you decide on that?

E: I thought that Nagg and Nell were the old folks in their second childhood, and basically happier than the younger ones who were still battling with life. They've given up the battle. They can certainly remember far happier days, but they're sort of living in the golden sunset of their lives. They seem to enjoy life and they entertain each other. Well, he entertains her really, but she doesn't want to be entertained. The generation thing is very important there to me, that in a way the old people at the end of their lives have more real life in them than the young people.

K: What was your work with Peter Evans like? How, for example, did you come up with his walk?

E: All we tried to do was interpret Beckett's stage directions. Beckett describes his walk as stiff and lurching, and he complains about the pain in his legs and the fact that he can't sit down. So we simply tried to bring to physical life exactly what Beckett had described, and from that Peter evolved what you saw.

K: At the beginning he walks into the wall. Was that intended as a joke?

E: Walking for him is not easy, and again, according to Beckett's description, his eyes are fixed on the ground. It's not really a gag, but of course it's funny. Because walking is difficult and his eyes are fixed on the ground, he doesn't see that he's walking into the wall until he hits it. So he walks until something stops him, and it's the wall. It only happens when he's waking up. He hasn't had his coffee. He hasn't gone out to the kitchen yet and he has things that he has to do: he has to draw the curtains and look out of the window, and in order to do that he also has to get the ladder so he can get up to the window, and he's still out of it, not fully conscious.

K: My impression of it, as an audience member, had to do with the well-known idea that the characters in *Endgame* are actors who are aware they're playing before people. It seemed as if this Clov wasn't necessarily a bungler, but someone performing rehearsed mistakes. Was that the intention?

E: That wasn't exactly the intention; let's say it was meant to be ambiguous – but we did deal very much with the performance aspect of the play. They talk about their routines and the things they do in life as being part of their performance. Beckett plays games with the audience. He even has Clov look directly into the theater and say, "I see a multitude in transports of joy." Hamm desperately wants to perform, needs an audience, forces Clov alternately to perform with him or be his audience, and later the same with Nagg. Is he performing because there is, hopefully, a real paying public in the theater where *Endgame* is being presented, or because he needs to people his depleted universe of three other people in one never-to-be-left room with a "public"? So we never tried to make it a fourth-wall performance where it really goes on in some remote space. It's going on on the stage of the theater where it's going on, etc., etc.

K: Which did you prefer to play as an actor, Clov or Hamm?

E: I preferred to play Hamm, simply because by the time I got to play Hamm I was much more familiar with Beckett's work, and I was much older and understood more about it, so I felt more fulfilled by it.

K: What about the ending in your production? There was a very distinct change in Evans' Clov near the end. It's as if he throws a tantrum, he bursts out laughing, and has even more trouble than before standing up. Can you talk about that?

E: I think toward the end of the play he's becoming desperate; he can't stop obeying, so he obeys with a sort of crazy, self-deriding mania. He's having an hysterical fit because he can't stop, and because Hamm won't let him stop, and he can't get out of there. Or he thinks, "If I do this then I'll be able to leave. If I just do this, get this over with, finish this, then I can go." Beckett doesn't say anything like that in his stage directions, but it seemed clear from the development of the play that that's where it was going.

K: Did you decide as a director, or did Peter decide as an actor, that Clov leaves?

E: No, he doesn't leave. He stands there. He's all set to go, but he doesn't go, and we don't know what happens. I'm now a firm believer in not answering questions that Beckett doesn't answer. If Beckett leaves it open it's because he doesn't want it answered, and in a deeper sense he isn't even asking – the question is irrelevant. Clov is neither Hamm's son nor not

Hamm's son. And I think it may be because he wants *Hamm* to be uncertain. I mean, if anyone would know Hamm would know. Maybe Hamm doesn't know.

K: Maybe Beckett doesn't know.

E: I think Beckett really doesn't know. The longer you live, and the more you remember, and the more you have in your background, the less sure you are that any of it ever happened exactly that way. I think the subjectivity and unreliability of memory in linking the characters to each other are themes in *Endgame*.

K: Can you tell me about the genesis of your performance as Reader in *Ohio Impromptu*?

E: I didn't originate that role. I came into the production to replace David Warrilow, who had been directed by Alan Schneider, and then Alan directed me in it. I had already seen David's performance; they were in the middle of their run. I accepted immediately. But I had minimal rehearsal time with Alan. I think I had three or four rehearsals with him; of a few hours each, and I also had to be put into the other plays, *Catastrophe* and *What Where*. Mainly I had to fit into an existing production where everything was already set. Before I began to rehearse I went to see the production. I got a lot of ideas from David's performance, ideas that I didn't necessarily understand at all. I just thought, "that's good and I want to do it that way," because I didn't know what else to do. I hadn't the vaguest idea what else to do. I wasn't going to start from scratch; there was no time to start from scratch. So I said, "I'm going to do as much of that as I can," thinking all the time, "Oh, I can't do that at all, I'll never bring it off. But they say I can, Alan believes that I can, so all right I'll do it, I'll try, I'll see." As it turned out, I think that my performance was very different from David's. It became very personal. I was able really to perform the part as if it were my own. I wasn't anymore imitating anything. I love that play. Certainly of the three in that program it was my favorite.

K: What kind of reality does the actor playing Reader have to create for himself, and how is that different from the sort of reality you have to create for yourself with Lucky or Clov or Hamm?

E: I would say that it's much more ambiguous than Hamm or Clov or Lucky. Those characters exist in an identifiable reality – the reality of the play. In *Endgame* there are two men who live shut up in a room with two old people in ashcans, and one is the master and one is the servant, one is older and blind, the other is younger and crippled. So you know who they are and you know where they are. In *Ohio Impromptu* there are no such easy answers. But again you get them from the text, because the text is a perfect receptacle for Beckett's vision, for what he's writing about. The identity of the two men becomes clear; one seems to be a figment of the other's imagination, and then toward the end of the play you're not sure which is the real one and which is the figment. But as long as you know that possibility exists, that's already something you can deal with, that you can act.

K: So what did you use as an actor? You say you get some answers from the text.

E: First of all, to understand the "story," which is what the Reader reads out of the book. The "story" begins with a man, unnamed, unidentified, who is grieving for the loss of a loved one, and who has moved out of the place where they lived together to try to forget, and who can't forget and then wants to move back, but can't. And that grief never goes away. Then one day a man arrives wearing a long black coat, draws a book out of his pocket, sits down and reads all night until dawn, and then disappears. Then on other nights he comes back, and he always reads from the same story. Eventually you realize that the man who comes is the man who's reading, and that this is another night of reading the book through the whole night until dawn. So that the man who is reading is obviously the character who arrived, is not the man who was bereaved, but the man who says to the bereaved in the story, "I have been sent by – and here he named the dear name – to comfort you." But he looks – and this is Beckett's stage direction, and it's described in the story – exactly like the man he's reading to. He doesn't come in the guise of the dear one, who has disappeared and presumably died, but in the guise of the man he's reading to. The possibility that's awakened in my imagination is that, out of extreme loneliness, the man who is alone and bereaved invents a companion who is himself, a sort of an alter ego who comes and reads the sad tale over, to have company, and to have someone share the grief.

K: So this is not the first time the reading happens.

E: No. It's endless. It's a picture within a picture within a picture within a picture. It's just endless. Except that it gets very ambiguous, and beautifully so, at the end when he reads, "I shall not come again." Does that mean this is the last time? But since he is reading the printed page, each time is the "last" time! Etc., etc.

K: Why is Reader stopped by Listener when he tries to turn to "page forty paragraph four"?

E: That's the point where the story is talking about the "dreadful symptoms," the awful insomnia. I guess he had visions or experiences out of insomnia, as described in detail on page forty paragraph four, and the Reader is turning the pages back to page forty to read those details which are now referred to. It's like "see footnote on page forty." And the Listener's hand stops him because he doesn't want to hear those terrible things; he can't stand the idea that he's going to have to listen to his own nightmares.

K: So it's himself who stops him.

E: No, it's the other man. It's the Listener who stops him, but who is the Listener? Who is he?

K: How much do you have to answer those questions, resolve those ambiguities, to do the part?

E: There are different schools of thought about this. Some people won't even consider such questions as legitimate. They say Beckett is pure poetry and just music, and that you don't ask yourself these questions, but I think that's a load. Somewhere in themselves they had to have asked those questions, and they had to have answered them. That they don't want to talk about it is perfectly legitimate, that they don't want to have to say that I decided this or that is legitimate. But no matter how abstract and disconnected you want to keep yourself from the meaning of the text, it still has meaning; it's not notes in music, where you can keep your distance. These are specific words, they say things, they have referential meaning, you relate to them in a different way than you relate to just sounds. And so I think that it isn't quite sincere to call it "music." On the other hand I don't think there's any hard-and-fast rule about it. You find certain questions that you feel, for personal reasons, need to be answered or decided upon, and others that you don't want to answer. I come down more on the side of ambiguity. I certainly, as I said before, don't think we should answer questions Beckett doesn't answer. If Beckett makes it ambiguous, all you have to do as an actor is to understand what the ambiguities are: what are the possibilities? What are those two or three or four possible choices? A single possibility is not ambiguous, but with two there is already ambiguity.

K: What do you do with that as an actor? I mean, you come up with an ambiguity, then what?

E: You deal with the ambiguity. Find a way to deal with it. Obviously it depends on what kind of ambiguity you're talking about. If Hamm is telling a story about a man who came crawling on his belly years ago and asked Hamm to take him in with his child, up to that point it's merely a story, but the hint is that that's how Clov got there. Was the child Clov?

K: Are you saying that the actor who plays Hamm has to understand that it mustn't be clear.

E: Yes, that maybe it's Clov and maybe it isn't Clov. Hamm asks Clov, "Do you remember your father?" It's very possible that the whole story is a lie, and that Hamm is the father, and this never happened. But it's also clear that if it is a lie, or if it isn't a lie, he's tantalizing Clov with it. So in the ambiguities there are things that are not ambiguous. And maybe he doesn't know himself, doesn't remember anymore. He's told the story so many times that maybe he now believes it really happened. But maybe it never did, and maybe he doesn't know anymore whether or not it happened. Maybe he's not sure if Clov is really his son. It's important for the actor to realize that it's not ambiguous because Beckett was too vague to write something precise and needs to be clarified by making one choice or the other. Beckett is writing precisely about a man who doesn't remember, who can't be sure if he's telling the truth or not.

K: I wonder if I could get you to be a little more specific about *Ohio Impromptu*. You talked about a couple of ambiguities in Hamm that the actor has to carry with him and understand. Which ones have to be understood with Reader? What ambiguities in that script have to be carried by the actor in order not to simplify it?

E: First of all, did this happen to me? Is it my story I'm reading, or is it his story I'm reading? And that of course is related to acting, if you become very involved in your role. Is this really happening to me or not? If I'm feeling things, if I am emotionally involved, then something is happening to me. There's an ambiguity there, in acting, and I think that's also in the play. Beckett's always doing that. I mean even in *Catastrophe* where the protagonist is standing on a pedestal, on display, and the director is directing, and the assistant is like the assistant director, and they're arranging him for a performance, and the performance is going on while you're doing it. At the end the director is out in the hall, out among the audience, talking about a future performance, but there's a performance going on now. So he plays games, the same as in *Godot* and *Endgame*. End-Game.

K: Yes, but I'm curious about how you deal with that.

E: If you decide that something is an ambiguity that mustn't be resolved, then it's also something you ignore. The question of whose story it is becomes moot, it doesn't matter – I mean, if you identify with the character. I'm reading the story, and whether or not it's mine, I identify with it. At the end of the play, when you, the Reader, close the book, you both, Reader and Listener, in mirror image look at each other, suddenly stare at each other after not having seen each other throughout the whole play. Both characters are described in stage directions as appearing identical and sitting in identical positions. It's suddenly looking into a mirror; only which is the reflection, which is the reality? So you know that you're not just reading a story about somebody else that means nothing to you; the grief is real, whether it's yours or his. You characterize a man to whom this has happened.

K: And do you have to understand anything about who the other person is?

E: Well, in this play, it's sort of ambiguously clear who the other person is: the other person is the person to whom it happened *if it didn't happen to me.* It's like an Escher drawing – architecturally precise black-and-white lines, except you don't know how this staircase leads to that landing, because if you follow the staircase upwards it should lead to the next highest landing, but it turns out to be the one below!

K: What did it mean to you to look into Listener's eyes?

E: Saying goodbye, saying farewell. At the end of the story he seems to say that he's finished reading; the dear one has told him – the Reader – not to come again to the Listener: "No need to go to him again." So to the lonely one, the Listener, who is receiving this announcement from the dear one not only that the Reader won't come again but that he *need* not, I believe it's tantamount to an announcement of death. You need not go back because he's going to die. He won't be there anymore, so there's no point in going back to read to him. It's like a foreknowledge of one's own death.

KLAUS HERM has performed in three West Berlin productions under Beckett's direction: *Waiting for Godot* (1975), *That Time* (1976) and *Play* (1978), all at the Schiller Theater Werkstatt. He has also performed in Beckett's radio and television plays, including the author's productions of *Ghost Trio* (1977) and *... but the clouds ...* (1977) at the Süddeutscher Rundfunk in Stuttgart. This interview took place in West Berlin on April 13, 1987. (Translated from German by Jonathan Kalb)

Jonathan Kalb: When did you first meet Beckett?

Klaus Herm: In 1965 during the first production of *Waiting for Godot*, which Deryk Mendel directed – the first not for Berlin but for me. The rehearsals had gotten quite complicated and [Horst] Bollmann said, "For God's sake, we have a living author. He should just come." So Beckett was contacted, and about fourteen days before the premiere he came. He gave some decisive suggestions, in his reserved way, but otherwise didn't interfere in rehearsals.

That production went on to become a success, but at the opening party Beckett said, "Yes, it's splendid that it went like this. But you know, I'd really like to do *Godot* myself – not today, not tomorrow, but at some point. I need a little time to prepare myself, maybe in six months." That just amazed me. I thought, "My God, he wrote the play and yet he needs preparation?" Then he asked, "And if I do it, would you play Lucky again?" Well! I floated at that moment, I may say, like a small balloon. I was happy. And *ten years* later, when I'd already left the Schiller Theater, I got a call from the Intendant telling me that Beckett wanted to direct *Godot* himself and would like me again as Lucky. Typical for Beckett . . . after ten years!!

K: And except for Pozzo they were the same actors in 1975.

H: Yes. Only Vladimir and Estragon exchanged roles – which was not all that simple at first because both had already made up their minds about the roles learned ten years before.

K: What did you think of Beckett as a stage director?

H: The work was wonderful and stimulating, and you never felt stifled. Despite that, though, I wouldn't say he could direct other plays. And he doesn't want to, anyway. He said, he's no director.

K: Do you have a particular Beckett technique? What I mean is, is it different to play Beckett than to play other authors?

H: Yes, absolutely. On the one hand it's a severe reduction, primarily of the comedic elements. You have to minimize expression severely. The art of leaving out. There's a Chinese anecdote in which someone draws a rooster, first with all the feathers, then with fewer and fewer, and at the end the rooster is drawn with a single stroke but one nevertheless sees it's a rooster. I've always tried out my roles exuberantly and overflowingly, and then reduced during rehearsals. The comedic element lay underneath, but it wasn't "exhibited." You try through reduction to come to a strong concentration on the essential, and through that a small gesture takes on enormous power.

K: Did that process differ between the two productions of *Waiting for Godot?*

H: Mendel is a choreographer, and he comes at things very much in a choreographic way – which is, incidentally, also the case with Beckett. I asked him once why he wanted to direct *Godot* himself, and he answered, "The play is messily written." It's messy not in its words but in its visuals, and in fact his *Regiebuch* looks like a mathematics text. Now that all may sound pretty silly, but it isn't by any means. He always asked, "Is that also your feeling, to make this movement, or walk this way?" He never grafted anything on. To insert comedic devices in order to bridge over your own "shallows" has nothing to do with Beckett texts. Nothing is approximate; his world is always a complex.

K: Was there no improvisation?

H: No. Never. That's just not done, and there's also nothing there to improvise. Take this sentence of Lucky's, for example, which is so monstrous. You stand at the beginning of it again and again, and it raises more and more associations and associative images. They come naturally. That's the imagination, no? You can't just play or express one of these and expect it to become plastic for the public.

K: Honestly now, how did you react, at the beginning, to Beckett's exactitude?

H: That really presented no difficulty for me, strangely enough, because I'm always a bit picayune. I work quite slowly. Everything isn't always immediately at my disposal; I don't have that skill. For the most part, I make choices only after I've understood the word and the situation. And that's really what it means to work on Beckett texts: you have to understand the inner situation through the word. And in fact Beckett loves comedians, the comedic element; it pleases him. It's superficiality in the comedian that troubles him.

K: To make the question a bit more specific, in his rehearsal diary for *Godot*, Walter Asmus wrote that Beckett started out by reading Lucky's whole monologue aloud, very precisely. Was that, for example, okay with you? That doesn't always happen with directors.

H: Yes, it does sometimes. But here it so happened that the other actors were still busy with another production, so I was alone with him right away at the first rehearsal. Beckett said, "Under the circumstances, we'll start right in with this sentence, if that's all right with you." Well, I was flabbergasted. I thought I'd at least have some time to acclimatize myself. And he went on to divide the sentence this way: "From here to there it's the indifference of Heaven, and from here to there it's the shrinking of Man, seen spiritually I mean, and from here to there it's the petrifaction." In my preparatory work, I'd already chosen signposts for myself, and it happened that they coincided exactly with what Beckett said. Naturally, that gave me a pretty good feeling, and I thought, "Aha, I already know what he means." These points – "indifference of Heaven," "shrinking of Man," "petrifaction" – are not at all abstract for me, but rather concrete. I know what to do with these things.

K: Can you say a bit more about your approach to Lucky? What work did you do on your own?

H: Since I knew in good time that I'd be playing the role, I learned the sentence early and "carried it around" with me. And I wondered, why is he called Lucky, the happy one? He walks on the rope, must carry constantly, is tormented, why happy? Well, it's because he's the only one of the three [sic – four?] who has a concrete task, or who presents himself with a task. He exists because he does something. Pozzo says, "In reality he carries like a pig. It's not his job." But he does it. That is a declaration of existence. And one naturally extrapolates from that and asks, why do we live? Why are we here, anyway? You'd die if you had no *raison d'être*, so Lucky clings to his task. That's why he kicks Estragon when he wants to take the bag away; he's defending his task.

K: So it really didn't bother you at all that Beckett spent little or no time on psychological motivation or naturalistic backgrounds for the characters?

H: I understand that in him. He did, after all, write the play. And if I'm going to realize it somehow, I should go in this described way. I think Asmus also wrote, in *Theater heute*, about how I approached the text, about how "Herm" imagines concrete situations, develops them for himself first, and then lets them drop to go Beckett's way. I always try to imagine concrete situations with Beckett texts, to go not into abstractions but rather into wholly conscious situations. For instance, in *That Time*, the Voices A, B, C describe a man going into a museum, looking at paintings, traveling with a streetcar "to the end of the line." He remembers his love "on the stone together in the sun," etc., a tapestry of life woven out of three voices. That was wholly concrete for me, and so I worked on it wholly concretely, colorful and varied, in order afterward to reduce everything as Beckett wanted it. He wanted these memories to be in uniform gray, a continuous stream and flow of words. I understood that. I did say to myself, though, that if you start out bubbling forth a continuous stream and flow of words, purely technically, the image won't come across at all. In my work, I have to establish the images first of all for myself, in order then to put them onto this single plane.

K: But *That Time* is really very different from *Waiting for Godot*. In *Godot* you have more of a real "character" to play. It sounds as though, even with the more traditional character, it's a question of how much psychological motivation one needs *in general* as an actor, not just in a Beckett play. Is that true?

H: Yes. I like to have psychological motivations in other roles, too, but it also helps me when I can imagine how someone moves, or what his demeanor is. In *Godot* Beckett describes that absolutely. The entrances are described; the walk is described; the carrying is described. At one point, the walk was different. He wanted to have it slouching at first; then we agreed that it be utterly light, like something gliding over the floor, so the movement wouldn't become massive. Moreover, Lucky stands in one spot for the most part, bent over for about a half-hour, never setting down his bags, and that gets to your back. So I thought, "wavering gently, like a leaf in the wind." I imagined a Calder mobile moved by a current of air, and I moved lightly sometimes – even when others spoke to me. Beckett approved.

K: So could one say that, in a sense, you reversed the usual process, since you received specific physical instructions first and then moved on to psychological considerations?

H: Well, I always try to duplicate what the director says. Beckett never just said, "Do it that way." It simply happened that way. In other situations I'm very easily irritated, or prone to getting "set," and I'm unfortunately also often prone to believing the director strongly. Here there were no restrictions, though, or rather something gave me the feeling that I should carry out something that Beckett, and not I, imagined.

K: You speak Lucky's monologue much slower and more sensibly than most other actors. Why is that?

H: Because Lucky wants to express himself clearly. That's his desperate attempt, now that he is obliged to talk: to clear something up. And when one wants to put a thing especially clearly, one invariably ends up rambling without end. So he's always trying to reorganize, concentrate on the next point. His aphorisms overwhelm him; he's overrun by them. A lot of people said at the time, "Great, you needn't be afraid if you 'go up.' Just say anything, then." But I thought, there's no period or comma in the sentence – it's written without punctuation – so if you say one syllable differently, one small word, leave out an "and," it's like a nuclear explosion. That's the problem with this sentence: you can't peel off the tiniest piece or the whole awesome structure collapses.

K: How did you think of your relationship with Pozzo? Asmus has said that the actor who played that role had a great deal of difficulty with the play. Did this situation affect you?

H: No. I know the actor, Carl Raddatz, somewhat. He has a certain type of naiveté that is good for this role, and I believe it fascinated or impressed Beckett, too. Raddatz is a difficult "rehearser"; I know that from other plays. He always has to know everything, even the psychological. That the psychological never came into question here was perhaps the difficulty. Really, I didn't find there to be such great difficulties back then, though; the ones with Minetti [who played Pozzo in 1965] were another story entirely.

K: The reason I ask is that I'd like to know what the actor playing Lucky needs from the one playing Pozzo in order to do his role.

H: It's an interrelationship, a tandem, like that of Estragon and Vladimir, who also can't get free of one another. "We're not tied?" Of course we're tied. Therefore we belong together, like a mirror with two sides.

K: Did you have such a relationship?

H: Yes, I had it. And if I didn't, I would've had to imagine it. You can't just pick and choose as an actor: "I like him," or "I'm not playing with him." Eventually it'll happen that you have a love scene with a woman you altogether can't stand. You have to play the scene, anyway. Raddatz is a very precise actor, and that is important. With Beckett one can't improvise, and certainly one can't improvise as a comic.

K: It seems as if you accepted Beckett's working method, with all his exactitude, etc., very easily. Would you have accepted it so easily with another director?

H: That's a good question and not so easy to answer. Offhand I'd say,

"Yes." Beckett didn't really do anything special at all. He didn't make a big fuss but rather tried to direct his play. I'm a little old-fashioned in that I always like to know first of all what the author or poet wants, what's in the play, and then see how I can get it across. To start out saying, "We're going to do great things – cast the men's roles with women and the women's roles with men": that I find terrible. That's so chic, and so much the trend. So I'd say that if a director made it as simple as Beckett did, extracting the humor, not making it ponderous but letting the existential element remain, then absolutely, I would've accepted it in exactly the same way.

K: You've already talked about this a bit, but I'd like to hear more about the differences between working on *That Time* and working on *Godot*. What are the actor's concerns when performing a later play like *That Time*?

H: That's, of course, something else entirely. Strictly speaking, *That Time* isn't a play. It's not classifiable. It moves, in a manner of speaking, beyond legality. Thus, for the most part there are no possibilities of play; it's mind work. You stand on the stage, only your head is visible, and you listen to your own voice – which presents a crazy problem: sometimes you hear only your own mistakes! That's how I imagine purgatory!! I helped myself through it by trying to think of the current sentence a split second *before* it came up on the tape. I love this play very much. It's a text-of-the-century, and it was a pleasure to work on, but it was not a pleasure to perform. *That Time* – and *Footfalls*, which is also short – are an absolutely experimental kind of play, barely classifiable in theater practice. They're variations about the theater, about how far one can go. Beckett said once, "I really don't know whether one can do this to the public." And in some way he was right.

K: The published rehearsal diary for *That Time* speaks of your reading the text for sense at the beginning and then later for fluidity. Can you talk about that transition? What was the problem and what was the goal?

H: His goal was to have it without emotion. At first I thought these three versions – A, B, C – were supposed to contrast with one another. I had imagined it more colorfully; that was my problem. But he said, "No, look, the thoughts you think, they're without emotions. They're at the same level." He wants to have this stream of words, and he doesn't care whether people get the story or not. What matters to him is the flow of words. And, strangely, some spectators with whom I spoke said that, at the beginning, one starts to listen and tries to attend to the sense. Then one loses oneself, hears only this trickle of words, and thinks suddenly, "God, those are my thoughts being spoken." Naturally, that made me happy. That is to say, I believe that, through the depersonalization and neutralization of the text, he wanted to give the public the chance to think something of their own. I had

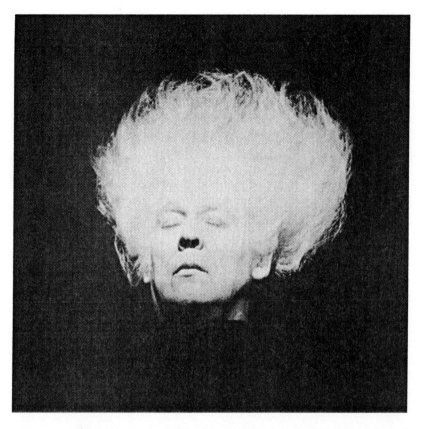

27 Klaus Herm in *Damals* (*That Time*), directed by Samuel Beckett, Schiller Theater Werkstatt, West Berlin, 1976. (Photo: Anneliese Heuer)

difficulty adjusting to this uniform flow, in addition to the fact that there was always the technical difficulty of speaking without breathing. The breathing was cut out by the sound technician. Beckett didn't want any pauses except for the three specified in the text. Without period or pauses, and as much as possible without breathing! And technically that was exceedingly difficult. I always spoke a replica of what I'd done, stopped, breathed, went back a little, and then spoke further. The problem was to speak further at exactly the same level, which is extremely difficult. And though I spoke steadily and didn't shade things, I always tried to imagine the images.

K: Asmus told me in an interview that Beckett wanted no color, but in the end there was color, a picture in fact.

H: Yes, yes. It's altogether possible that it then became somewhat colorful, but it was not colorfully spoken. If you're really in touch with what you want to express, you can express it without comedic effects.

K: You've been quoted as saying that you and Beckett worked together with particular joy on this play. Why was that?

H: I also enjoyed working together with him on *Godot*. In *That Time* it may have been due to us being alone. I sensed that it contained a lot of his own nature. But since I knew about his shyness, I never spoke about that and so we drew closer to one another. Maybe that was typical of the work.

K: I'd like to ask a few questions about the television plays, *Ghost Trio* and *. . . but the clouds . . .* Was the work with Beckett in the TV studio different from the work with him onstage?

H: Not really. No.

K: How much rehearsal time did you have for these plays?

H: For television we had enough time. There you are reduced as an actor. You have no possibilities to modulate, colors or characters to indicate.

K: What, specifically, does that reduction mean? In *Ghost Trio*, for example, what are the actor's concerns in a play where he doesn't say a word and where he shows his face only twice, briefly?

H: I tried to concentrate fully on the music and then on the woman's words.

K: But the woman's voice speaks mostly with the spectators.

H: Yes, of course, but it affects me despite that. I have to accommodate myself to it, imagine why he sits there. Again, this problem of waiting, of longing. You see, I believe that what one thinks or feels is in some way transmitted. Why does one look at children who are simply there and don't want to prove anything to you? Why does one look there? What is so interesting? It can only be that they are fully at peace in themselves. And as an actor one tries again and again, desperately, to produce that quality. I also bought the Brendel recording [of Beethoven] that we used and played it at home a million times. As if learning a role, I learned to hear. One can't just think, "Oh wonderful, there's no text, and the visuals are also no problem. I'll just sit there bent over." I believe Beckett would perceive that in a minute.

K: In *. . . but the clouds . . .*, did Beckett say anything about the character, about what he does, etc.?

H: Not a thing. For him the problem was figuring out how to make all the steps the same: in other words, almost a mathematical problem. The rest didn't interest him, what one thinks about it. It didn't really matter to me, either, I realized. What was exceptionally difficult was that I always had to step through this circle and hit exactly the same point. If the circle isn't marked, and it wasn't, you lose the direction and go suddenly this way instead of that. Only by means of a tiny point of light outside the playing space could I keep the direction. Furthermore, the steps had to be counted. And with which foot do you begin to walk? And on which do you stop in the middle of the circle? With Beckett the repetition is what matters, the reflection and the repetition, and then again the same.

K: So you don't need to think about why he walks?

H: No. It says in the text, he comes from somewhere outside, goes into his little sanctum, gets dressed again, and goes out again. I took that as completely real. Absolutely as in life. I mean, I would dress differently in life, not necessarily put on a night-cap, but one always has to take it as concretely as possible.

FREDERICK NEUMANN, one of the original members of Mabou Mines, has adapted and directed three Beckett prose works: *Mercier and Camier* (1979), *Company* (1982) and *Worstward Ho* (1986). He has also acted in other Becket plays and adaptations, among them JoAnne Akalaitis' *Cascando* (1976) and the American premieres of *Theater I* and *Theater II* (1985), and has performed various Beckett texts as readings. This interview took place in New York City on May 13, 1986.

Fred Neumann: When I first started doing pieces with JoAnne Akalaitis and the others in Paris in the 1960s, before Mabou Mines existed, Beckett was one of the first authors we worked with. In fact, it was after *Play* that it was decided we were going to bite the nickel and start a theater in New York City. In 1976 we went on a tour with some pieces we had developed, a bill of Beckett and Breuer: *Cascando*, *The Lost Ones* and *B-Beaver Animation*. We took them to Berlin and there, lo and behold, we met Beckett, who had been advised that some of his texts were strongly stretched to adapt them to the stage.

Jonathan Kalb: He saw those pieces?

N: He didn't see them, no. He looked at the sets and, looking especially at the set of *Cascando*, said, "You have adapted it, haven't you!" That started my relationship with him. Because I made a living dubbing and narrating films and so forth, I had reason to go back to Paris and, for an hour or an hour and a half, we'd drink coffee, beer, wine, smoke cigarillos. I was certainly intimidated when I went on to ask him to adapt his first novel, *More Pricks Than Kicks*. I dropped that on him and he said, "Well, we'll see." I came back to America to work with Mabou Mines, and four months later I got a note from him that said, "Dear Fred, Please leave the poor little thing alone. But as to the other work you inquired about . . ." You see, I'd really wanted to do *Mercier and Camier*, and in 1978 I did it.

K: Why do you think he allowed you to do that, when so many people have been (and had been) turned down for the same request?

N: I don't know. We talked a lot, and we had some past in common – you know, way back, with many of the expatriates after the war. Beckett had talked some about Roussillon, though never about any heroic deeds he might have done. And we had the Europe of World War II hanging over our spirits.

K: So you think it was because of this old connection, thin as it might have been at the beginning?

N: Well, I think he was also impressed with some of the work Mabou Mines had done, even though he didn't agree with some of the outcome.

K: But what did he see of that work?

N: He didn't. Stuff filtered back to him. He knew about it one way or another. When I say, "Why don't you see your productions done here and there?" he says, "What would I do, sit in the back row?" And who knows if he didn't see any of them or not? He sometimes peeks into a theater – during *Endgame*, for example. He told me years later that that's what he tells everybody but in fact he does sometimes look in. I think, frankly, that Beckett arranged everything in his life so he could write. Though he wasn't the recluse to the extent that some people said he was.

So, no, he didn't see those pieces in Berlin, but they certainly played a part in his willingness to let me do a prose text without knowledge of how I would stage it. After it was up I said, "This is probably going to be too much of a muchness for your taste," which it was even for mine. It was "Designers go!" and they had fun with it, and the Philip Glass music was wonderful. He got reports about it and said he'd "heard very good things, but with some reservations." And that's how I started working on his prose. You see, I understand his texts as not just written words but as something almost three dimensional, and meant to be experienced in space if only with the ear. There are always voices and always something representing the stage, also darkness and something like day, an announcement of the beginning of things, as in Genesis – the void, the emptiness and some kind of spark of something there that takes place, to be seen and heard, and perhaps even ignored.

K: Was Beckett's permission for *Worstward Ho* and *Company* also given to you as a personal favor?

N: They were confided to me in a personal way but also as between professionals. In fact, he gave me another one, which I haven't done yet. It's a rather short piece called *From An Abandoned Work*, which he refers to as FAAW.

K: Speaking as an actor, do you approach Beckett differently from the way you approach other authors?

N: Well, I'm also a Mabou Mines actor, you know; there's a distinction there. It's a different kind of theater, more presentational. Mabou Mines people generally don't have a fourth wall, generally talk face to face with the audience. I went to the Actors' Studio in 1954. I thought there were going to be theater opportunities there, but there weren't yet. The Off-Broadway Theater movement was just beginning. So I lived in Europe all that time, worked in theater in France and Italy. And I look at some of the work I did there, especially in the classical vein, differently from Mabou Mines' approach to things. With Beckett there seems to be a combination of the classical and the personal, moments of the exhibitionistic and moments of withdrawal, of turning inward, but never in an emotional sense. The will to get at excruciating truth.

K: That "will" sounds like a result of text analysis, or at least of some sort of critical response, which is usually the province of the director. How does it affect your performance when you have to think directorially because you're the director as well as a performer?

N: Well, disastrously, because (à la Mabou Mines) at the beginning a piece is developed in performance in front of a public, got through, and then you say, "My God, I haven't done all I should." But one really does that on the stage everywhere. A lot of actors have good manners; they learn to shut up and do their bit. Nevertheless, you can feel the wheels turning. Some directors know some actors think directorially, at least during rehearsals. That's been part of my upbringing, I may say, in Mabou Mines, where we all consider ourselves directors/actors or actors/directors. Even when we first started out and Lee Breuer was the only director, we all contributed directorially to the making of "pieces." We were asked to use our intelligence on the stage as directors, and also as writers – not *just* as actors who submit. I've had to unlearn some of that.

I think that Beckett's work, especially the way I've seen it done here, has been focused too often with an exaggerated sense of awe for the author, the work as the ultimate emotional tenor of a piece. Not to be ignored. But somehow you've got to maintain a perspective on the work, from a distance. "Awe" is then left to the eye of the beholder. I think, in Beckett's writing, he sees from the inside as well as from the outside; you detect this double vision happening all the time in a more and more refined style as the writing develops. There is this critical intelligence always functioning, this taste, this ear, and these perceptions are missing often from many of the Beckett productions I've seen.

K: You seem to be saying that the actor has to understand the text both very closely from moment to moment and also in a broader way.

N: When I say critical intelligence, I don't just mean understanding with the mind; I mean with the senses, too: sight, hearing, touch, the whole presence of one's body in the body of the work. One is constantly aware of what one is doing while one is doing it; one tries to produce the thing, but with some distancing, look at oneself as one does it. I find this inherent in Beckett's writing: the player is somehow watching the writer or vice-versa.

Beckett lets this go its way, then stops it, plays with it, and so forth. Beckett's prose sometimes requires a kind of "toning down" when done on the stage, a simplification of the ways in which the characters are "aware." And that is the problem with anyone else coming in to stage the pieces with me. I'd have to try to communicate all I thought about them, all the minute details of my interpretation. It would become an interpretation of an interpretation. So, I'm sort of bound to carry out the direction of my conception of a staging. With *Company*, I would have loved to have had someone else perform it. I ended up having to do it, though.

Another kind of example is Opener, the character I played in *Cascando*. Just to tell you what I brought to that piece, again it's this business of the language, the critical intelligence. I modeled my character on the person of Kenneth Burke, whom I knew and who is a wonderful, wonderful character. He has a very distinctive voice and a distinctive language, and I must say that he inspired me. [Imitates him.] "Damn it, Fred," he says, "Jesus Christ, what are we trying to say? What are we trying to *say*?!" He was a dead ringer for this character of Opener, who's old and reads everything; he'd turn on his thinking machine, turn off his thinking machine, the voices would happen, the voices would go. As one plays one has this impulse to want to "tune in" to one's thoughts, but I also had to allow that to happen on cue. And then "tune in" to the thoughts of others. The cello player and Opener sort of alternated with the voices of the others around the table, speaking in chorus. And I just played *my* cello; I was just part of the music, I think.

K: The piece, *Company*, obviously had a very different beginning from *Cascando*. For one thing, you talked about it with Beckett first. Could you tell me about those discussions and the inception of the piece as theater?

N: Well, *Mercier and Camier* was a fortunate precedent because it was cluttered and not very simple. I did *Company* first as a reading at the Loeb in Cambridge, and the staging became a question of when to use this voice or that voice. The "I" had little to say, the accusative second-person "you" much more, as did the "he," and that's a lot of what Beckett and I spoke about. Beckett said, "I don't know, Fred, what you could do with it. It all takes place in the dark." And I said, "Like the theater, in the dark." "Touché," he said. I told him about the reading and he said, "How long did it take, Fred?" And I said, "fifty-nine minutes," and that was really going fast for eighty-nine pages. And he said, "I think it could go to sixty." We talked like that, you know?

And then he said, "But what are you going to *do* with it, Fred?" It put me on the spot, whenever he'd get around to that question. And I told him I find in *Company* an awful lot to do with sound, with aural perception. In fact, he's always talking about the voices, the sound of voices being distant, near or far. And that's why I turned to the satellite dishes. With satellite dishes we sort of listen to space, to capture the voices of space, to "see" them. That's why I had them listening to the emptiness, the void, the darkness. Nothing happening there, they turn in on themselves, those huge twelve-foot diameter dishes, forming sections of the inner surface of the skull. An early idea was to create a huge iris, through which the audience would see the piece. You know, a Mabou Mines thing, the idea of seeing it as if from inside a head. Then I realized that I didn't need to do that, that the spectators all had their own "mental irises" through which they would see it. The dishes were like portholes on the universe, because of the lack of light on the specially painted surfaces, then a turning inward *with* light, revealing these same bone-white surfaces.

I think at first I made a big mistake with *Company*. I felt that Beckett was deliberately making this text much longer than he would ordinarily make texts. This is hard to express, but it seemed as if he wanted to make a point about the laboriousness of the whole process, the problem the character presents for himself, the problem the writer presents for himself, and the problem of life itself, "getting through it." So I felt that laboriousness was essential to the piece. In other words, like Richard Foreman, who said early on about his work, "If there had been only two people left in the audience at the end of a piece, I would have considered it a success." Somehow he intended to drive them out of his "hysterical-ontological" theater.

K: Ontological-hysteric.

N: Yes, I'm calling it hysterical, meaning awesomely humorous. But I think I made a mistake. I was trying to be part of that process, making a point of the labor of it.

K: So you weren't necessarily worried about whether it was accessible, whether people were going to follow it.

N: That's right. And I think that was wrong. I found out that it was much more accessible, much easier, and much funnier than I'd thought. The last thing I have to say about *Company* is that I was very worried about using music – even that of Philip Glass. But when I asked Beckett about it, with trepidation, he answered, "I think there are the proper interstices."

K: You may feel you've answered this question already, but why have you been so preoccupied with this Beckett material for so many years? What is it you can't get away from?

N: I guess it goes to why Beckett and I started up a friendship. It has to do with a vision of our time, and with the experience of trying something really new, and I think Beckett is really new. I think he is going to be recognized by a broader public in the years to come. Language has always been fascinating to me, that's why I was in Europe, and Beckett and I were in the same boat, seeing French as a wonderful kind of medium, devising how to say things in few words, or even in one. Language, his language, *compelled* him to a study of literature, and the more I dealt with it the more I wanted to speak it, interpret it, share its creative fire.

EKKEHARD SCHALL, one of the leaders of the Berliner Ensemble, is known internationally for his performances in Bertolt Brecht's plays. In 1986 at the Theater im Palast, he played in the German Democratic Republic's first Beckett production, *Krapp's Last Tape*. This interview took place in East Berlin on March 7, 1987. Also present was Barbara Brecht-Schall, Schall's wife and Brecht's daughter. (Translated from German by Jonathan Kalb)

Jonathan Kalb: Was Krapp your first Beckett role?

Ekkehard Schall: Yes, my first. Until then I'd only read Beckett, his plays, his prose, and was always very impressed. Although I'd know less where to begin performing some plays than others, in general I think he's quite a marvelous dramatist, a writer-of-the-century.

K: Can you say more about what you think of Beckett as a writer? Why do you think he's important?

S: Yes. For example, here in *Krapp's Last Tape*, as in other plays, he depicts a condition but no development, a condition that's become immobile. In spite of that, I find that a movement still exists in his plays: namely, a recognition. Krapp has basically concluded his life by preserving it on tapes for a long time. And on this birthday, his sixty-ninth, he remembers a point in his life that he once spoke of on a tape. He's now of the opinion that since then, thirty years ago, his life hasn't really developed, because he couldn't resolve back then to start a family, or to stay together with this particular woman. Indeed, he pushed this woman away from him and determined his fate thirty years ago. It becomes apparent at the beginning that he knows something important occurred back then. He looks for a very particular point on the tape, the point with the woman in the boat, her offer and his refusal, and in the end surprises himself by coming to a strongly emotional realization – suddenly and for the first time – that he can't bear any more.

There *is* a development in the play. It's not a more or less unchangeable stagnation or repetition. I don't think that's what's going on here. For me, it's a tremendously lively play. A man says, "I bear that which I realize. I have lived my life wrong." That's what he says, or claims, and with this attitude he enters the play, wanting to bring it to a close. That's how I read the play, or rather interpret it. In the end, a horror arises suddenly that is wholly new to him, and the play leaves him there, aghast. According to David Leveaux [the director], Beckett is supposed to have said once at a rehearsal, "The man is dead the next day." It really is the last evening. One could assume that, and that's the way I think of this play. Moreover, his professional failure comes out in the course of all this – not explicitly

28 Ekkehard Schall in *Das letzte Band* (*Krapp's Last Tape*), directed by David Leveaux, Theater im Palast, East Berlin, 1986. (Photo: Maria Steinfeldt)

played, for the most part, but rather referred to in a sentence or two. At one point right in the middle, as he dictates the last tape, comes this peculiar, sparing, but horrible remark: "Seventeen copies sold, of which eleven at trade price to free circulating libraries beyond the seas. Getting known." "Getting known": at sixty-nine he says that! And then he quotes the exact price, the sum he ultimately earned, namely: "One pound six and something, eight I have little doubt."

K: So it's "movement" that is especially important to you.

S: Yes.

K: In that case, how is it different to play this kind of drama, or this particular drama, from what you usually play? Or is it different?

S: For me it wasn't different. I'm now at work, for example, on a fragment of Brecht's, *Fatzer*, that Heiner Müller put together. Heiner Müller
assembled the pieces and we all, so to speak, entered newly into the
unknown, although we know Brecht better than most dramatic writers
since we've been dealing with him for decades. In spite of that, it's an
adventure, this play, in which people also back out. Four soldiers back out
of World War I, they desert, but they also go into a new movement – and
that's where it's similar to Krapp. That is to say, they don't return home as
deserters in order to find revolutionaries there, in order to join the revolution, but rather to hide themselves until the revolution comes and they are
truly liberated. They remain inactive for that reason, but in the hope of a
revolution. They don't take part, they don't seek any contact with the
revolutionaries – which is interesting and worthy of consideration. And
they perish; all four of them perish.

There are certainly similarities between *Fatzer* and *Krapp's Last Tape*,
where a man says to himself, "I listen to myself once again. I want to
consult myself once again about that first cause, about where the exact turn
was after which my life didn't go further than where I am now. What have
I waited for?" And he converts this resolution into action, energetically and
in rather sovereign style, as he probably did on all preceding birthdays, in
order to gather strength for the coming year. Only this time he doesn't
succeed. He loses his sovereignty. He remains in the end sitting on the
stage, capable of nothing, truly at the end of his life: "last tape." And one
can safely assume it is the last day. He won't live to see tomorrow, and if he
did it would be inconsequential.

K: How and with whom did the idea begin to play Beckett in East Berlin?

S: I'm not the first to have the idea to play Beckett. Brecht already had
the *Godot* idea before 1956. Brecht didn't want anything to do with some of
Beckett's ideas, but he did want to do something with *Godot*. The clown
technique in *Godot*, which applies also to other plays, only makes the
situations seemingly motionless. The pretension or insight of the individuals (and play characters are always individuals, even when they're generic
representations) says, "I'm not moving any more. I'm not stirring from
this spot. I'm not taking part." But that persistence leads to nothing if it
doesn't arrest the overall movement of nature and society, which of course
moves on. In fairness one should show that, too, though in *Krapp* it's not
necessary because, in my opinion, the play contains a self-sufficient tragic
development and crisis.

K: But this was the first Beckett production in the GDR?

S: Yes.

K: Does that mean you received permission to do it suddenly?

S: I didn't receive the permission suddenly, just when I needed it.

K: Really?

S: I didn't carry on a great battle there. Difficulties are sometimes simply a question of hard and soft currency exchange rates [*Devisenfrage*]. Formerly money was not the only consideration, that I admit, but now and certainly for some years we want to and will perform good and important plays from all countries. And hopefully that depends on us, and on our carrying it out. One can of course perform all plays by different means.

K: Then why has Beckett never been performed before?

S: If something doesn't burn under someone's nails, that means he's not strong enough to realize it or succeed with it. In Dresden *Godot* is being performed, and I presume further Beckett plays will follow. There are also other plays and authors that used to be played little or never. Formerly, there was a quarrel between the viewpoints of the Theater of the Absurd and Social Realism (especially in the 1950s), whose demands were partly dogmatic. In bad times opposing positions are not really examined and appraised ideologically and technically, but rather superficially classified and privileged accordingly, or even forbidden. I believe this time is now past. I've never performed Ionesco, but *Rhinoceros* is really a good play that should be performed, or Pinter and others.

K: I had no idea they were permitted.

S: I wanted to perform Beckett's play and have consequently performed it. I coupled it with a poem by Brecht, and the reason for that was that I thought of this common idea, this title, *Lebensabende*, and in doing so had no interest – and I hope that comes out – in playing different positions against one another. I don't think at all about playing Brecht off Beckett or Beckett off Brecht, using them that way. I polemicize with the contents of the texts about my experiences with reality; that's enough. The confrontation in the theater of socialism/capitalism doesn't interest me. At the moment I'm considering whether I won't change the order of *Krapp* and *The Education of Millet*, but only because the Beckett play naturally makes a stronger impact than the Brecht poem which I merely recite and sing.

K: Do you see a connection between *Krapp's Last Tape* and *The Education of Millet*? Or between Brecht and Beckett in general?

S: Both describe conditions in bourgeois society. In the poem *The Education of Millet*, Brecht describes a man who reaches the contentment of old age under the circumstances of the revolution and the beginning of the building of socialism in the Soviet Union. But this Tschaganak Bersijew is, for the length of his life, altogether no revolutionary, none whatsoever. It's his own decision to cultivate millet in the desert and to irrigate parts of the desert. It's a decision that came out of his conscience, out of his own insight and stubbornness, before the revolution struck. He has a premonition, so to speak, about the new social circumstances that occur there, and he lays claim to them. He simply puts the new circumstances at his disposal by saying, "If they're there now, then they should help me." Thus, he enters the cause not because he is changed by the revolution, but rather because he predicted beforehand – through his customary way of life, and his acquaintance with nature and his environment – meeting no difficulties in the new circumstances.

And with Krapp, it seems to me that from early on he obviously eluded a constant compulsion to decide and a responsibility that seemed threatening to him: namely, to work continuously and give his life continuity. What probably happened was that, while eluding the capitalist order, he eluded his environment more and more. The play's description of his relationship with women is fairly strong. And through that it suddenly comes out at the end that this attempt Krapp made to prevent and repeatedly break off communication with other people, especially women, also obviously contributed to his not investing enough in his work, and thereby remaining unsuccessful.

Barbara Brecht-Schall: He broke everything off for the sake of his work, I think, and consequently the work also lay paralyzed. It wasn't worth it, so to speak.

K: So the connection is in work and difficulty with work.

S: For me. That exists in *Krapp* but is not specified, because when he listens to the old tape, it goes on and on with the description of women with whom he could have imagined a life together, perhaps could have begun one as well, but every time he seems to have said to himself, "No, that's getting too intimate for me. That's probably taking away my strength." He broke off his relations with other people again and again; even the death of his parents, in particular that of his mother, he refers to without sorrow. Then he hears on the tape, which he dictated thirty years ago and now listens to at sixty-nine, that back then on his thirty-ninth birthday he had just listened to a tape made twelve years earlier, at about twenty-seven, which describes the same thing: that in fact he has found no real and lasting contact with women, or for that matter with people in general.

BBS: A long life, and the high point is a short love story from many years ago. That's the saddest part for me. He practically lives off that his whole life. One has the feeling that this one tape comes up again and again; that was the high point of his life, and so paltry.

S: At first we got hold of the so-called "Berlin Version" of *Krapp.* That's the version Beckett prepared during his production at the Schiller Theater, with Martin Held as Krapp. I considered that first, and then I read the original version and realized I liked it better. I realized suddenly how much the Berlin version was influenced by the actor.

K: Did you also see the version with Martin Held?

S: I can't say definitely. I think so. I did perceive from reading it and comparing, though, that Beckett is a real man of the theater, and Martin Held is a vital actor who got this role deservedly. Beckett worked along with him well and made use of his corporeality and expressive possibilities. I just felt that the original version of the play was still, so to speak, unused by the actor. So I used that first version, published by Suhrkamp in the translation by Elmar Tophoven.

K: Is it possible to buy Beckett here, or must one go to West Berlin?

S: A great deal has already been published here *about* Beckett. This year an anthology will appear with texts by Beckett. So far Beckett has not been printed, but he will be printed now, after which I hope a large edition will also come, a large collection with many plays.

K: I know that you've performed often in West Germany and other Western countries. Have you seen many Beckett performances during these trips?

S: No. My trips are working trips, you know. When I was last in America, where I played at the Clurman Theatre in New York, which is in the same house as the Beckett Theatre, I performed almost every evening. I performed there twenty-four times, and that's really exhausting. I've seen little. Most of what I've seen has been on television. I've seen too little. But I'm also not in favor of watching something in order to know how you're supposed to do it, or still worse, watching so that you can do it differently. I'm for polemical theater concerned with thoughts and reality, but not for polemical theater concerned with the performances of other actors or theaters.

K: Obviously the spectators here in the GDR are not used to Beckett or to this type of play. What do you think the general opinion is of this production of *Krapp's Last Tape?*

S: I think the people are astonished that this play by this author, of whom they've probably heard, is moving in human terms. I have the impression that many spectators are very moved by this aged fellow, with his recognition and confession of having failed. I have that impression, and it's a strong impression. There are also objections. A few people have written me who didn't approve of my characterization – that I, for example, didn't bring out the intellectual strongly enough. But I can only answer that the intellectual doesn't interest me inasmuch as it's not important to the development of the stage character [*Figur*] in the play's plot. It's exactly the same thing with Galileo (you know, I don't just play Krapp the writer). I'm not interested in Galileo the physicist but rather in Galileo the stage character, who in particular situations displays particular behaviors. Or I've played Oppenheimer with texts from the original examination. There as well I'm not interested in the scientist but rather exclusively in modes of behavior in situations the stage characters enter.

K: I would think, for example, that some people would be happy simply because something new is being played. Is that true?

S: Yes. As I said, I'm of the opinion that it left behind a great impression on many people. Of course, the people who come to my performance expecting a sensation to emerge, or to be shown suddenly how Beckett and his way of writing now overturns the whole theater world here, they're not satisfied. That's also not my intention. I find it a wonderful play, he is a wonderful writer, but I don't say, "That is now the way to an absolutely new land." I can perform this play with my methods.

K: Can you speak a bit more about the plans Brecht had to adapt and direct *Waiting for Godot*?

S: He didn't get very far into them. The only thing I still remember is, of course, that he felt one must in some manner show that while these people continue to wait for someone on whose arrival nothing material depends – and they not only come to terms with that, so to speak, but also feel good about living statically, remaining where they are and what they are – at the same time, the entire society changes in any number of ways: wars are waged, revolutionary movements press forward, another land degenerates into barbarism. Not to be agitational, but if one shows that the behavior of these characters is therefore absurd, because it suppresses or reverses reality in an absurd way, then it's good. And I believe Brecht would have tried it in this manner.

K: Why did he stop?

BBS: He returned in 1948 and died in 1956. In that period he had to bring the plays he had lying in the drawer onto the stage. He never accomplished that; he was in the midst of work. There was a huge amount of plans for new productions and new plays; for example, *The Chariot of Ares*. He worked here with great fun and great momentum. He had to introduce a new kind of theater that he particularly had in mind, with a (frankly) rotten pile of actors. And also, all the respectable people were infected with the thousand-year-old style and manner of performing theater.

S: It was by no means a cessation. Brecht had many ideas, and *Godot* was one of them. But only what he himself had brought onto the stage was, for him, a provisionally final playtext.

DAVID WARRILOW, one of the original members of Mabou Mines, first performed Beckett together with some of the other original members in a Paris production of *Play* (1967) that pre-dated the company's formation. He went on to perform in Mabou Mines productions of *The Lost Ones* (1975), for which he received international acclaim, *Cascando* (1976) and *Mercier and Camier* (1979) – though he withdrew from the company in 1978.³ Beckett wrote *A Piece of Monologue* (1980) for him, and his other Beckett work includes the world premiere of *Ohio Impromptu* (1981), a stage version of *Eh Joe* (1981), the New York premiere of *Catastrophe* together with the world premiere of *What Where* (1983), a French production of *Cette Fois* (*That Time*) (1985) and radio productions of *All That Fall* (1986) and *Words and Music* (1987). This interview took place in New York City on May 18, 1986.

Jonathan Kalb: Could you review the history of your relationship with Beckett – when and how you met him, and the high points over the years?

David Warrilow: We have been friends for ten years, corresponded for over twenty. This is the way it went. I was in Paris doing a job at a magazine. However, some people had tracked me down and were sort of luring me back to theater, which I had chosen not to pursue seriously. One day a caller asked me if I'd go and meet this author, Samuel Beckett, who was approving casting of a production of *Endgame* which was to be done in Paris in English.⁴ That was about all I knew. So I was taken to an apartment on the Boulevard du Montparnasse, introduced to him, and it was then that I learned that I was to understudy the role of Nagg. Well, I was about thirty, you know, and I thought it was very, very strange, but there you are. He looked at me and nodded and that was that. Eventually, that production was directed by him and performed by Jack MacGowran and Patrick Magee at the Studio des Champs-Elysées. It was a dazzling, absolutely extraordinary production, and the first Beckett I'd seen. That was the first actual meeting.

There was some correspondence because I wrote and asked for the rights, on behalf of Lee Breuer, for *Come and Go* to be done at the Edinburgh Festival, which was turned down because John Calder had other plans for it. That was sort of the beginning of an exchange. And then came the incident of *The Lost Ones* which, as you may know, was a stage adaptation of a prose piece, which was against the rules. We'd intended to do a staged reading, but in three weeks of rehearsal it turned into a performance. It was really a sort of runaway experience, amazing, and we had to decide whether to go on or stop, to have it reviewed or not. We asked that it not be reviewed; however news of the performance got to Mr. Beckett. At first his reaction was angry, I think, and I offered to stop doing performances. But he didn't ask for that. He, I think, became curious. When it was known that Mabou Mines was going to be in Berlin in 1976 and he was going to be there directing *Footfalls*, he wrote me and suggested that he meet with the company. We were also going to be doing JoAnne Akalaitis' *Cascando* on that tour, about which he was also curious. So he came one day to the Museum of Modern Art where we were performing, and he met with not only the whole company but everybody on that tour – children, baby-sitters, tech people, about twenty-three people he met that day (you know, Mr. Recluse), and he was wonderful, very open. And it was tremendously exciting to be in his presence that way. He asked to see the set of *The Lost Ones*, to examine the figures, the ladders and so on, he asked a lot of questions, including the big one, "did you cut the text?," which I was dreading. I was just dreading that one, but it was fine; I said yes we had and he just nodded. He said to me privately, "I'm sorry but I won't be able to see a performance because I have a phobia of public situations." I was relieved, I think, because I was afraid of what might happen if he *did* see a performance. I did not assume, along with everyone else, that it would please him. For one thing, I feel that perhaps his major experience is over when he puts his last period on a text.

This April, in Paris, our first taste of working together, I could see that he was excited by the physical, technical work in the theater, because after having completely rethought and reworked *What Where* for television in Stuttgart, he decided to try to effect the same thing onstage for the French premiere of *Quoi Ou*. So his work with the director [Pierre Chabert] was a matter of how to realize the television image on the stage. I'm told it was very successful. The piece lasted about six minutes and seventeen seconds, for which we had two hours of make-up, and it was a great success. In that particular case obviously the writing had not completed the experience; the experience for him was going to be complete when he saw a particular image realized.

K: You act in many different kinds of drama – Shakespeare, *The Golden Windows*, *The Count of Monte Cristo*. Do you approach Beckett differently from other authors? Do you have a theory of Beckett or a process for performing Beckett?

W: There's a place in me that does Beckett, a place I go to in myself. The process of working on his material is no different from working on any other writing, great writing, in terms of the way one sets about the work. But I know that there's a place in me which is for his work. I don't know how else to explain it. Everybody has in themselves a sanctuary that they can go to when they need deep guidance. It's a place of natural knowing and inspiration. I have a place in me like that for his work.

K: Why do you think you are so often singled out as a great Beckett actor?

W: I don't know the answer to that. I really don't. For one thing, I can't see myself perform. I don't know what experience people have when they do see me perform. I occasionally hear statements that I'm forced to listen or pay attention to. My doctor is a man I admire and respect and love deeply; when I first met him, he declined to send me a bill. I said, "why?" He said, "because I saw you do *The Lost Ones* three times." Now what he says to me is, "I'm not concerned with whether other actors are better than you or not. I only know that when I hear you do it, I know what it is." I still don't know what that means; however, it's a statement about somebody's experience, which I accept and must pay some attention to. You see, when I see somebody in tears after a performance and they don't know what it is that's making them cry, then I have to assume that something happens with the combination of his words and my voice, but I don't know what that thing is. I don't know what it *is*. I know that certain pieces of music touch a chord in me somewhere that I can't analyze or describe, and often tears can result from that touching inside, and there doesn't have to be a logical, analytical explanation of how that is, why that happens.

I have of course tried to pay some attention to the fact that my mother's family is Irish, to the fact that when I was first doing *The Lost Ones* and using an Irish accent something happened. When I saw photographs of that piece I saw things that I have not seen in myself before. It was as if a transformation was taking place. For most of my life I had been at great pains, I think, to ignore the Irishness. My mother was born in England, but her parents were from Cork. I didn't know them, and I'd never been to Ireland, no one in my family had an Irish accent, so it's not something I was exposed to. It was something I was sort of conscious of, something my mother was romantically attached to, but it rather irritated me that she was romantically attached to it. It didn't seem real to me. She wanted it to be very real in her life but it didn't seem very real to me. However, I do think that when I started to sound that way, parts of me began to open up that had been closed down. And since a great deal of the key to Beckett's writing is a very oblique humor, which I find extremely Irish, those elements began to open up as well. Again, that's just part of the picture, and I don't know why it is that sometimes people seem more able, with me, to accept the experience that they have with the work. That's the only way I know how to put it.

K: Do you think you understand what you're doing better, or more deeply, than others?

W: When I'm being totally honest I have to tell audiences that I do not understand what it is I am doing. I don't understand the writing. I'm not a stupid person, but if somebody were to say to me, "What is *Ohio Impromptu* about?" I either cannot give a true answer or I don't want to. I don't know quite which it is. I think it really is, I can't. I don't know how. I did have a short discussion about that play with a young director in Paris, and his attitude (and maybe it's Beckett's as well, I don't know) was that it's totally simple and straightforward, not complicated at all, and the questions I have about it are irrelevant and have no bearing on anything. That is not my experience. My experience of that piece is that there are questions but no answers to any of them, that it is on a level of mysteriousness which defies entry except on a soul level. The questions I have, the sort of academic questions – Who is this person? What is this book? What is this story? When is this taking place? How many times has it taken place? – none of them is answered. There are no answers to those things. One can make assumptions, but those are only assumptions, that's all. It's just like opinion.

K: How much do you, as an actor playing Reader, have to decide where you are, what the book is *for you*, etc.?

W: What's *your* answer to that question?

K: Well, I'm not acting it; I'm just watching.

W: How much do I need to decide those things for you to have an experience of the play?

K: How much?

W: Well, I'm telling you I made none of those decisions.

K: What kinds of decisions do you make?

W: That I will read the text. And that I will read at a certain pace, using a certain kind of voice, and that there will be an intention. Now, the most useful intention that Beckett gave me early on in the *Ohio Impromptu* experience was to treat it like a bedtime story and let it be soothing. It wasn't always that way in performance. But I do think that that can be a very satisfactory way of approaching the text. It's also a very beautiful idea, for Reader to be telling Listener a bedtime story.

K: It sounds like *Rockaby*.

W: Yes, very much like that. And, incidentally, the way Samuel Beckett reads it is very much the way the actresses do *Rockaby*; there's a similar lilt.

K: It sounds as though all of the issues for you are musical issues . . .

W: Yes, they are.

K: . . . and none of them is within any reality of a character.

W: Right. I barely deal with psychological reality. I don't have to. I mean, I can have ideas about that but it isn't what works. What works is finding what musicians have called the "right tone." By "right" I mean what works for me. I then have to trust that it'll work for somebody else – that if I get it right, if I sing it "on key," "in tune," it's going to vibrate properly for somebody else.

K: How do you know when something's "working?"

W: It pleases me, and it makes me listen harder and pleasurably to myself. When the note is not quite "on," it makes me physically uncomfortable, it makes me nervous, it doesn't sit right, I start to get negative feedback from my system. And I then have to do whatever I have to do to adjust, to get back on track. It does take a considerable amount of daring and discipline to hold to that line; it means that I can't allow myself to rush out of fear or anxiety. Once I've chosen the tempo, then that's what's going to be and I must hold to it and be faithful. I want to be more open to other ways of trying to do the material. However, I did just try one in Paris and I can't say that I was very satisfied with the attempt. It had to do with *Ohio Impromptu* in French. French is no problem for me; the language is another of my tools. The issue was tone and tempo, because the way the author hears that piece is somewhat different from the way it lies in my being. So I was making certain adjustments to attempt to give him a satisfying experience. I'm not at all sure that what happened was really artistically acceptable to me – and that's okay, that's fine. It was a birthday present to him.

K: There is another actor onstage with you in *Ohio Impromptu*, and there are several actors in *Catastrophe* and *What Where*. How do they affect what you just said about coming to your tone?

W: *Catastrophe* is such a realistic play if one is doing the Director, which I did in Paris this time, that that question almost doesn't enter in. *Catastrophe* is like a classical structure, and there's real psychology in the playing of it. I make a big separation between that play and plays like *Ohio Impromptu* that are like art songs. In *Catastrophe*, for example, I would give myself over to a more traditional form of theater and play it out that way. I far preferred to play the Protagonist in *Catastrophe*; that's a much more interesting role to do, much more interesting. For one thing because it's sculptural, and there's an infinite amount of delicate muscular work to be done. It's also very interesting to deal with the problem of not feeling like a victim. He can look whatever way he looks to the audience, but not to be involved in self-pity while standing on that block is a very interesting task.

K: I'm curious about Listener. Do you have to have any thoughts about him, the other person sitting there onstage with you?

W: One certainly has feelings about that person. I've been through a lot of changes over that one, it's very interesting. When you first do a piece of work, especially if you care a lot about it, then everything that contributes to your feeling comfortable in the situation is of tremendous importance. I can get very manic about certain things; I want things to be where they're supposed to be, lit the way they're supposed to be lit, and sound the way they're supposed to sound. I don't have, yet, an enormous amount of flexibility in that area. And in the beginning with a piece of work I really need those things to be "as agreed" so that I can go deep inside. As long as I make sure everything's in place I can go in. Then over years of doing it like that many times in different places and with different people, I start to get strength about my performance, and it doesn't have to be about everything being in place and that person being just the right person for me to do the piece with. I did become very attached to doing the piece with Rand Mitchell. My most recent experience, with Jean-Louis Barrault, was a shift.

K: What was special about Rand?

W: His total devotion to the work. His ability to surrender ego to the piece. You know, there are not many actors who are willing to give of themselves, of their time and their energy, to so seemingly thankless a task: sitting at a table with their head down, hidden, saying nothing, from time to time knocking on the table. There aren't many actors who want to do that. And he was tireless in his attention, in his concern that everything be just right. I mean, I'm sure that in many ways we just went overboard about this; one can just go crazy about these things. But, you see, I want people to care about the work as much as I do; that's important to me. What I personally feel about the relationship between those two men is unimportant. I *feel* it's unimportant. I've had flashes about those pieces, but I checked with Beckett about one of them and it turned out to be nothing, nowhere; he didn't know what I was talking about.

K: What was that?

W: The Ellmann biography of Joyce tells a story of Joyce, toward the end, being visited in Zurich by a man called Ruggiero, who was a friend of his. This Italian would apparently come into the room, and always take off his broad-brimmed black hat and throw it on the bed. Joyce would say to him, "Please don't do that, it means somebody's going to die." When I read that story, I immediately saw *Ohio Impromptu*. I saw that black hat sitting in the middle of that space, and the fact that it was being construed as a presage of death, the fact that *Ohio Impromptu* is supposedly about Beckett and Joyce, and so on. I just thought I was putting two and two properly together. Well, he didn't know what I was talking about. So you see if one wants to get into speculation about that kind of thing, and draw conclusions and make deductions, one can just keep on ending up at a brick wall. Then what happens? You go back to the word on the page. That's all you have. That's all anyone ever has. Billie Whitelaw said to me one night in Los Angeles, "How can you know how to do his work without his telling you how?" I said, "The way any actor will have to when he's no longer with us. What will an actor have but what is on the page? What does one have in Shakespeare but what is on the page, and then that place in oneself which is a place of trust and inspiration where you go to have it happen?" You see, lots of actors want to believe that the answer is outside them, and that they can pay for it, go to school for it, or hire it. Well, I don't believe any of those things. There is help, but the place is always inside, and everybody has what it takes to get the job done.

K: Can you talk about the rehearsal process for *Ohio Impromptu* with Alan Schneider?

W: I was unwell at the time, so rehearsals took place here in my apartment. We had, I think, four or five, maybe a few more, of probably three hours. A great deal of the work on that piece has to do with decisions about wigs, book, lights, make-up. And I now see, from having just been in a working situation with Beckett, that we all give ourselves a great deal of unnecessary headache trying to obey the instructions, when in fact they are quite malleable in his head. For example, one of the designers in Paris said to me, "He says that we might as well cut the table down; now he thinks it's too long." And if you remember, the instructions for that are quite specific. And, for example – another of these insights – he specifies in *Ohio Impromptu* that the table is made of deal. I remember being with an Irishman in Edinburgh at the time of the festival, and we were talking about these things, and I said to him, "Tell me something, why do you think that Samuel Beckett would specify that the table be made of deal for this play?" And he said, "Oh, it must be because the poorest coffins in Ireland are made of deal." All right, so I said, "Sam, does this have anything to do with it?" And he said, "Is that so? They're made of deal. I didn't know that." So here we go again.

K: Are you saying there was an attempt to get a table made of deal and it turned out it didn't matter?

W: Yes. Anyway, you can't get deal, I think, in this country. The wood doesn't exist here. So then you ask, what's the closest thing to deal, what does it really look like, why would it have to be deal? And then, what does the long white hair mean? And on and on, these decisions, decisions, decisions. I think the New York production was more striking than the Paris one because of specificity of choice. For example, the look of the wigs was almost immaterial in Paris. They didn't seem to care at all, he didn't seem to care either; it was amazing, amazing. It means that when I talk to people from now on about mounting productions of his work, I shall really suggest that they allow themselves a little more latitude. But if they start to change radically certain things about the staging he has indicated, then they're going to be in trouble.

K: In trouble about it working?

W: No, I mean about his response. If somebody said, "We can only get blue light in this theater," that's okay – I'm sure in the last resort that would have to be acceptable. But he does not understand the need of a JoAnne Akalaitis, say, or an Andre Gregory, to alter the rules, as he sees them, of *Endgame*. But there you are, at a certain point one begins to think that it's all fairly arbitrary.

K: I'm a little bit surprised that you had only four or five rehearsals.

W: Well, you see, I'm now talking about the rehearsals for the original performance in Ohio, the very first performance of that play.

K: But what about the knocks? There was no stage time for that?

W: Well, we drilled a lot. There was a lot of drilling. But Rand was very quick, and he knew his cues. The real work was to determine the quality of the knocks.

K: Can you describe that?

W: Well, I know what Alan worked on, and then I saw Beckett do it himself, so I know that they were very different. What Beckett asked Jean-Louis Barrault to do was to take only the fingernail of the right index finger and tap it very lightly on the table. Now it was a bit silly because Beckett was standing on the theater floor where there were footlights from another production with a metal casing, and when he tapped with his finger on this metal casing it made quite a loud noise. Jean-Louis Barrault was attempting to do this on a big table made of wood, and it didn't make the same sound at all. So it was very strange what was going on. It was like they were at odds, you know, and I decided not to interfere with any of this, but to let go and only do my job, not become a co-director. Beckett was saying that the first knock was to be sharp and quick on top of the word, but not very loud. Then there would be this pause, which he said really could depend on the actor, while he listened to the repeat of the phrase. Only when he was totally happy about what he received, what he felt about it, would he then knock, signaling, "You may go on." Rand used knuckles, one knuckle I think. Therefore, the knocking in the New York production was more violent. I mean, it had more presence and noise to it. It was more commanding, more peremptory, sometimes angrier possibly, possibly. What Beckett was doing was much more intimate, having much more to do with Listener being satisfied.

K: What you've said implies that Beckett distinctly intends the knocks to be an interruption, that Listener should not anticipate them.

W: Oh, absolutely. I always warn the actor I'm doing the piece with: "You know, if you don't knock, I will be going on, because I will be into the next word." So they really have to be on their marks. They must cut me off. I would usually get to the first consonant.

K: Which of course keeps that actor on his toes.

W: Yes. It gets to be really vibrant, alive. And it means that the Reader must be stopped in his impulse, that he then has to breathe to decide to say again what he just said – all that is involved. A sense of present necessity.

K: An issue in Billie Whitelaw's work with Beckett, in both *Not I* and *Rockaby*, was "color." Beckett kept saying, "no color, no color," and though she wanted to do what he wanted, when she was up there onstage she couldn't help inserting emotion. She said there was too much "umph" in it to remain completely neutral. I presume you had a similar experience with him. Can you talk about that?

W: Well I think the *Ohio Impromptu* difference of opinion probably could be resumed in the color problem. It's true that my reading of *Ohio Impromptu* does contain quite a lot of color. I had no problem with that concept with *What Where*. In fact, that was what I always wanted to do with the New York production, make it as gray as possible, uniform and gray. This time I think I really achieved it. When I listen to *Rockaby*, which I just did several times in French over there, I must say that it really did seem to me to be most effective when there was almost no color coming out of the actress' energy, when the energy went into maintaining a level of uniformity about the speaking. Just occasionally as the piece went on there would be slight rises in tone, in the note of the voice. There is something very important about that.

K: I'd like to press you a little bit about something you've said. You describe your work with Beckett much as Whitelaw does, as an instrument out of which his words, his art, emerges. You say you don't know what you're saying or what it means. Yet, I know that you've been an editor, and it's obvious that you're very intelligent, as is Whitelaw, though she's always reminding us that she left school at fifteen. Could there possibly be some slight disingenuousness in your saying that intelligence doesn't go into it? To be frank, I perceive both of you understanding the texts better than many other people. Maybe that's not how you act them, but does it really have *nothing* to do with it?

W: I truly don't want to get into a pose about this. That doesn't interest me. I'm still trying to be very clear and articulate about the experience. It could be that we *do* understand, and then we choose to let go of that aspect of the experience to be able to perform. I know that if an actor gets up onstage and starts to play the meaning of the thing it dies, it just dies. Meaning is whatever happens in the viewer's experience of it. I don't feel that there really is intrinsic meaning. I also think that ideas are valueless; everything happens in action. The action in performing a Beckett play is making the instrument resonate. You know, one of my difficulties doing *What Where* was that I was to maintain absolutely the same note and an absolutely identical rhythm of speech throughout, and the other actors were to match me; they had to find the note, no matter which one I used. We would start to do the piece, something would go off, and the director would say, "Stop, stop . . . okay, pick it up." Well, what was going on in me was this constant anxiety that I wasn't going to be able to get the note again, that I would have lost my note, and I would be out of tune with myself. That was a constant preoccupation. Nobody else really cared, I don't think, whether I picked it up on the right note, but it was totally important to me. It had to do with doing that piece, with knowing that I was able to do that. I didn't care what it meant. I didn't care. I really didn't. I mean, I *did not* care what the line, "We are the last five," means. I don't know what that means.

K: This sounds a lot like the way actors describe their experiences in *Play*. They cannot think about even the meaning of their sentences because they're only concerned with the light. Is that the way you felt in *Play*?

29 JoAnne Akalaitis, David Warrilow and Ruth Maleczech in the Mabou Mines production of *Play*, Public Theater, NYC (production 1967, revised 1971, date of photo unknown). (Photo: Tony Kent)

W: Oh, absolutely. The only thing that's more terrifying than *Play* is *Not I*. And I don't have to do that because I'm not a woman.

K: Otherwise you would have to do it.

W: I'm sure that if I were of that gender I would feel somewhat obliged to have that experience.

K: I'd like to return to *The Lost Ones*. You spoke before about the story behind the group's permission to do that piece, and it sounds as if what you had was permission to do a reading but in rehearsal it became something else.

W: Yes, it was just a startling experience. I mean, we really did start to do a staged reading. I would have the book, and Lee would say, "Suppose here we do this," and I would say, "Well, I can't really do that and hold the book," and he'd say, "Well, just put the book down on that seat, and then you'll go and pick it up again." I kept having more and more tasks to do. And then the idea of the model came in, then the idea of the little people – I would sort of move them around – and all this time I couldn't get to pick up the book. So finally I thought, "I can't really do this unless I learn the text." And suddenly I was learning the text – it was the last week – and then we were doing it. It was all very confusing because I thought everyone was going to hate it, be bored by it and walk out, all that stuff.

K: How did you come up with the idea of the Irish accent?

W: Lee asked me to do it. Because of the nature of the text – it's so precise, so precious in many ways, the way it deals with measurement and volume and mass and surface and so on, and the fact that so much incredible emotional power is suppressed like that – he wanted it to be like a lecture demonstration, a combination of Rembrandt's "Anatomy Lesson" and a lecture in an amphitheater at the Sorbonne, which dictated the shape of the seating in the cylinder. Therefore something minute, kind of microscopic, would be going on while the text was being spoken – that's how we got to have the tweezers, etc. We started out with a character: the kind of man who was a guide at Versailles, who probably was something in his life, then fell on hard times and found himself doing this rather menial task, but bringing to it a great deal of knowledge and grace. On top of that, Lee then said, "Let's see what it sounds like with a bit of an Irish accent." Well, what it did was really highlight the humor in that piece. Beckett doesn't want to agree that there's a great deal of Irishness in his writing in English, but there is, there really is. I mean, he was surprised that we had done *All That Fall* with Irish accents. Now, *All That Fall* is a deeply Irish play; I've even seen the railway station where it's set, and it's very much of that play. So the Irish accent came in for *The Lost Ones*, and what it did was to provide a sort of distancing and a strange intimacy at the same time; it gave a quality to the storytelling which was deceptively comfortable. It was seductive, and I think it drew people into the story. So when it really started to get horrendous, people were already in the trap. They were already in there; they couldn't really get out.

K: So the conceptualization of it as theater really happened in those three weeks and not before. There was no preconception of it at all?

W: We decided we needed a third piece of work to complete the evening, and we simply didn't know what. Lee and I went to bookstores and went through all the novels and so on, and we talked about this and that. And finally, sort of in despair, I said, "I have this book on my shelf, but I couldn't bear it, I couldn't read it." I'd bought it about a year before, and it was called *The Lost Ones*, and I'd read about two pages and then put it down. I thought it was unbearable. So I put it in his hands and he took it home; he called me the next morning and said, "This is it."
     "What do you mean, this is it?"
     "This is it. It's fantastic." So I felt rather stupid, and we got together and read it. And it was literally three weeks before opening night. You see, three weeks to do a reading of a piece is plenty of time. But what happened was so phenomenal it hardly bears description. Some people still talk about that piece as being the most important theatrical experience of their lives.

K: With many, perhaps most, attempts to adapt Beckett's prose to the stage, a lot of people go away saying, "Why don't they just leave this alone, on the page where it belongs?" *The Lost Ones* really is an example of successful theater being made out of it.

W: Something obviously very unusual happened with *The Lost Ones*. One can quote chapter and verse through history on any number of attempts to represent in the flesh the experience that is brought about by reading. And there are all kinds of levels to that experience. Usually what happens when people take the prose and put it onstage is that they indulge in front of other people their own pleasure in reading it. Now you know already, from what I've said about *The Lost Ones*, that that was not what was involved at least with my part of the process. For people who had read the book, something was unlocked by seeing it, hearing it done. The sculptor Bruce Nauman once said to some collectors that if they wanted to understand more about his work they should read Samuel Beckett's *The Lost Ones*. Those same collectors came to see a performance in New York and afterwards they told me that they had read the work four and five times, and that hearing it, seeing it that way, had given them a deeper understanding.
     If I had any real misgivings about *The Lost Ones* it was this: there is no way to speak the text without punctuating it, which means that one has to be

unfaithful to the writing, since the only punctuation is a period. That is lost. One can poo-poo that and push it aside, but it stayed with me. Also what stayed with me was finally an unwillingness, in a way, to come between the written word and the spectator. Which is one of the reasons why I asked – when he wrote *A Piece of Monologue* and asked me what I had in mind – for a specific of the image to be that you couldn't see the person's face. You didn't have benefit of the eyes and therefore had to listen if you wanted any clues at all. That still seems to me very important. Because in *The Lost Ones* people would get very involved in who I was and what I looked like. Well, all right, so that's what happens with an actor. But there's something about that – I suppose the responsibility of it – that really got to me after a while. In that sense, I feel that Beckett's on to something when he takes away all that, takes away a lot of that aspect of personality, so that something about the essential experience can come through, without the warmth. It's sort of a perverse point. I'm not really sure what it is I'm saying, but I do know that I didn't want people to say to me after *A Piece of Monologue*, "I just want to see your eyes, I want to see your eyes on the stage, I want to see what's going on when you say these things." You don't get to. You get to listen and you get to look at this image.

K: Your face can't be seen when you do radio plays. Did you have a positive experience with the recent production of *All That Fall*?

W: Oh, I'm quite happy with the work I did in that. What was very funny was that, when I saw Beckett in January, one of the first things he said was: "What do you think of *All That Fall*?" I said, "I don't know. I haven't heard it. Have you?" He said, "Oh yes. I just received a copy." And I said, "Oh. Well, what do you think of it?" And he looked down and said, "Well, a number of weaknesses." I said, "Do you mean the production?" He said, "No, no, no. The writing." And then he said, "What I really was waiting for was the rain at the end."

K: That's a wonderful story.

W: It says an awful lot. Part of it says, "the less the better." In other words, when you get the sound of the rain that's when you're getting the real stuff, on your way to silence. Once my friend Rocky Greenberg asked him, "What are you writing at the moment?" And the answer was, "Another blot on silence."

BILLIE WHITELAW'S first experience performing Beckett was in *Play* (1964) at the Old Vic. Subsequently, in the course of playing Winnie in Beckett's London production of *Happy Days* (1979) and appearing in three Beckett premieres – the London premiere of *Not I* (1973) and the world premieres of *Rockaby* (1981) and *Footfalls* (1976), which Beckett wrote for her – she became known as the author's "chosen actress." Her other Beckett work includes a radio production of *All That Fall* (1986) and tours of the triple-bill *Rockaby, Enough* and *Footfalls* (1984 and 1986). This interview took place in Purchase, New York, on August 1, 1986.

Jonathan Kalb: You've spoken many times about the fact that Beckett reads his work to you. Can you talk about the process of moving from that reading to your own performance? How does it become yours?

Billie Whitelaw: It takes a little while. The main thing that I have, the main thing I need – and so I feel I'm a bit of a cheat, but never mind – is him. I've never worked without him. Once I've heard him say albeit two or three lines of a piece, then I have some idea of the area he's working in, the tempo of it. I then take that and go over and over it, and gradually like topsy it starts to grow. Everyone's got to find their own hook to hang the play on. Me, I recognized an inner scream in *Not I*, something I'd been sitting on for a long time, and whatever it was connected with me very fundamentally, very deeply. But the words that I've got scribbled all over my texts are: "No color," "Don't act," "No emotion," "Just say it." And if in doubt – and this applies to acting wherever, on whatever – don't do it, do nothing. That's a Golden Rule of acting. I think when he says, "No color, no emotion," he means, "Don't act, for God's sake."

K: Yet you are doing something even when you are, as you say, doing nothing. And that something *is* that "hook" or "connection" to you.

W: Yes. In *Rockaby* I'm not just sitting in the chair listening to a recording of my own voice. I do find *Rockaby*, even sitting in a chair and listening to my thoughts on tape, quite emotionally draining and depressing, to be honest. These three short pieces – *Enough*, which I read, *Footfalls* and *Rockaby* – I find doing them far more difficult, exhausting and emotionally draining than doing twelve hours a day of the Greeks at the Royal Shakespeare Company. These three short pieces are like all of that condensed into an hour.

K: How would you characterize the difference between you and other actors? Why can't anyone listen to Samuel Beckett read his work and produce the same result you do?

W: I will totally accept what he has written, and I will then try just to give him what he wants. This is a long-winded way of answering your question, but I don't think he just writes a play. I think he's a writer, a painter, a musician, and his works seem to me all these things rolled into one. I remember once he said to me in my home, "I don't know whether the theater is the right place for me anymore." He was getting further and further away from writing conventional plays. And I know what he meant. I thought, well perhaps he should be in an art gallery or something. Perhaps I should be pacing up and down in the Tate Gallery, I don't know, because the way the thing looks and the way he paints with light is just as important as what comes out of my mouth. Therefore, I will not argue with him and say, "What does this mean, and what does that mean, and why do you want it like this, and wouldn't it be a good idea if I made this sentence a question instead of a full stop?" If he wanted a question he wouldn't have put a full stop there. So I will just go along with whatever it is. And I will turn myself inside out, and I have made myself ill, trying to complete the image he has in his mind's eye and in his ear.

K: So in a way you are the theater person he can't be.

W: Yes. I feel that I place myself totally at his disposal, and I can be a tube of paint or a musical instrument or whatever. I won't argue, I won't argue, because I trust him totally, and have absolute respect for his integrity and his artistic vision. So really I just do as I'm told. A lot of actors do say, "Well what does it mean?" I've never asked him what anything meant, apart from one question in *Footfalls*: "Am I dead?" And I think you know the answer, don't you? "Let's just say you're not quite there." And I understood exactly what he meant. I then knew I was in a sort of strange no-man's-land, gray, neither here nor there. That could be going over from life to death, the no-man's-land of drugs, the no-man's-land of unconsciousness and anaesthetic, whatever hook the actor wants to hang it onto. Me, I hung it on the no-man's-land of life and death, this gray area. But that's all I used.

K: In *Not I*, Beckett kept saying, "No color, no color," to you, and in the *Rockaby* documentary you said that, though you wanted to give him what he asked for, the piece held such emotion for you that it was impossible for you to do it in a totally gray tone – that's not how it came out.

W: No. It did to begin with, but then it grew different. Now, when he did it, it didn't come out without color either. I'd say, "All right, say that for me," and he would and then I'd say, "You may not know it but you are an absolute powerhouse of emotion." One thing I've learnt about Beckett is that to arrive where he wants you to arrive, it's got to be step by step. It's

got to go through the proper stages. When working with Beckett I am
working with material that I don't necessarily want to have explained to
me, so I start off by being like a robot, saying, "out . . . into this world . . .
this world . . . . tiny little thing . . . before its time." I just tap it out like a
robot. But gradually something happens after a few days of doing this. I
mean, one's own terror takes over of course, but it also takes on a life of its
own. The walk in *Footfalls* – it's not just seven or nine paces depending on
the size of the stage, it's not that. I have actually twisted my spine by doing
Footfalls, because in fact something happens whereby my spine starts to
spiral down as though I am disappearing. And it's physically very painful to
do. Each play I do, I'm left with a legacy or scar. Now, perhaps I'm being
silly, perhaps I shouldn't do that, but I feel that the shape my body makes is
just as important as the sound that comes out of my mouth. And that's the
shape my body wants to take, of somebody who's spiraling inward.

K: It sounds as though your primary experience in productions is with
Beckett. What then did Alan Schneider do for you? How did he help you?

W: Well I do need, just as an actor, someone to say, "Now look, you're
falling in love with the sound of your own voice." It's very easy with
Rockaby and *Footfalls* in particular to pretend that one is a sort of latter-
day Ella Fitzgerald and start to bend notes here and there, and to quite
enjoy the actual process of making it. And that's the actor's indulgence
which we're all guilty of and Sam hates, hates. I was very grateful on the
evenings that Alan would come and sit in front and just watch it, sort of
indomitable.

K: Can you tell me about how the prose piece *Enough* got added to the
performance? Did you work with Beckett on that, too?

W: He hates it. Alan presented it to me as a package: "Would you do
Enough and *Rockaby* in New York?" These things happen often not out of
any great feeling of artistic merit; I think they just needed something else
to pad out the evening.

K: So he didn't read it to you and go through your usual process?

W: No, and I don't want him anywhere near it, because I'm very bad in
it. I'm a little better now; at least I keep my hands still and I don't make
funny faces. I've learnt it, and I stand still and say the lines. I was very
ashamed of myself before. But I get nervous like most actors, and when I
get nervous I move. It's better now than it was. I do now say before each
performance that Samuel Beckett does not like his prose being read out
loud.

30 Billie Whitelaw in *Footfalls*, directed by Alan Schneider, Samuel
Beckett Theatre, NYC, 1984. (Photo: Martha Swope)

K: I'd like to return to a point I asked you about before. You say one has to go through the right steps, but is it really true that everyone could go through those steps?

W: I think you've got to trust him, and think perhaps he's right, perhaps he does know better than you. I say, "Trust the words." Because to me it seems that Beckett doesn't write *about* something – about an emotion, about some old lady rocking herself to possible death in a chair – he actually writes it, he writes the thing itself. And you don't have to add to that. He's done ninety percent of the work for you by writing the actual emotion on the page as a composer will write an emotive passage in a piece of music. It's there. And by the time you've gone through the process of learning it, which is no mean feat, of getting the words out so they're articulate, so that all the notes and "ts" and vowel sounds are actually there, you don't have to do anything, because he's done it. Something weird and extraordinary does happen, as long as you the actor don't get in the way. But in order not to get in the way you have to be incredibly disciplined. Because an actor wants to act, and a servant wants to serve. When we were doing *Not I* with students at Oxford, one girl thought it'd be a marvelous idea if there were a couple of laughs or screams or if something very noisy happened with the mouth wide open. And she thought it'd be a good idea if when that happens there were screens all around, so there would be about thirty mouths. And I said, "Well, I would give it a whirl as written first, because I think simplicity is what will make it work and not all that Cecil B. deMille."

K: You were once quoted in the *Village Voice* as saying that you didn't know *Waiting for Godot* or *Endgame*.

W: I'm not a great reader.

K: So it's true that you don't know those plays?

W: Well, I've seen *Waiting for Godot*, I've seen his production of it in German at the Royal Court. And I was knocked out by it, and I didn't understand a word of the language.

K: That was your first experience with *Waiting for Godot*?

W: Yes.

K: That's obviously his best-known play. Have you never been curious to see it in English?

W: Well, I'm not very proud of any of this, and I'm sure a psychiatrist, if I ever went to one, would have very good explanations about why I live this recluse-like sort of existence: I never go to the theater. I only go to the theater through the stage door, so I have no idea what other actors do.

K: You must have gone to the theater before you went into it professionally.

W: Well, I've been to the theater occasionally, but I'm not a theater-goer, and I'm not a reader of plays. No, I went into the theater long before I ever went to the theater.

K: How often do you do non-Beckett roles?

W: Well, Beckett is just a very small part of my career. At the moment it seems all-consuming because this year seems to have been devoted to it. I'm delighted about that, although I do find it very exhausting to do these two little plays, I have to say. But they're just one small part of my life, the part that gets the most attention. I have to earn a living.

K: Is there a Beckett process for you that's different from the processes you use with Shakespeare and Sophocles, etc?

W: Ideally, the way I work with Beckett is the way I feel one should work with any play. And that is, allow it to grow, don't get in the way, see what comes off the page, trust the writer. Sometimes one needs to throw a few pyrotechnics in there.

K: But Shakespeare, obviously, is not here to read his works aloud.

W: No, but I find that more and more I'm getting involved with rhythm. When we were doing the Greeks there seemed to be, not always but often, a pattern of three going through the lines. And I said to John Barton about some four- or five-page speech, "Give me time just to let this grow, because in here is something very beautiful, but I don't want to start acting being beautiful. I would like something beautiful to come out of these words because I know it's in there. And therefore at rehearsal I'm just going to say it and tap out the rhythm of three and stand stock still."

K: Are you saying that even with these other writers the primary thing is the sound, the music?

W: I think so. That seems to happen more and more. Actually, I never wanted to be an actress at all. If I had any ideas about going into the theater – and I'm not sure I did – it was to be in vaudeville song and dance. That's what I would have loved to do. So perhaps it's come round in some strange, funny way.

K: In *Rockaby* you have only four one-word lines to say, and you have one stage direction, "a little softer each time." When you're up there doing that, what are you thinking?

W: I'm saying the thoughts. I say the dialogue in my head, because I have certain lines where I open my eyes and certain lines where I close them. Sometimes I open them very fast; I have no idea why. But I go along with it. And the "Mores" do vary from night to night, I think – I suppose it's just the degree to which I'm concentrating. Because I'm not just sitting in a chair, I'm very glad when it's over.

K: Why does it get softer? I'm asking you what you use for that as an actress.

W: This is only my opinion. I think it's because she's getting weaker, and the rock of the chair should be lessening, and the light is lessening. In *Footfalls* the same thing happens; she gets lower and lower and lower until it's like a little pile of ashes on the floor at the end, and the light comes up and she's gone. In fact, the woman in *Rockaby* is actually going further and further down that steep stair. So with the last "More" she knows she's on the way out. And as long as that rocker keeps rocking she's all right. Once it stops she's gone – I think, but I don't know. I would like to say that's what it is, but that's what I use. Somebody else could use something else.

K: So your woman knows she's going out – that's terrifying.

W: Yes, and I do find it very frightening to do. And I find it desperately lonely to do. I feel very, very lonely in that chair. And I'm not a very good companion to have in the theater backstage afterwards, because I'm rather depressed.

K: It's interesting that in order to do your "Mores" properly you have to think of the tape as something that you are saying.

W: It's in my head. I think they're my thoughts. I put the tape in my head. And I sort of look in a particular way, but not at the audience. Sometimes as a director Beckett comes out with absolute gems and I use them a lot in other areas. We were doing *Happy Days* and I just did not know where in the theater to look during this particular section. And I asked, and he thought for a bit and then said, "Inward." And it was the most marvelous, succinct piece of direction I've ever been given. So although my eyes are opening and closing, I take the tape in with me, everything in with me.

K: What makes you decide to open or close your eyes on particular lines?

W: The text usually dictates everything that I do. I mean, it's as simple as a line like "all rise/famished eyes." It would not, to me, make sense to speak a line like that with my eyes shut, so I make sure that my eyes, unless I've forgotten, are open just before that. So that when I say, "famished eyes," there are famished eyes there to look at.

K: Since you hear the voice in your head, is your terror mostly that that voice is going to stop?

W: It's the chair I'm frightened of stopping. As long as the chair rocks my thoughts will continue. And so when the chair stops, that is like terror for me, Billie Whitelaw, sitting in the chair. And once the chair starts to rock, then my thoughts can start again, but if that chair doesn't move I have no thoughts, have no existence. That's what it feels like.

K: You speak about the character as being both in your control and outside your control, which might be seen, in a sense, as an interpretation. Is it possible that some sort of understanding does happen to you after a while with a Beckett text, just because you need to apply it to yourself in some way in order to do it?

W: Yes, that has to happen with every play. But with Beckett it's purer in some way. Do you remember two marvelous Irish actors, Patrick Magee and Jack MacGowran? They were Sam's terrible twins, he adored them, and then I came along and we were terrible triplets. I remember Pat Magee said to me one time backstage when we were both doing Beckett at the Royal Court – and he was marvelous, a fine intellect, a fine mind when he wasn't drinking – he said, "Ah, Billie. You can't fool around or cheat with this man." With other things you could sort of fool around and say, "Well, I see what's required here. It's not in the text, but I'll apply it." One can just apply it like a coat of paint. And I don't think you can apply things to Beckett like that. There again, I use a metaphor from the wallpaper industry; we have a phrase, "grin through." If you put paint on wallpaper without taking the wallpaper off, the wallpaper pattern will "grin through" the paint. Well, what he has written will "grin through" like the wallpaper through the distemper.

K: I don't mean to accuse you of disingenuousness, but it does seem as if you interpret despite yourself.

W: Yes. That's the way I act. Unless I can actually touch the feeling of the character I'm playing, I find I'm in big, big trouble. But I have to be patient. I do envy actors who can just get a script, read it once, leap straight in there and do it. I'm open-mouthed.

K: All of these physical effects you've described – the back pains with *Footfalls*, the terror with *Not I*, the depression with *Rockaby* – how do you feel about all of these things? What's your attitude toward them?

W: I feel miserable, miserable. That's why I don't do them all that often. A theater tour of *Rockaby* and *Footfalls* is now being talked about, but it's going to have to be thought about very carefully. I mean, I can't do eight performances a week. Those two matinees at the Clurman really gave me sort of chronic health problems, so if I do a tour it's got to be worked out that at some point I have some days off just to recuperate and get some of this black and gray out of my psyche. Especially in *Footfalls*: this creature does sort of take over.

K: So you do it because of Sam?

W: Yes, and also because I respect his work very much. I was deeply honored and privileged to be asked to do it, and he's trusted me with it. I would quite enjoy it, if I got the energy, to relearn *Happy Days*. I'd be quite happy to do that again, because I'm quite fond of Winnie. She's quite jolly in a way; there's a bit more light and shade there. But I'm not a Beckett actress; I'm just an actress who tries to earn a living, and Beckett by some grace of God happens to have crossed my path and the process of my work. I mean, I haven't, like you, read his plays and thought, "My God, I've got to meet this man." All I knew about him was that he wrote this play in which poor Brenda Bruce sat up to her neck in sand.[5] That's all I knew.

Notes

1. Introduction

1. Richard Gilman, *Common and Uncommon Masks* (NY: Vintage, 1971), p. 90.
2. Samuel Beckett, "Dante . . . Bruno. Vico . . Joyce," in *Disjecta*, ed. Ruby Cohn (NY: Grove Press, 1984), p. 27.
3. Patrice Pavis, *Languages of the Stage* (NY: PAJ Publications, 1982), p. 99.

2. Rockaby *and the art of inadvertent interpretation*

1. Charles R. Lyons, "Perceiving *Rockaby* – As a Text, As a Text by Samuel Beckett, As a Text for Performance," *Comparative Drama* 16, Winter 1982/83. Page numbers in parentheses refer to this article.
2. All *Rockaby* quotations are from *The Collected Shorter Plays of Samuel Beckett* (NY: Grove Press, 1984).
3. In fairness I should mention that in a later article ("Directing/Acting Beckett," *Comparative Drama* 19, Winter 1985/86, pp. 289–304), Lyons and a co-author, Barbara S. Becker, do write about Whitelaw, but do not relate her acting to Lyons' earlier ideas about audience perception. They acknowledge that "the text in performance becomes a more independent artifact than the text in reading," but fail to explore that independence with due specificity.
4. John Russell Brown makes a similar observation about recorded sound in *Breath* in his article "Beckett and the Art of the Nonplus," in *Beckett at 80/Beckett in Context*, ed. Enoch Brater (NY: Oxford University Press, 1986), p. 36.
5. David Edelstein, "Rockaby Billie," *Village Voice*, March 20, 1984, p. 81 – hereafter designated *VV*.
6. Whitelaw is not the only actor who has depended on Beckett's line-readings. Jack MacGowran, for instance, convinced the author to record Lucky's monologue for him before rehearsals for the 1964 Royal Court production of *Godot*, and when the actor made his Claddagh Records album, *MacGowran Speaking Beckett*, he dutifully obeyed Beckett's instructions to speak in monotone. See Jordan R. Young, *The Beckett Actor* (Beverly Hills, CA: Moonstone Press, 1987), pp. 98, 106.
7. In her interview with me in part three Whitelaw acknowledges that *Enough* was the weakest part of the evening, which also included *Footfalls*.
8. Deirdre Bair, *Samuel Beckett: A Biography* (NY and London: Harcourt Brace Jovanovich, 1978), p. 561.
9. Mel Gussow, "How Billie Whitelaw Interprets Beckett," *New York Times*, February 14, 1984, p. C13.

10.   Here again, Lyons and Becker's article partially rectifies an omission in the earlier piece. For instance, the authors state that in *Happy Days* "the rhythms of Winnie's repetitive speech and actions provide the primary energy of the actor's performance." I have no interest in denigrating such points; though unconnected to Lyons' perceptual model, they are sound, and perhaps they represent legitimate second thoughts about this subject. (See, however, Lyons' essay "Beckett's Fundamental Theatre: The Plays from *Not I* to *What Where*," in *Beckett's Later Fiction and Drama*, ed. James Acheson and Kateryna Arthur [NY: St. Martin's Press, 1987], pp. 80–97, which generalizes ideas in the earlier essay to apply to all the late plays.) My purpose, in any case, is not to attack Lyons ad hominem but to point out that the omissions in "Perceiving *Rockaby*" remain typical of even the best dramatic criticism on Beckett.

11.   The one survey of this kind of which I am aware is Colin Duckworth's, described in his book *Angels of Darkness* (NY: Barnes & Noble Books, 1972), and it is based on only three productions at two different theaters. Even the audiences at those two theaters, however, disagreed on whether Beckett's impact was intellectual. See the compilation of Duckworth's findings, pp. 116–143.

12.   Lyons quotes this passage from Martin Esslin's "A Theatre of Stasis" in *Mediations* (NY: Grove Press, 1982), p. 123, saying that Esslin would probably disagree with the intricacy of his description of spectating in Beckett's theater, but I think their disagreement, if it exists, stems from speaking of different kinds of spectators. In every age and every art form there are those who are satisfied with initial impressions and those who think past them; Beckett's theater is no exception and has a wide range of viewers.

13.   Mark Matousek, "Schneider on Beckett, Understanding, Differently," *Village Voice*, July 3, 1984, p. 97.

3.   Considerations of acting in the early plays

1.   Alain Robbe-Grillet, "Samuel Beckett, or Presence on the Stage," in *For a New Novel*, trans. Richard Howard (NY: Grove Press, 1965), pp. 120–121.

2.   Alan Schneider, *Entrances* (NY: Viking, 1986), pp. 227–228.

3.   John Lahr, *Notes on a Cowardly Lion* (NY: Alfred A. Knopf, 1969), p. 266.

4.   Herbert Berghof, who directed *Godot* in New York after the Miami fiasco, had a much easier time working with Lahr than did Schneider, and one reason sometimes given for that is his different casting choice for Vladimir.

> [Berghof:] I did feel it was wrong to cast Tom Ewell with Bert. Their type of comedy is too similar – naive, simple, innocent. Bert has this same radiance or innocence. I thought the character should be played by somebody who had comedic elements but was a sharper player, more intellectual. I suggested E. G. Marshall. He had a kind of New England acuteness, a cerebral quality to contrast with Estragon's vulnerability.   (Lahr, *Notes*, p. 274)

Lahr considered Marshall's contributions in rehearsal "brilliant," and developed his stage relationship with him further than he had with Ewell. Berghof's comment, however, does not satisfy as an explanation of the improvement in Lahr's performance (if in fact there was one – see *Entrances*, pp. 235–236). Since Roger Blin's original casting of Pierre Latour and Lucien Raimbourg, every production has had a Didi and Gogo who intentionally contrast in some way. (See Ruby Cohn, "Growing (Up?) with *Godot*," in *Beckett at 80/Beckett in Context*, pp. 13–24.) The common practice of casting opposite types is worthless if the actors fail to justify their modes of contrast as aspects of Didi and Gogo's interdependency. What really happened, as his biography states, was that Lahr grew more comfortable with the play and eventually came to understand and trust it.

5. See for example the 1971 videotaped interview between Alan Schneider and John Lahr in the Lincoln Center archives.

6. "MacGowran on Beckett," interview with Richard Toscan, *Theatre Quarterly*, vol. 3, no. 2, July–Sept. 1973, p. 17.

7. Enoch Brater, "Brecht's Alienated Actor in Beckett's Theater," *Comparative Drama* 9, Fall 1975, p. 197. See also Clas Zilliacus, *Beckett and Broadcasting* (Abo [Finland]: Abo Akademi, 1976), p. 142, for similar comments on radio drama in an otherwise very intelligent study.

8. Bernard Dort, "L'acteur de Beckett: davantage de jeu," *Revue d'Esthétique*, special number 1986, pp. 227–234. All subsequent references to this special number, guest-edited by Pierre Chabert, are designated *RE*.

9. Beckett's preference has always been faithfulness to genre. (See his 1957 letter to Barney Rossett, excerpted in chapter 7.) He has, however, occasionally granted permission, with misgivings, to those who want to try the works in other media, and Schneider filmed his 1961 production with such authorization. Beckett knew nothing about the PBS telecast of the Los Angeles Actors' Theatre production I refer to later. See Ruby Cohn, *Just Play: Beckett's Theater* (Princeton: Princeton University Press, 1980), p. 208, 286, n. 3.

10. Cohn, *Just Play*, p. 209.

11. As several critics and Beckett himself have pointed out, most of Lucky's speech makes sense if one picks out the main grammatical elements. It is really two clauses elongated and strung together with the detritus of an eroded mind: "Given the existence . . . of a personal God . . . who from the heights of divine apathia divine athambia divine aphasia loves us dearly . . . it is established beyond all doubt . . . that man . . . wastes and pines . . . and . . . what is more . . . in spite of the strides of physical culture . . . fades away." A third clause follows, concerning the earth's appearance as an "abode of stones," but it never resolves grammatically and suggests that, in Lucky's head, analysis has succumbed to an assault of visual images. If the actor emphasizes these points of cohesion in his delivery, both the audience and the other characters will have what they need to follow logically until about two-thirds of the way through. For an alternative view, however, see Anselm Atkins, "A Note on the Structure of Lucky's Speech," *Modern Drama*, vol. 9, no. 3, Dec. 1966, p. 309.

12. Interestingly, there was also an English television production in 1961, directed by Donald McWhinnie, with Jack MacGowran as Vladimir and Peter Woodthorpe as Estragon, about which McWhinnie said, "Jackie was excellent, but the play didn't work on television . . . I don't think it can. When you put *Waiting for Godot* on the small screen it loses the artificiality; it's too realistic. We tried to give it some kind of stylization by doing it all with one camera. Beckett wasn't too happy about it."

(Quoted in Young, *The Beckett Actor*, p. 77.) I see this comment as consistent with what I've said about the realism within Mostel and Meredith's fantasy world.

13.   Vivian Mercier, *Beckett/Beckett* (NY: Oxford University Press, 1977), p. 46.

14.   Schneider/Lahr interview. Three of Schneider's *Godots* up to this time are mentioned in this chapter. The fourth was a 1959 production at the Alley Theatre in Houston, Texas, in which the actors – John Astin (Vladimir) and Sidney Kaye (Estragon) – wore full clown make-up. Schneider tells John Lahr that Beckett knew of this production, did not object to the make-up, but did question its being staged in the round. Beckett had, in fact, written to Schneider about this issue three years earlier: "I don't in my ignorance agree with the round and feel 'Godot' needs a very closed box." ("Beckett's Letters on Endgame," in *The Village Voice Reader*, ed. Daniel Wolf and Edwin Fancher, [Garden City, NY: Doubleday, 1962], p. 183.) A photo of the Alley production accompanies Schneider's article "'Any Way You Like, Alan': Working With Beckett," *Theatre Quarterly*, vol. 5, no. 19, Sept.–Nov. 1975, p. 33. See also Roger Blin's comments about why he rejected "the circus element" in the world premiere of *Godot*, in "Blin On Beckett," interview by Tom Bishop, in *On Beckett*, ed. S. E. Gontarski (NY: Grove Press, 1986), pp. 228, 231.

Concerning Schneider's comment about eliciting "a sense of waiting," I should mention that Beckett made a similar remark directly to his actors during his 1975 Schiller Theater rehearsals. Asmus reports that in explaining the *Wartestellen* (Beckett's word for twelve pre-planned points of stillness where the actors were told to pause and stand in place), he asked them to "try to make the frozen picture of waiting into a major motif of the play." (Walter Asmus, "A Rehearsal Diary," in Dougald McMillan and Martha Fehsenfeld, *Beckett in the Theatre: The Author as Practical Playwright and Director* [London: John Calder, 1988], p. 143.) To be sure, this is exactly the type of comment one *cannot* make to most actors, especially American ones, because it abstracts a situation which they need to imagine as concrete in order to act it. As I discuss further on, though, one reason Beckett can direct in this way is that certain actors try harder for him than for other directors. Asmus told me that, when he tried to transfer Beckett's *Godot* production to the Brooklyn Academy of Music stage in 1978, using American actors, he "had a very hard time." See his interview in part three. There is also an unpublished letter at the University of Texas, Austin, in which Beckett expresses his sympathy with Asmus' dilemma and his awareness that the process used in Berlin would not work with American actors.

15.   There is a poor-quality videotape of this production in the Beckett Audio-Visual Archives at the Bobst Library, New York University.

16.   Asmus says that Bollmann and Wigger were able to form such a close onstage relationship partly because, being colleagues for many years at the Schiller Theater, they had their own friendship offstage. In addition, they knew the script of *Godot* extremely well before rehearsals even started, having already played it together (with reversed roles) ten years earlier, in a production directed by Deryk Mendel with Beckett's assistance. See Asmus' interview in part three. Similar observations were made in the 1960s about Magee and MacGowran; see Young, *The Beckett Actor*, p. 94.

17.   Asmus, "A Rehearsal Diary," p. 140.

18.   McMillan and Fehsenfeld, *Beckett in the Theatre*, p. 99.

19.   It is worth mentioning that Beckett began rehearsing with Lucky's speech,

which Klaus Herm says was due to the fact that the other actors were still involved in another production. See Herm's interview in part three. Nevertheless, in light of the fact that Herm was offered an unusually detailed logical structure around which to construct his delivery, it does seem as if the author attributes special importance to this speech. See note 11 above and Asmus' "A Rehearsal Diary."

20.   Scholars and critics may object that the more important dichotomy is surely Stanislavsky/Meyerhold, and that is true from the standpoint of theater history. For actors, however, particularly in America, Brecht is the name around which non- or anti-naturalistic performance philosophies are grouped. Among performers, any technique that departs from psychological realism performed as if behind an imaginary fourth wall, requiring the actor to acknowledge the audience's presence, is called, loosely, Brechtian. Part of what I am objecting to in this section is that loose usage.

21.   Michael Goldman, "Vitality and Deadness in Beckett's Plays," in *Beckett at 80/ Beckett in Context*, p. 76. See also Goldman's comments on the Beckett actor in *The Actor's Freedom: Toward A Theory of Drama* (NY: Viking, 1975), p. 107.

22.   In his essay on Artaud in *Towards a Poor Theater* (NY: Simon and Schuster, 1968), Jerzy Grotowski also speaks of a kind of acting allied neither with Stanislavsky nor with Brecht but using certain principles from both:

> [Artaud] touches something essential, of which he is not quite aware. It is the true lesson of the sacred theatre; whether we speak of the medieval European drama, the Balinese, or the Indian Kathakali: this knowledge that spontaneity and discipline, far from weakening each other, mutually reinforce themselves; that what is elementary feeds what is constructed and vice versa, to become the real source of a kind of acting that glows. This lesson was neither understood by Stanislavsky, who let natural impulses dominate, nor by Brecht, who gave too much emphasis to the construction of a role.   (p. 121)

It is beyond the scope of this chapter to discuss Grotowski's theories in connection with Beckett, though there is much to say on that subject despite Beckett's famous disclaimer, "Not for me these Grotowskis and Methods." In chapter 8 I pursue a parallel between Beckett acting and Artaud that relates indirectly to Grotowski. William Worthen discusses this topic in *The Idea of the Actor: Drama and the Ethics of Performance* (Princeton: Princeton University Press, 1984), pp. 207–208. See also Eugene Ionesco's comments about being dissatisfied with both realism and the alternative offered by Brecht and Piscator, in *Notes and Counter Notes*, trans. Donald Watson (NY: Grove Press, 1964), pp. 18–19.

23.   Quoted in Colin Duckworth, "Beckett's New *Godot*," in *Beckett's Later Fiction and Drama*, p. 189. See also Worthen's discussion of this subject in *The Idea of the Actor*, pp. 213–214.

24.   Pierre Chabert, "The Body in Beckett's Theatre," *Journal of Beckett Studies 8*, Fall 1982, p. 25.

25.   A detailed account of the intentions behind this *Endgame* production – which went through various evolutionary stages and was the outgrowth of Chaikin's long preoccupation with the play – may be found in Eileen Blumenthal, *Joseph Chaikin* (Cambridge: Cambridge University Press, 1984), pp. 188–207.

26.   Interview with Peter Evans, New York City, June 26, 1986.

27.   Interview with Asmus in part three.

28.   *Ibid.*

29.   Madeleine Renaud, "Laisser parler Beckett ou le sac de Winnie," *RE*, p. 172. This and all other translations from French and German are my own unless otherwise noted; original texts appear in the notes.

> Mais le texte est si beau, si évocateur, que je ne me soucie pas des gestes en jouant, ou des objets, ou de la position des bras – est-ce que je ne tourne pas mon cou un peu trop à droite, un peu trop à gauche? – ou de la fermeture des yeux . . . Je ne m'en fais pas. Je suis tranquille. Car il n'y a qu'à laisser parler Beckett.

> J'ai travaillé ce texte en le sublimant. Je ne distingue pas entre les paroles, les gestes, les objets . . . Pour moi c'est un tout, c'est l'état intérieur qui compte. Et ce qui domine, c'est la joie, un don de soi total.

Pierre Chabert, "Beckett as Director," *Gambit*, vol. 7, no. 28, 1976, p. 41.

30.   Samuel Beckett, "Dante . . . Bruno. Vico . . Joyce," p. 19.

31.   It is worth pointing out that devotees of Brecht also sometimes execrate comparisons with Beckett, as can be seen in this opening of an article by Werner Hecht on Brecht's planned adaptation of *Godot* – "Brecht 'und' Beckett: ein absurder Vergleich," *Theater der Zeit* 14, Aug. 1–15, 1966, p. 28.

> Natürlich kann man eigentlich alles vergleichen: die Banane mit dem Nashorn, die Eierschale mit der Urne, das Tonband mit der Palme.

> Man kann natürlich auch Brecht mit Beckett vergleichen.

> Of course, one can compare virtually everything: the banana with the rhinoceros, the egg-shell with the urn, the recording tape with the palm tree.

> One can, of course, also compare Brecht with Beckett.

For a much more developed comparison, however, which argues specifically against Hecht, see John Fuegi, "Beckett und Brecht," in *Das Werk von Samuel Beckett: Berliner Colloquium*, ed. Hans Mayer and Uwe Johnson (Frankfurt-on-Main: Suhrkamp, 1975), pp. 185–204.

32.   Martin Esslin, "'Godot,' the Authorized Version," *Journal of Beckett Studies* 1, Winter 1976, p. 99.

33.   Goldman, "Vitality and Deadness in Beckett's Plays," p. 76.

34.   Harold Pinter, "Beckett," in *Beckett at 60: A Festschrift*, ed. John Calder (London: Calder and Boyars, 1967), p. 86.

35.   Quoted by Harold Hobson, "Samuel Beckett – Dramatist of the Year," *International Theatre Annual* 1 (London: John Calder, 1956), p. 153.

36.   Brater, "Brecht's Alienated Actor in Beckett's Theater," pp. 195, 203.

37.   Bertolt Brecht, "A Short Organum for the Theatre," in *Brecht On Theatre*, trans. John Willet (NY: Hill and Wang, 1957), p. 192.

38.   Robbe-Grillet, "Samuel Beckett, or Presence on the Stage," p. 16.

4.   Considerations of acting in the late plays

1.   By "late Beckett" I mean dramatic works since *Happy Days* (1961), which for the most part have dispensed with even the provisional types of naturalism Beckett used when he started writing for the theater. This stylistic distinction, which sees the later

works as more concerned with verbal music and finely wrought tableaux than with psychologically understood exchanges among characters, is not foolproof. Some recent works such as *Catastrophe*, for example, do not fit the pattern. It applies sufficiently well, however, to be used for the sake of argument.

2. Quotations from *Ohio Impromptu* are from *The Collected Shorter Plays of Samuel Beckett*.

3. Enoch Brater points out in his book *Beyond Minimalism: Beckett's Late Style in the Theater* (NY and Oxford: Oxford University Press, 1987) that the line in *Ohio Impromptu*, "White nights now again his portion," may be a pun referring to an archive in England where Beckett has deposited many notebooks, manuscripts and other paraphernalia relating to the composition and production of his works.

> The counterpart through literal translation of the French *nuit blanche*, a sleepless night ["White nights"], is also a pun on Whiteknights, the location of the Beckett Archive at the University of Reading. Such a meaning would be truly apposite for a play originally performed in America before an audience of Beckett specialists, many of whom had spent hours poring over the rich holdings at Whiteknights.

> (p. 132)

4. Samuel Beckett, *Malone Dies*, in *Three Novels by Samuel Beckett* (NY: Grove Press, 1965), p. 194. Another interesting forerunner to *Ohio Impromptu*, specifically to Listener's knocks, is an early holograph of *Not I* in which, in S. E. Gontarski's words, there is a "corrective Auditor" who "interrupts Mouth to insist on a specific narrative, to correct errors in fact, and tacitly to urge Mouth to identify a bit more with her story" (S. E. Gontarski, *The Intent of Undoing* [Bloomington: Indiana University Press, 1985], p. 145).

5. Alan Schneider, "'Any Way You Like, Alan': Working with Beckett," p. 35. Unfortunately, I did not have an opportunity to speak with Schneider about these or any other performances before his death. See Epstein and Warrilow's comments, in their interviews, on how much time each of them spent with him.

6. Ben Barnes, "Aspects of Directing Beckett," *Irish University Review*, vol. 14, no. 1, 1984, p. 86.

7. When Warrilow made this comment, he quickly added that he does feel a special inspiration for Beckett. His statement that "there's a place in me which is for his work" is similar to certain comments of Billie Whitelaw's: e.g. "It's almost as if he were writing about me – even down to the little jokes one has with oneself" (to me in conversation).

8. A similar process seems to occur with the television plays, which have many structural and temperamental similarities to the late stage works. One example demonstrating this is the Jean-Louis Barrault performance in *Dis Joe* discussed in chapter 6, and another is *Was Wo*, Beckett's 1986 German television adaptation of the play *What Where*. As Asmus explains in his rehearsal diary for the latter production, "All Gimmicks Gone?," *Theater heute*, April 1986, pp. 28–30, Beckett began by asking the actors to speak in an exhausted, resigned manner, every sentence delivered on a heavy exhale, but eventually changed his mind and instituted a hard, robot-like monotone, indicating defeat or resignation visually with sunken heads; the result was a much more mysterious and compelling work that some critics think is more tightly crafted even than the original stage play.

9.   Walter D. Asmus, "Practical Aspects of Theatre, Radio and Television: Rehearsal Notes for the German Premiere of Beckett's 'That Time' and 'Footfalls' at the Schiller Theater Werkstatt, Berlin (Directed by Beckett)," *Journal of Beckett Studies* 2, Summer 1977, pp. 82–95. All following quotations regarding this production, unless otherwise noted, are from this article.

10.   Interestingly, Beckett even found Warrilow to be too much of an identifiable character during 1986 rehearsals for *L'Impromptu d'Ohio* in Paris. The author felt that Warrilow's delivery contained too much "resignation" and "color," and asked him to use instead a clipped, matter-of-fact voice without major intonations, which significantly inhibited him. (This information comes from a conversation with Professor Tom Bishop on May 16, 1986. Compare the actor's comments about the matter in his interview.) The story was also described to me in terms similar to Bishop's by Pierre Chabert, "nominal director" (Chabert's phrase) of the production, who agreed with Beckett that Warrilow's voice was too slow and deep, adding:

> It's a reading. It's just a reading. Afterwards, David did a reading with just a microphone at the Pompidou Centre, and at that time I think he found what we were looking for. I think the fact of the microphone was important. It was fantastic, because he wasn't forced to speak forcefully and loudly.

(Conversation in Paris, November 15, 1986.)

When I asked Beckett about this affair, he said that he didn't remember any disagreement with David but that he also didn't think "he was at his best here in Paris." He then added that he thought the major problem with the production was Listener, played by Jean-Louis Barrault, who he said "was just doing his job." Warrilow also spoke of difficulties working with Barrault.

11.   While directing *Play* in Berlin in 1978, Beckett requested a piano in order to give each of the actors their own note, which they were to maintain in speaking, but he eventually had to give up the idea because they found it impossible to attend to anything other than pitch while performing. (See the rehearsal diary for the production: Walter Asmus, "Beckett inszeniert sein 'Spiel,'" *Theater heute*, Dec. 1978, pp. 6–10.) See also Asmus' additional comments on the incident in his interview.

5.   *Underground staging in perspective*

1.   Beckett to me in conversation, November 16, 1986.

2.   Alan Schneider, "What Does A Director Do?," *New York Theatre Review*, Spring/Summer 1977, pp. 16–17.

3.   "Blin on Beckett," interview by Tom Bishop in *On Beckett*, ed. S. E. Gontarski, p. 235.

4.   Michael Bakewell refers to a similar remark by Beckett regarding *Eh Joe*: "I met Beckett to talk the play over . . . On the back of an old envelope he drew the set, the exact placing of the furniture (what little there was), the movements of the actor and the tracking line of the camera. These were presented not as absolutes but as the only way in which the play could work" (Michael Bakewell, "Working with Beckett," *Adam* 337–339 [1970], p. 72).

5. Bert O. States, *The Shape of Paradox* (Berkeley, Los Angeles, London: University of California Press, 1978), p. 32.

6. Käthe Rülicke-Weiler, *Die Dramaturgie Brechts* (Berlin: Deb, 1966), p. 156. Das Ende der bürgerlichen Welt, das uns die absurden Autoren als Ende der Welt und der Menschen einreden wollen, indem sie beide in ihren Stücken sterben lassen, spiegelt sich in dieser bürgerlichen Dramatik in einer erstaunlichen, da vollständigen, Selbstauflösung. Über die namenlosen, auf die Stimme reduzierten Krüppelwesen Becketts kann es keinen Schritt mehr hinaus geben. Alle spätere Dramatik kann nur noch zurück in die Gesellschaft der Menschen. Nachdem sich die absurde Dramatik selbst ad absurdum geführt und ihren Bankrott erklärt hat, muß sie sich wieder als Drama herstellen, da sie keine andere Wahl hat, als ihren Leichen wieder Leben einzuhauchen oder aufzuhören, zu existieren. For another example, markedly less propagandistic, see Darko Suvin, ''Beckett's Purgatory of the Individual,'' *TDR*, vol. 11, no. 4, Summer 1967, pp. 23–36.

7. Theodor Adorno, ''Trying to Understand *Endgame*,'' trans. Michael T. Jones, *New German Critique* 26, Spring/Summer 1982, p. 122.

8. Details of Brecht's plans may be found in Rülicke-Weiler, *Die Dramaturgie Brechts*, and in Werner Hecht, ''Brecht 'und' Beckett: ein absurder Vergleich,'' pp. 28–30.

9. Quoted from Volker Canaris, ''Einen klassischen Text muß man überprüfen,'' *Theater heute*, April 1971, p. 24: ''Wenn ich so einen gesellschaftlichen Bezug in das Stück einziehen könnte, wäre mir wohler.''

10. For a more detailed discussion of this production, see my article ''Krapp at the Palast'' (*Theater*, vol. 19, no. 1, Fall/Winter 1987, pp. 73–77). Interestingly, the GDR premiere of *Godot*, which took place in Dresden in March 1987, apparently did not have the same polemical atmosphere and was very well received by audiences. Director Wolfgang Engel had originally wanted to cast women for that premiere, but Beckett promptly protested and the parts were played by four men. I did not see the production, but Engel's comments in a subsequent interview (''Warten auf Gorbatschow?,'' interview by Horst Thiemer, *Theater heute*, May 1987, pp. 58–59) indicate that he did not follow Brecht's plans at all or indeed see the play agitationally in any way.
Dieses Herr-Knecht-Verhältnis [Pozzo-Lucky]: Zunächst könnte man denken, ach, das ist der böse Kapitalist und sein Sklave oder wie auch immer. Das erschien uns im besten Falle brauchbar für ein böses Märchen, aber nicht für die Assoziations-Möglichkeiten, die ein Beckettscher Text liefert.

This master-slave relationship [Pozzo-Lucky]: to begin with one could think, oh, that's the bad capitalist and his slave, just as always. That seems to us at best useful for a vicious fairy-tale, but not for the possibilities for associations that a Beckettian text affords. (p. 58)

11. Clas Zilliacus, ''Three Times *Godot*: Beckett, Brecht, Bulatovic,'' *Comparative Drama* 4, Spring 1970, p. 13.

12. *Ibid.*, pp. 13–14.

13. In her article ''Quoting from Godot,'' *Journal of Beckett Studies* 9, 1984, pp. 114–115, Anne C. Murch describes an Australian production in which Didi and

Gogo were played as "'no-hopers' wandering aimlessly in the bush," Pozzo was "the *icon* of the colonial oppressor," and Lucky was "an Australian aborigine, the colonial slave." These characterizations present a much more direct politicization than those in Howarth's production, and yet Murch says:

> The audience, entirely white and urban, had no difficulty in transcending the regionalist *parti-pris* and identifying with the plight of the *personae*. It was experienced as their own malaise in a rootless culture in which they groped unsuccessfully for some life-giving, structuring principle in a big city, urban but not urbane.

This would seem to be another example demonstrating my point further on, that Beckett's plays often prove stronger than attempts to politicize them.

14.   My impression (unverified statistically) is that *Endgame* has been subjected to even more directorial changes than *Godot*, which is not to say, though, that *Godot* lags far behind. For descriptions of several concept *Godots*, see Georg Hensel, "Da es so gespielt wird . . . spielen wir es eben so," in *Beckett in Berlin*, ed. Klaus Völker (Berlin: Fröhlich & Kaufmann, 1986), pp. 10–25.

15.   Peter von Becker, "Das 'Endspiel' immer weiterspielen?," *Theater heute*, Dec. 1978, p. 13: "Ist's nicht doch eine Torheit, in unseren Theatern Beckett, der mit dem Spielen und dem Erzählen und dem ewigen Reden Schluß machen will, so selbstverständlich weiterzuspielen? Wenn man's nicht *weiter* spielen kann."

16.   See Alain Piette, "Beckett After the Deluge," *Theater*, vol. 15, no. 3, Summer/Fall 1984, pp. 54–57, for an account of Delval's production. I had been misinformed when I wrote my review of Akalaitis' *Endgame* (note 22 below) that Beckett knew about Delval's production. He told me himself that he did not. The author apparently did know about George Tabori's 1984 *Godot* at the Münchner Kammerspiele, however: see note 34 below and Georg Hensel, "Da es so gespielt wird . . .," p. 14.

17.   Barney Rossett writes, for instance, that "we did make very strong objections to Andre Gregory's production of ENDGAME in 1973, although we didn't learn about it until after the production had started. The affair was amicably settled by their agreeing to cease performances" (letter to me, November 5, 1986). See also Clas Zilliacus, *Beckett and Broadcasting*, p. 173, for the story of Grove's objection to Sydney Schubert Walter's production of *Embers* at the Café Cino in 1963. As is well known, Beckett has also taken a firm position against "sex-blind," or cross-gender, casting. In fact, the majority of his official objections to German productions seem to have been prompted by cross-gender casting: seven of ten examples listed in letters to me of Sept. 9 and Oct. 2, 1987, from Dr. Susanne Wolfram of S. Fischer Verlag, which handles rights to the major plays in Germany.

18.   Adorno, "Trying to Understand *Endgame*," p. 123. Interestingly, this passage by Adorno comes close to recognizing what S. E. Gontarski was to demonstrate conclusively in his 1985 study of Beckett's manuscripts, *The Intent of Undoing*: that in the process of composition, Beckett considers and then rejects many of the "clarifying" changes suggested by directors.

19.   Adorno, "Trying to Understand *Endgame*, p. 125.

20.   *Ibid.*, p. 120.

21.   See the section of Akalaitis' interview in which she insists that "this *is* the play; it's a production of *Endgame*" and implies that she does not distinguish

between the importance of Beckett's stage directions and those of Noel Coward.

22. For a fuller description of the production, see my review, "The Underground *Endgame*," *Theater*, vol. 16, no. 2, Spring 1985, pp. 88–92. Any discrepancies between the opinions expressed in that review and those in this chapter may be attributed to my reaction to Akalaitis' interview.

23. Richard Goldman, "*Endgame* and its Scorekeepers," *Twentieth-Century Interpretations of Endgame*, ed. Bell Gale Chevigny (Englewood Cliffs, NJ: Prentice-Hall, 1969), p. 35.

24. Thomas Kilroy, "Two Playwrights: Yeats and Beckett," in *Myth and Reality in Irish Literature*, ed. Joseph Ronsley (Waterloo, Ontario: Wilfrid Laurier University Press, 1977), p. 188.

25. The opening credits of the broadcast did briefly announce that it was an adaptation, but I saw no mention of that fact in any press listings or advertisements.

26. Samuel Beckett, *Glückliche Tage/Oh les beaux jours/Happy Days* (Frankfurt-on-Main: Suhrkamp, 1975), pp. 36–37.

27. Cohn, *Just Play*, p. 286, n. 1. The comment is quoted in context in chapter 7.

28. *New York Times*, June 1, 1979, p. C10.

29. *New York Post*, June 14, 1979, p. 39.

30. Katharine Worth, "The Space and the Sound in Beckett's Theatre," in *Beckett the Shape Changer*, ed. Katharine Worth (London and Boston: Routledge & Kegan Paul, 1975), p. 198.

31. For a list of the changes made in the script at BAM, see McMillan and Fehsenfeld, *Beckett in the Theatre*.

32. Worth, "The Space and the Sound in Beckett's Theatre," p. 196.

33. As already stated, Akalaitis' *Endgame* does have the benefit of openly declaring its atextuality, as one imagines Brecht's *Godot* would have had. But if one suspects, as I do, that Brecht gave up the idea of adapting Beckett because he saw it was an ill-fated project (or that he would have come to that realization had he started to work on it in the theater – Heiner Müller's opinion), one wonders why Akalaitis did not do the same. For she has displayed in the past, particularly in her direction of Franz Xaver Kroetz's work, an uncommon sensitivity to the limits to which dramatic language and physicalization may be stretched before their relevancy to the play begins to break down. One thinks especially of the unforgettable externalizations of internal frustrations in *Through the Leaves* (1984). With scripts considered classic, however, such as *Endgame*, Genet's *The Balcony* and Büchner's *Leonce and Lena*, she seems to take a different attitude. She encountered identical difficulties to *Endgame*, for instance, the following season at ART when she returned to direct *The Balcony*, setting it in Central America. A visually stunning set placed the action in a specific time and place, resolving several of the script's important ambiguities in order to justify its severe theatricalism. And as I discuss more in depth in my review of the production ("Whose Text Is It Anyway?," *Theater*, vol. 17, no. 3, Summer/Fall 1986, pp. 97–100), that resolved ambiguity then backfired on her by working against the interests of the specific setting, blocking all possibility of direct political meaning. The unfortunate truth is that her contemporizations of classics cancel their potential for pointed political statement in the course of their very attempt at political relevance.

34. It was indeed very atypical of Beckett to tolerate such a production. He seems

to have done so out of personal affection for Tabori but was later horrified by what he heard about the production: "I shuddered" (letter from Georg Hensel to me, May 30, 1987).

35.   States, *The Shape of Paradox*, p. 34.

36.   Adorno, "Trying to Understand *Endgame*," p. 143. As already described in chapter 3, Beckett also sees his plays musically, and Roger Blin says this was true from the start of his practical work in the theater: "At first, he looked on [*Fin de partie*] as a kind of musical score. When a word occurred or was repeated, when Hamm called Clov, Clov should always come in the same way every time, like a musical phrase coming from the same instrument with the same volume" ("Blin on Beckett," p. 233).

37.   Hugh Kenner, *Samuel Beckett: A Critical Study* (NY: Grove Press, 1961), p. 160.

6.   Eh Joe, Dis Joe, He Joe: *toward a television icon*

1.   Vivian Mercier, *Beckett/Beckett*, p. 237.

2.   Copies of all three versions of *Eh Joe* discussed in this chapter, and many of Beckett's other television plays, may be found in the Beckett Audio-Visual Archive at New York University. Some examples of stage versions are: David Warrilow's *Eh Joe*, directed by Alan Schneider at the Festival d'Automne in Paris in 1981; Rick Cluchey's *Eh Joe* at Chicago's Goodman Theatre in 1983, and the Noho Theatre Group's *Quad I+II* at the American Folk Theatre in New York City in 1986. Both *Eh Joe* adaptations were done with special permission of the author, as was Jack Garfein's 1988 adaptation of *Nacht und Träume* at the Kreis-Theater in Vienna.

3.   Martin Esslin, "A Poetry of Moving Images," in *Beckett Translating/Translating Beckett*, ed. Alan Warren Friedman, Charles Rossman and Dana Sherzer (University Park and London: Penn State Press, 1987), p. 74. Esslin uses the phrase "visual poetry" specifically in regard to *Quad* and *Nacht und Träume*.

4.   Beckett told me that, in the SDR production, the *Lied* was peformed by an amateur singer who worked in the studio's technical crew and did not want his name to appear in the credits.

5.   The religiosity in *Nacht und Träume* is salient and has been commented on by a number of critics, but it is not typical of the television plays and so is not relevant to the discussion in this chapter. The following passage from an interview with Jim Lewis is nevertheless worth quoting. Jim Lewis, "Beckett et la caméra," interviewed by Sandra Solov, *RE*, p. 379:

> SS: *A-t-il jamais parlé des allusions bibliques dans le contexte de* Night and Dreams?
>
> JL: Quand on essuie les gouttes de transpiration sur le front du personnage, Beckett a simplement dit que le tissu fait allusion au voile qu'utilise Véronique pour essuyer le front de Jésus pendant le chemin de Croix. L'empreinte du visage du Christ reste sur le tissu.
>
> SS: *Did he ever speak of biblical allusions in the context of* Night and Dreams?
>
> JL: At the moment when they wipe the drops of perspiration from the brow of

the character, Beckett simply said that the cloth made an allusion to the veil that Veronica used to wipe the brow of Jesus on the Way of the Cross. The imprint of Christ's face remains on the cloth.

6. Lewis, "Beckett et la caméra," p. 376: "que c'était difficile pour lui d'écrire encore des mots, sans avoir le sentiment que c'est un mensonge."

7. Zilliacus, *Beckett and Broadcasting*, p. 194.

8. All English quotations from *Eh Joe* and Beckett's other television scripts are from *The Collected Shorter Plays* (NY: Grove Press, 1984). Quotations from *Dis Joe* are from *Comédie et actes divers* (Paris: Les Editions de Minuit, 1972). Quotations from *He Joe* are from *Film/Eh Joe* (Frankfurt-on-Main: Suhrkamp, 1968). Page numbers in parentheses refer to these editions.

9. Israel Shenker, interview with Beckett, *New York Times*, May 5, 1956, section 2, pp. 1, 3.

10. See my discussion of this movement in chapter 8.

11. Tom Driver, "Beckett by the Madeleine," *Columbia University Forum*, Summer 1961, p. 25.

12. Linda Ben-Zvi, "Samuel Beckett's Media Plays," *Modern Drama*, vol. 28, no. 1, March 1985, p. 36.

13. Esslin, "A Poetry of Moving Images," pp. 70–71.

14. Asmus interview in part three.

15. Beckett to me in conversation, January 30, 1987.

16. S. E. Gontarski, *The Intent of Undoing*, p. 120. John Fletcher and John Spurling, *Beckett: A Study of his Plays* (London: Methuen, 1972), p. 99.

17. Siegfried Melchinger, "Regie Samuel Beckett," *Theater heute*, May 1966, p. 15:

"Haben Sie sich die Stimme als eine konkrete Person gedacht?"
BECKETT: "Es ist eine konkrete Person für Joe."
"Aber er erfindet doch selbst, was er zu hören glaubt?"
BECKETT: "Sie flüstert wirklich in ihm. Er hört sie. Nur wenn sie lebt, kann er den Wunsch haben, sie zu töten. Sie ist tot, aber in ihm lebt sie. Das ist seine Passion: die Stimmen zu töten, die er nicht töten kann."

Beckett has made similar comments to me and to others in conversation, saying explicitly that the reason for the final smile – which remains absent from all the published texts, as does the final smile in *Ghost Trio* – is that Joe has "won," succeeding finally in strangling the voice.

18. Gontarski, *The Intent of Undoing*, p. 117.

19. Zilliacus, *Beckett and Broadcasting*, pp. 186–187.

20. *Ibid.*, p. 187.

21. Gontarski, *The Intent of Undoing*, p. 113.

22. I should mention that Beckett returned to Stuttgart in 1979 to remake *He Joe* with the well-known German actor Heinz Bennent. He was "terribly disappointed" with the result, however, and is very candid about saying so. He told me he thinks the production "deeply beside the point."

23. Melchinger, "Regie Samuel Beckett," p. 14: "Nein. Aber mit anderen Schauspielern wird es anders." Neither Lewis nor Nancy Illig (Voice) had seen the BBC production at this time (letter from Jim Lewis to me, May 24, 1987).

24. Lewis, "Beckett et la caméra," p. 374:

> JL: . . . La lumière est toujours faible. Et je n'arrive jamais à la rendre assez faible pour Beckett. On est là, assis, et on regarde l'écran de contrôle et il me dit: "Jim, tu ne peux pas réduire la lumière encore un peu plus?" . . .
>
> SS: *Mais pourqoui la lumière est-elle toujours faible chez Beckett?*
>
> JL: Dans la plupart des cas, on évoque le passé, la mémoire, la nuit et les rêves aussi.

25. Beckett seems to have changed his mind quite a bit about the length of the nine camera moves and the initial distance from Joe's face. The English text specifies moves of exactly four inches starting from one yard away, the German text moves of exactly five centimeters starting from fifty centimeters, and the French text moves of a "dizaine" centimeters starting from "un mètre environ." In a letter to me (note 23 above) Jim Lewis commented: "As far as I know we never discussed measured moves . . . I simply cannot remember us spending much time with centimeters and meters, etc. . . . the voice dictated the starting and stopping of the camera, perhaps we felt that rigid adherence to strict measurement wasn't necessary – it wouldn't be the first time that Sam abandoned his usually very exacting instructions."

26. Samuel Beckett, *Stories and Texts for Nothing* (NY: Grove Press, 1967), p. 9. Samuel Beckett, *Three Novels*, p. 273.

27. Some of Beckett's unpublished letters at the University of Texas, Austin, show that he did intend to help with this French version. Deirdre Bair, however, quotes a letter from Beckett to "John [sic] Knowlson" from Feb. 8, 1971, in which the author states that he and Mitrani had "one or two conversations before shooting, nothing more" (Deirdre Bair, *Samuel Beckett: A Biography*, pp. 600, 717, n. 30).

28. James Knowlson, "*Ghost Trio/Geistertrio*," in *Beckett at 80/Beckett in Context*, p. 201.

29. Esslin, *Mediations*, p. 151.

30. Beckett was on the set during the entire shooting of *Film* (1963), and in an essay on the shooting process the director, Alan Schneider, credits him with many production decisions. (Alan Schneider, "On Directing *Film*," in Samuel Beckett, *Film* [NY: Grove Press, 1969], pp. 63–94). Considering the array of technical and logistical problems that project encountered, however, I venture to guess that Beckett was not eager to work in film again afterwards, and the harmonious conditions at SDR figured importantly in his decision to direct for television. Of course, some of his reasons were undoubtedly more profound than that, and we can speculate on those as well. There is something decidedly appropriate about this author having turned late in his life to television, a medium whose history has been almost entirely a story of limited ambition. To bring expectations of painterly precision to an arena where coarseness has long been the norm (not only in programming but also in image-resolution, despite increases over the years in the number of lighted dots per square inch) is almost to insure a degree of failure.

> . . . to be an artist is to fail, as no other dare fail, that failure is his world and the shrink from it desertion.
>
> (Samuel Beckett, "Three Dialogues," in *Disjecta*, p. 145)

All of old. Nothing else ever. Ever tried. Ever failed. No matter. Try again. Fail again. Fail better.

> (Samuel Beckett, *Worstward Ho* [NY: Grove Press, 1983], p. 7)

7. The gamble of staging prose fiction

1. Georg Hensel, "Da es so gespielt wird . . .," p. 10:
Ohne das Theater wäre Samuel Beckett ein ziemlich unbekannter Schriftsteller. Seine Romane sind vor 1953, vor seinem Welterfolg "Warten auf Godot," kaum gelesen worden und sie sind noch heute eine esoterische Lektüre für einen kleinen Kreis. Becketts Schritt auf die Bühne war auch ein Schritt in die Popularität: man liest ihn nicht, man sieht ihn im Theater.
2. Quoted from Zilliacus, *Beckett and Broadcasting*, p. 3. See also Beckett's letter to Jack MacGowran (Dec. 13. 1967) in response to the actor's request, on behalf of Roman Polanski, to film *Godot*:
I'm terribly sorry to disappoint you and Polanski but I don't want any film of *Godot*. As it stands it is simply not cinema material. And adaptation would destroy it. Please forgive me . . . and don't think of me as a purist bastard.
> (Quoted in Young, *The Beckett Actor*, p. 120)
3. See MacGowran's biography – Young's *The Beckett Actor* – for information on the extent of Beckett's involvement with the actor's one-man performances.
4. Cohn, *Just Play*, p. 286, n. 1.
5. Bair, *Samuel Beckett*, p. 555.
6. See Cohn's chapter "Jumping Beckett's Genres" in *Just Play* for excellent descriptions of these performances, and of *The Lost Ones* which I discuss below. Descriptions of other cross-genre events can be found in *Beckett on File*, comp. Virginia Cooke (London and New York: Methuen, 1985), pp. 66–83.
7. Interview with Neumann in part three.
8. Samuel Beckett, *Three Novels*, p. 307.
9. Samuel Beckett, *Company* (NY: Grove Press, 1980). Page numbers in parentheses refer to this edition.
10. Samuel Beckett, *Three Novels*, pp. 343, 360.
11. I describe a performance of *Company* I saw at the Public Theater in New York City in early 1983, the program for which credits Honora Fergusson, Neumann's wife, as co-director. In this version Fergusson made a brief appearance in the piece, entering during the summerhouse section from behind one of the disks and sitting motionless, staring forward.
12. S. E. Gontarski, "*Company* for Company: Androgyny and Theatricality in Samuel Beckett's Prose," in *Beckett's Later Fiction and Drama*, ed. James Acheson and Kateryna Arthur, p. 193.
13. Pierre Chabert told me that in his 1984 staging of *Compagnie* with Pierre Dux at the Théâtre du Rond-Point in Paris he felt very strongly about making sufficient cuts to keep the performance to about an hour. All such cuts were made by Beckett, who also attended several rehearsals. See Maryvonne Saison's article on this adaptation, "Mettre en scène l'irreprésentable," *RE*, pp. 85–87. Chabert's concept was subsequently used in another American adaptation by Stanley Gontarski with the

actor Alan Mandell. Gontarski gives a detailed account of this version in his article "*Company* for Company . . ."

14.   Interview with Gerald Thomas, New York City, Feb. 3, 1986. Thomas told me that *All Strange Away* was his seventh adaptation, preceded by *Fizzles*, *Texts for Nothing*, *Embers*, *Lessness* (for stage and radio), *Echo's Bones* (for stage and radio) and *Company* (for radio). I could not verify his claims about these productions, except regarding *All Strange Away*, which I saw, and about which Barney Rosset told me, "he must have had permission."

15.   *All Strange Away* originally opened at La Mama with the actor Ryan Cutrona and enjoyed a successful run there; Cutrona was not available at the time the production moved uptown. This move involved more than a change of actor, however; there was also significant development in the directing concept. For instance, "*All Strange Away 1*," as Thomas refers to it, contained far less voice-over and did not include the final scene with the old man. "*All Strange Away 2*" was slightly shorter, about seventy-five minutes, due to the cut near the end, and a video of it exists at Lincoln Center. Thomas told me he would like some day to stage another version, "*All Strange Away 3*," in which he would "remove the speaking actor altogether. I would have the whole thing over tape recorders and have a live human figure in the cube."

16.   Samuel Beckett, "All Strange Away," in *Rockaby and Other Short Pieces* (NY: Grove Press, 1981). Page numbers in parentheses refer to this edition.

17.   It seems Beckett uses the words "Fancy" and "Imagination" interchangeably in *All Strange Away* as a conscious fillip to Coleridge, who made a distinction between them and held it to be of the utmost importance. In *Frescoes of the Skull* (NY: Grove Press, 1980), John Pilling writes, "Beckett hereabouts resuscitates the category of Fancy which the great Romantic poets considered decidedly inferior to Imagination, reminding us implicitly that he is a good deal less interested in the Sublime than they were" (p. 138).

18.   James Knowlson and John Pilling, *Frescoes of the Skull*, p. 144.

19.   Samuel Beckett, "Peintres de l'Empêchement," *Disjecta*, pp. 136–137. (See note 23 below.)

20.   Samuel Beckett, *Watt* (NY: Grove Press, 1953), p. 77.

21.   The cube used for the set of *All Strange Away* was originally a sculpture by Daniela Thomas, the director's wife.

22.   Quoted from Stanley Kauffmann, *Persons of the Drama: Theater Criticism and Comment* (NY, Hagerstown, San Francisco, London: Harper & Row, 1976), p. 212.

23.   Samuel Beckett, "Peintres de l'Empêchement," pp. 136–137: "Un dévoilement sans fin, voile derrière voile, plan sur plan de transparences imparfaites, un dévoilement vers l'indévoilable, le rien, la chose à nouveau. Et l'ensevelissement dans l'unique, dans un lieu d'impénétrables proximités, cellule peinte sur la pierre de la cellule, art d'incarcération . . ."

24.   In *Just Play* (p. 224), Ruby Cohn states that *The Lost Ones* began in 1972, but David Warrilow's recollection is that work on it began in March 1974. The "Performance History" given to me by the Mabou Mines Development Foundation, Inc., states that the work premiered at the Theater for the New City in October 1975. See note 3 in the Conversations section.

25. Two questions relating to *The Lost Ones* were never answered to my satisfaction by any of the parties involved, so I simply mention them here as seeming contradictions in its history. First, if Beckett really never saw *The Lost Ones*, as he insists (or, for that matter, any other production of Warrilow's), then how did he come to think so highly of Warrilow's acting that he would decide to write a play for him in 1979 (*A Piece of Monologue*)? When I asked Warrilow about this he responded as follows: "Yes, strange, I know, but he never did see me perform. But then, some actors have made him wince, & he's still let them go on doing his work" (letter to me July 2, 1986). See, in this regard, Frederick Neumann's comment, in his interview in part three, that Beckett "sometimes peeks into a theater."

Second, since Beckett eventually granted permission for *The Lost Ones* personally, when he asked to see the set and meet the Mabou Mines company during their 1976 trip to Berlin, why did his American publisher continue to treat the production as reprobate until it closed? (Breuer says he was denied the rights to make a film of it.) Barney Rosset responded to an inquiry by stating that any of his decisions regarding the production were his attempt to fulfill what he understood to be Beckett's wishes, which he stressed were not and are not always unambiguously clear. What does seem clear is that we are all of us the poorer for the fact that Breuer has not directed another Beckett performance. Speaking candidly in an interview about his annoyance at Beckett's reaction to JoAnne Akalaitis' *Endgame*, Breuer said, "J'ai beaucoup de respect pour Samuel Beckett et je préfère renoncer à monter ses pièces pour l'instant plutôt que de lui déplaire ou de lui faire de la peine" ("I have a great deal of respect for Samuel Beckett and I prefer to give up staging his plays for the moment rather than displease him or cause him pain") (Lee Breuer, "Un théâtre narratif," *RE*, p. 96).

26. Samuel Beckett, *The Lost Ones* (NY: Grove Press, 1972). Page numbers in parentheses refer to this edition.

27. Ruby Cohn writes that the length of *The Lost Ones* was determined by Glass' music; the text was cut by "about a third" to fit the score's fifty-minute length (*Just Play*, pp. 224–225). A very poor-quality video of the piece exists at Lincoln Center.

28. Lee Breuer commented on this same topic in the interview "Un théâtre narratif," p. 96:

Je ne pense pas . . . qu'on puisse jouer Beckett avec un accent américain. Il faut le jouer en français ou avec un accent irlandais. La seule pièce qui me semble avoir un côté anglais, c'est *Comédie*. On l'a jouée avec un léger accent londonien. Quand aux œuvres lyriques de Beckett, elles doivent avoir l'ironie laconique, la délicatesse d'une voix irlandaise.

I don't think . . . that you can act Beckett with an American accent. It must be played in French or with an Irish accent. The only play that seems to me to have an English aspect is *Play*. It was acted with a slow London accent. As for the lyric works of Beckett, they must have the laconic irony, the delicacy of an Irish voice.

29. States, *The Shape of Paradox*, pp. 49–50.

30. *The Lost Ones* was performed as the final piece in a three-part "Beckett evening" that also included *Play* and *Come and Go*.

8.   *Conclusion: the question of context*

1.   A few examples. An essay such as Thomas Whitaker's "'Wham, Bam, Thank You Sam': The Presence of Beckett," in *Beckett at 80/Beckett in Context*, pp. 208–229, offers instances of younger authors such as Fugard, Mamet, Soyinka and Shepard inheriting modernist technical innovations from Beckett: e.g. isolated and paired characters, desolate landscapes and "ethically ambiguous social vision[s]." But Whitaker considers neither the value, theatrical or otherwise, of these playwrights' visions with respect to Beckett's nor the status of the playtext in contemporary theater, nor does he mention the New York avant-garde at all. Alternatively, Ronald Hayman's *Theatre and Anti-Theatre: New Movements Since Beckett* (NY: Oxford University Press, 1979) does, to its author's credit, deal with Artaud and the declining influence of the playwright over the last century, but, as its subtitle prematurely burying the corpus implies, it does not assign Beckett a place in the new order of directorial dominance and sees his influence as limited to stylistic impressions on dramatists such as Handke, Albee and Shepard. Presumably, all of these writers are anachronistic, their efforts doomed to obsolescence, or at least to subordination, in an era of Brooks, Grotowskis and Chaikins.

2.   Herbert Blau, *Blooded Thought* (NY: PAJ Publications, 1982), p. 148.

3.   I have taken these words out of context. See Whitelaw's interview in part three.

4.   Antonin Artaud, *The Theater and its Double*, trans. Mary C. Richard (NY: Grove Press, 1958), p. 24.

5.   Whitelaw's comment is from her interview in part three. Worth's is from Eileen Blumenthal, "Irene Worth Has Time on Her Side," *Village Voice*, Aug. 27, 1979, p. 81.

6.   Lee Breuer, *Sister Suzie Cinema* (NY: TCG Publications, 1987), p. 102. The quotation comes from an essay carrying the pseudo-Artaudian title "The Theater and Its Trouble."

7.   Richard Schechner, *The End of Humanism* (NY: PAJ Publication, 1982), p. 32.

8.   Charles Marowitz, *Prospero's Staff: Acting and Directing in the Contemporary Theatre* (Bloomington and Indianapolis: Indiana University Press, 1986), p. 184.

9.   This anecdote, related by Beckett to Avigdor Arikha, is taken from Dan Hofstadter's article on Arikha, "A Painting Dervish," *The New Yorker*, June 1, 1987, p. 45.

10.   See Esslin's introduction to Kott's *Shakespeare Our Contemporary* (NY and London: W. W. Norton & Co., 1964), p. xi.

11.   Gerald Rabkin, "Is There a Text on this Stage," *Performing Arts Journal 26/27*, vol. 9, nos. 2/3, pp. 152–153. Rabkin discusses the ART incident in connection with topics such as the history of copyrights, Gresham's Law and Proudhonian poverty, without considering any aesthetic ramifications of Akalaitis' choices. His article is typical of the bloodless critical responses the production provoked, which avoided direct evaluation of the "performance text" whose autonomy they defended, instead focusing on legal and economic side issues.

12.   Schechner, *The End of Humanism*, p. 107.

13.   *Ibid.*, p. 101.

14.   *Ibid.*, p. 96.

15. *Ibid.*, pp. 96–97.

16. Renato Poggioli, *The Theory of the Avant-Garde*, trans. Gerald Fitzgerald (NY: Harper & Row, 1968), p. 82.

17. *Ibid.*, pp. 61 and 66. There is, of course, another, more explicitly political definition of the avant-garde, formulated by Peter Bürger (and contrasted with Poggioli in a Foreword to Bürger's book by Jochen Schulte-Sasse – *Theory of the Avant-Garde*, trans. Michael Shaw [Minneapolis: University of Minnesota Press, 1984]), which does not equate it with modernism and which sees its essence in the impulse to attack "art" as an institution. For Bürger, the avant-garde originated not with the critical consciousness of language that arose in the mid-nineteenth century but rather with the shift from Aestheticism to Symbolism some fifty years later, which ushered in the first true reversal of some deeply ingrained artists' attitudes: acceptance of the social status of art and of the artist's separation from bourgeois society. Schulte-Sasse writes:

> Avant-garde artists were not just reacting to society with feelings of ennui, angst, weltschmerz, and a host of other pseudoexistentialist passions of the soul. Avant-garde artists weren't merely reacting to society with last-ditch efforts at breaking up and dislodging prevalent styles. American theories of modernism – like their French models – have emphasized the pathos and not the praxis of the modern artist. We should come to see that avant-garde artists were actively attacking the institution of art. Their effort was not to isolate themselves but to reintegrate themselves and their art into life. It is no accident that the active, even aggressive artistic manifesto – an address to fellow artists and society – became the preferred medium of expression for the avant-garde artist of the twentieth century.
>
> (p. xxxvi)

If this is indeed the essence of avant-gardism, however, then I see no theater artists today working in an avant-garde mode. In the 1960s, the Living Theatre and other communal groups tried to act outside the institution of "theater" with the express intention of undermining and replacing it. And as recently as the late 1970s Squat Theater declared its goal of destroying the theater as it is commonly known and did succeed in shocking audiences with the pieces *Pig! Child! Fire!*, *Andy Warhol's Last Love* and *Mr. Dead and Mrs. Free*. The Living Theatre is long since effectively defunct, however, and Squat is now doing narrative works such as *Dreamland Burns* and *"L" Train to Eldorado* in proscenium frames. Writing in 1974, Bürger recognizes a corresponding vacuum in the plastic arts and concludes that we have entered a "post avant-gardiste phase" in which the attacks on art institutions are recognized to have failed and the institutions remain "as something separate from the praxis of life" (p. 57).

18. See Poggioli, *The Theory of the Avant-Garde*, p. 145, and see note 21 below.

19. Peter Handke, "Ich bin ein Bewohner des Elfenbeinturms," in *Prosa Gedichte Theaterstücke Hörspiel Aufsätze* (Frankfurt-on-Main, 1969), p. 271: "Der fatale Bedeutungsraum (die Bühne bedeutet Welt) blieb unreflektiert und führte für mich zu lächerlich eindeutigen Symbolismen wie etwa die des Beckett'schen Pantomimen . . . Das war für mich keine Neuigkeit, sondern ein Hereinfallen auf die alte Bedeutung der Bühne."

20. In his article "Peter Handke and the End of the 'Modern'," *Modern Drama*,

Jan. 1981, Michael Hays makes a valid point when he says that it is important to note that Beckett's plays are often understood as depictions of "life as 'absurd,'" but he, writing in 1981, does not have Handke's excuse for failing to distinguish between early and late works.

21.   Pavis, *Languages of the Stage*, p. 185. From a certain perspective, this cul-de-sac is also traceable to Artaud. In calling both for the *Gesamtkunstwerk* – a total stage poetry of lights, settings, music, movement and words – and for a return to the purity of the Orphic Mysteries – a hallucinatory mode of communication prior to that of spoken language – Artaud recommended a theater that was intensely spiritual and intensely corporeal simultaneously. (See Naomi Greene, *Antonin Artaud: Poet Without Words* [NY: Simon and Schuster, 1970].) And he thus, in effect, sent directors on a generation-long wild-goose chase, in the course of which they had to discover for themselves that language was not so easily escaped in performance. In the past thirty years or so we have seen thousands of attempts to achieve a religious intensity in performance purely by means of "technique" and without recourse to words: incorporation of complicated lighting, video, dance and all forms of technical wizardry. One pure example of this is Robert Whitman's work on *Raincover* and *Eclipse*, which were efforts to create time-textures, to "define" discrete moments, so to speak, through tangible stimuli. The tradition, of course, culminates with Robert Wilson, in whose solo works (i.e. those in which he writes the texts himself) distrust of language finds its natural end in a refusal to use words seriously.

22.   Richard Foreman, interview by David Savran, *American Theater*, July/August 1987, p. 21.

23.   "Brief an Robert Wilson," program insert for *Death, Destruction & Detroit II*, Schaubühne am Lehniner Platz, 1987. I have translated and excerpted from these three sentences, which begin the letter: "Eine Woche lang habe ich versucht, einen Text herzustellen, der Deiner Inszenierung von DD & D II, einem Gebilde, das mehr als Deine Früheren Arbeiten aus seiner eignen Explosion besteht, als Gravitationszentrum dienen kann. Der Versuch ist gescheitert. Vielleicht war die Explosion schon zu weit gediehen, der Grad der Beschleunigung (ich rede nicht von Uhrzeit) schon zu hoch, als daß ein Text, der notgedrungen etwas bedeutet, in den Wirbel der Sprengung sich noch einschreiben kann."

24.   To explain briefly what I mean by "certain discernible meanings," *Hamletmachine* is, among other things, a critique of the coercive nature of plot, plot as metaphor for the way we organize our lives, destiny seen as inescapable simply because it has been foretold, all of which echoes Büchner's *Dantons Tod* and its implicit critique of the coercive nature of history. Wilson gave this idea visual form by staging the action as a series of rotating scenes, the actors playing alternately to front, stage right, back, stage left, etc., each time executing a nearly equivalent movement sequence. I do not mean to imply that Wilson is always a better director when he works with substantial texts (by Müller or others), but he sometimes is, partly because of an occasionally fine capacity for what I have called inadvertent interpretation. That this would seem to contradict the reasons Müller has given for his interest in collaborating with Wilson is not the director's fault.

The outstanding literary products of the century work toward the liquidation of their autonomy (autonomy=product of incest with private property), toward the expropriation and finally the disappearance of the author.

They [the Germans] don't respect the text as a reality in itself. They always try to interpret the text, which is not really what I want from theatre. The text can speak for itself. I don't need people to interpret my text. And Wilson never interprets. He just gets the text and tries to find room for it.

(Statements by the playwright quoted from the program to Wilson's 1988 production of Müller's *Quartet* at the American Repertory Theatre)

25. Blau, *Blooded Thought*, p. 142.

Conversations

1. Ruby Cohn describes the Mabou Mines productions of *Cascando* and *Mercier and Camier* in her article "Mabou Mines' Translations of Beckett," in *Beckett Translating/Translating Beckett*, pp. 174–180.

2. An interview with Sam Waterston, who played Vladimir in this production, appears in Joanmarie Kalter, *Actors On Acting: Performing in Theatre and Film Today* (NY: Sterling, 1979), pp. 141–167.

3. In several instances, Warrilow gives earlier dates for pieces than the Mabou Mines "Performance History." He says *Play* was first performed in 1964/65, *The Lost Ones* in March 1974, and *A Piece of Monologue* in 1979.

4. Warrilow's note: "Since the play was rehearsed in London, I was obliged to withdraw from the project."

5. Whitelaw is speaking of the 1962 London premiere at the Royal Court Theatre, directed by George Devine.

Bibliography

This list consists of published secondary sources mentioned in the notes and selected others. Articles from collections are not listed separately unless an article is the only one in its book relevant to this subject.

Acheson, James and Kateryna Arthur, eds., *Beckett's Later Fiction and Drama* (NY: St. Martin's Press, 1987).

Adorno, Theodor, "Trying to Understand *Endgame*," trans. Michael T. Jones, *New German Critique* 26, Spring/Summer 1982, pp. 119–150.

Artaud, Antonin, *The Theater and its Double*, trans. Mary C. Richard (NY: Grove Press, 1958).

Asmus, Walter, "All Gimmicks Gone?," *Theater heute*, April 1986, pp. 28–30.

"Beckett Directs Godot," *Theatre Quarterly*, vol. 5, no. 19, Sept.–Nov. 1975, pp. 19–26.

"Beckett inszeniert sein 'Spiel,'" *Theater heute*, Dec. 1978, pp. 6–10.

"Practical Aspects of Theatre, Radio and Television: Rehearsal Notes for the German Premiere of Beckett's 'That Time' and 'Footfalls' at the Schiller-Theater Werkstatt, Berlin (Directed by Beckett)," trans. Helen Watanabe, *Journal of Beckett Studies* 2, Summer 1977, pp. 82–95.

Astier, Pierre, "Beckett's *Ohio Impromptu*: A View from the Isle of Swans," *Modern Drama*, vol. 25, no. 3, Sept. 1982, pp. 331–341.

Bair, Deirdre, *Samuel Beckett: A Biography* (NY and London: Harcourt Brace Jovanovich, 1978).

Bakewell, Michael, "Working with Beckett," *Adam* 337–339, 1970, pp. 72–73.

Barnes, Ben, "Aspects of Directing Beckett," *Irish University Review*, vol. 14, no. 1, 1984, pp. 69–87.

"Beckett's Letters on Endgame: Extracts from His Correspondence With Director Alan Schneider," in *The Village Voice Reader*, ed. Daniel Wolf and Edwin Fancher (Garden City, NY: Doubleday, 1962), pp. 182–186.

Becker, Peter von, "Das 'Endspiel' immer weiterspielen?," *Theater heute*, Dec. 1978, pp. 12–13.

Ben-Zvi, Linda, "Samuel Beckett's Media Plays," *Modern Drama*, vol. 28, no. 1, March 1985, pp. 22–37.

Blau, Herbert, *Blooded Thought* (NY: PAJ Publications, 1982).

Blumenthal, Eileen, "Irene Worth Has Time on Her Side," *Village Voice*, Aug. 27, 1979, p. 81.

Joseph Chaikin (Cambridge: Cambridge University Press, 1984).

Brater, Enoch, *Beyond Minimalism: Beckett's Late Style in the Theater* (NY and Oxford: Oxford University Press, 1987).

"Brecht's Alienated Actor in Beckett's Theater," *Comparative Drama* 9, Fall 1975, pp. 195–205.

"The 'Absurd' Actor in the Theatre of Samuel Beckett," *Educational Theatre Journal*, vol. 27, no. 2, May 1975, pp. 197–207.

ed., *Beckett at 80/Beckett in Context* (NY: Oxford University Press, 1986).

Brecht, Bertolt, *Brecht On Theatre*, trans. John Willet (NY: Hill and Wang, 1957).

Breuer, Lee, *Sister Suzie Cinema* (NY: TCG Publications, 1987).

Bürger, Peter, *Theory of the Avant-Garde*, trans. Michael Shaw (Minneapolis: University of Minnesota Press, 1984).

Burkman, Katherine, ed., *Myth and Ritual in the Plays of Samuel Beckett* (Rutherford: Fairleigh Dickinson University Press, 1987).

Calder, John, ed., *As No Other Dare Fail* (London: John Calder, 1986).

ed., *Beckett at 60: A Festschrift* (London: Calder and Boyars, 1967).

Canaris, Volker, "Einen klassischen Text muß man überprufen," *Theater heute*, April 1971, pp. 24–29.

Chabert, Pierre, "Beckett as Director," *Gambit*, vol. 7, no. 28, 1976, pp. 41–63.

"Fin de partie ou les poubelles du sens," *Revue d'Esthétique* 8, 1985, pp. 173–180.

"The Body in Beckett's Theatre," *Journal of Beckett Studies* 8, Fall 1982, pp. 23–28.

Chevigny, Bell Gale, ed., *Twentieth-Century Interpretations of Endgame* (Englewood Cliffs, NJ: Prentice-Hall, 1969).

Coe, Richard N., *Samuel Beckett* (NY: Grove Press, 1970).

Cohen, Debra, "The Mabou Mines *The Lost Ones*," *TDR*, vol. 20, no. 2, June 1976, pp. 83–87.

Cohn, Ruby, ed., *Modern Drama* (Beckett issue), vol. 9, no. 3, Dec. 1966.

ed., *Casebook On Waiting for Godot* (NY: Grove Press, 1967).

"Beckett's German 'Godot'," *Journal of Beckett Studies* 1, Winter 1976, pp. 41–49.

Just Play: Beckett's Theater (Princeton: Princeton University Press, 1980).

ed., *Beckett: Waiting for Godot*, Casebook Series (London: Macmillan, 1987).

Cooke, Virginia, comp., *Beckett on File* (London and New York: Methuen, 1985).

Das letzte Band: Regiebuch der Berliner Inszenierung, herausgegeben von Volker Canaris (Frankfurt-on-Main: Suhrkamp, 1970).

Dietrich, Richard F., "Beckett's Goad: From Stage to Film," *Literature/Film Quarterly* 4, 1976, pp. 83–89.

Driver, Tom, "Beckett by the Madeleine," *Columbia University Forum*, Summer 1961, pp. 21–25.

Duckworth, Colin, *Angels of Darkness: Dramatic Effect in Samuel Beckett with Special Reference to Eugene Ionesco* (NY: Barnes & Noble Books, 1972).

Edelstein, David, "Rockaby Billie," *Village Voice*, March 20, 1984, pp. 81, 86.

Elam, Keir, *The Semiotics of Theatre and Drama* (London and NY: Methuen, 1980).

Elsom, John, "Samuel Beckett, Max Wall and Me," *Contemporary Review*, May 1983, pp. 261–265.

"Endzeit und Aufbruch: Ekkehard Schall in *Lebensabende*," *Tip* (East Berlin: Theater im Palast), Oct.–March 1987, p. 6.

Engel, Wolfgang, "Warten auf Gorbatschow?," interview by Horst Thiemer, *Theater heute*, May 1987, pp. 58–59.

Esslin, Martin, "'Godot,' the Authorized Version," *Journal of Beckett Studies* 1, Winter 1976, pp. 98–100.

    Mediations: Essays on Brecht, Beckett and the Media (NY: Grove Press, 1982).

    The Theater of the Absurd (NY: Pelican, 1968).

Fletcher, John, Beryl Fletcher, Barry Smith and Walter Bachem, *A Student's Guide to the Plays of Samuel Beckett* (London and Boston: Faber & Faber, 1978).

Fletcher, John and John Spurling, *Beckett: A Study of his Plays* (London: Methuen, 1972).

    Beckett the Playwright (NY: Hill and Wang, 1985).

Foreman, Richard, interview with David Savran, *American Theater*, July/August 1987, pp. 14, 19–21, 40–50.

Friedman, Alan Warren, Charles Rossman and Dana Sherzer, eds., *Beckett Translating/Translating Beckett* (University Park and London: Penn State Press, 1987).

Friedman, Melvin J., ed., *Samuel Beckett Now: Critical Approaches to his Novels, Poetry and Plays* (Chicago and London: University of Chicago Press, 1970).

Gaipa, Ettore, "Die grossen Pessimisten lieben das Leben zutiefst: Giorgio Strehler über Beckett," *Theater heute*, Feb. 1983, pp. 22–23.

Gilman, Richard, *Common and Uncommon Masks* (NY: Vintage, 1971).

    The Making of Modern Drama (NY: Farrar, Straus and Giroux, 1972).

Goldman, Michael, *The Actor's Freedom: Toward a Theory of Drama* (NY: Viking, 1975).

Gontarski, S. E., *The Intent of Undoing* (Bloomington: Indiana University Press, 1985).

    ed., *On Beckett: Essays and Criticism* (NY: Grove Press, 1986).

Gontarski, S. E., Morris Beja and Pierre Astier, eds., *Samuel Beckett: Humanistic Perspectives* (Columbus: Ohio State University Press, 1983).

Goodman, Randolph, *Drama: A View from the Wings* (NY: Holt, Rinehart and Winston, 1978), interviews with Alan Schneider and Hume Cronyn, pp. 644–651.

Graver, Lawrence and Raymond Federman, eds., *Samuel Beckett: The Critical Heritage* (London: Routledge & Kegan Paul, 1979).

Greene, Naomi, *Antonin Artaud: Poet Without Words* (NY: Simon and Schuster, 1970).

Grotowski, Jerzy, *Towards a Poor Theater* (NY: Simon and Schuster, 1968).

Guicharnaud, Jacques, *Modern French Theater from Giraudoux to Beckett* (New Haven: Yale University Press, 1961).

Gussow, Mel, "How Billie Whitelaw Interprets Beckett," *New York Times*, Feb. 14, 1984, p. C13.

Hampton, Christopher, "Staging *All That Fall*," *Drama at Calgary*, Nov. 1967, pp. 48–52.

    "*All That Fall*, Productions II and III, Final Report," *Drama at Calgary*, May 1968, pp. 37–41.

Handke, Peter, "Ich bin ein Bewohner des Elfenbeinturms," in *Prosa Gedichte Theaterstücke Hörspiel Aufsätze* (Frankfurt-on-Main: Suhrkamp, 1969), pp. 263–272.

Hayman, Ronald, *Theatre and Anti-Theatre: New Movements Since Beckett* (NY: Oxford University Press, 1979).

Hays, Michael, "Peter Handke and the End of the 'Modern'," *Modern Drama*, Jan. 1981, pp. 346–366.

Hecht, Werner, "Brecht 'und' Beckett: ein absurder Vergleich," *Theater der Zeit* 14, Aug. 1–15, 1966, pp. 28–30.

Hensel, Georg, *Beckett* (Munich: Deutscher Taschenbuch Verlag, 1977).

Hobson, Harold, "Samuel Beckett – Dramatist of the Year," *International Theatre Annual* 1 (London: John Calder, 1956), pp. 153–155.

Hoffman, Frederick J., *Samuel Beckett: The Language of Self* (NY: E. P. Dutton & Co., 1964).

Hofstadter, Dan, "A Painting Dervish," *The New Yorker*, June 1, 1987, pp. 37–56.

Homan, Sidney, *Beckett's Theaters: Interpretations for Performance* (Lewisburg: Bucknell University Press, 1984).

Ionesco, Eugene, *Notes and Counter Notes*, trans. Donald Watson (NY: Grove Press, 1964).

Kalb, Jonathan, "Krapp at the Palast," *Theater*, vol. 19, no. 1, Fall/Winter 1987, pp. 73–77.

"The Critical Beckett," *Theater*, vol. 16, no. 3, Summer/Fall 1985, pp. 81–84.

"The Underground *Endgame*," *Theater*, vol. 16, no. 2, Spring 1985, pp. 88–92.

"Whose Text Is It Anyway?," *Theater*, vol. 17, no. 3, Summer/Fall 1986, pp. 97–100.

Kalter, Joanmarie, interview with Sam Waterston, in *Actors on Acting: Performing in Theater and Film Today* (NY: Sterling, 1979), pp. 141–167.

Kauffmann, Stanley, *Persons of the Drama: Theater Criticism and Comment* (NY, Hagerstown, San Francisco, London: Harper & Row, 1976).

Kenner, Hugh, *Samuel Beckett: A Critical Study* (NY: Grove Press, 1961).

The Stoic Comedians: Flaubert, Joyce and Beckett (Berkeley and Los Angeles: University of California Press, 1962).

Kilroy, Thomas, "Two Playwrights: Yeats and Beckett," in *Myth and Reality in Irish Literature*, ed. Joseph Ronsley (Waterloo, Ontario: Wilfrid Laurier University Press, 1977), pp. 183–195.

Kirby, E. T., "A Projection Theatre Production of Samuel Beckett's *Molloy*," *Silo*, Spring 1969, p. 5.

Knowlson, James, "'Krapp's Last Tape': The Evolution of a Play, 1958–75," *Journal of Beckett Studies* 1, Winter 1976, pp. 50–65.

Light and Darkness in the Theatre of Samuel Beckett (London: Turret Books, 1972).

"State of Play: Performance Changes and Beckett Scholarship," *Journal of Beckett Studies* 10, 1985, pp. 108–120.

ed., *Happy Days: The Production Notebook of Samuel Beckett* (NY: Grove Press, 1985).

ed., *Samuel Beckett: An Exhibition* (London: Turret Books, 1971).

ed., *Samuel Beckett: Krapp's Last Tape: Theatre Workbook No. 1* (London: Brutus Books, 1980).

Knowlson, James and John Pilling, *Frescoes of the Skull: The Later Prose and Drama of Samuel Beckett* (NY: Grove Press, 1980).

Kott, Jan, *Shakespeare Our Contemporary* (NY and London: W. W. Norton & Co., 1964).

Lahr, John, *Notes on a Cowardly Lion* (NY: Alfred A. Knopf, 1969).

Lawley, Paul, "Counterpoint, Absence and the Medium in Beckett's *Not I*," *Modern Drama*, vol. 26, no. 4, Dec. 1983, pp. 407–414.

Lyons, Charles R., "Perceiving *Rockaby* – As a Text, As a Text by Samuel Beckett, As a Text for Performance," *Comparative Drama* 16, Winter 1982/83, pp. 297–311.

Samuel Beckett (NY: Grove Press, 1983).

Lyons, Charles R. and Barbara S. Becker, "Directing/Acting Beckett," *Comparative Drama* 19, Winter 1985/86, pp. 289–304.

MacGowran, Jack, "Interview with Jack MacGowran," interviewers Kathleen McGrory and John Unterecker, in *Yeats, Joyce, and Beckett: New Light on Three Modern Irish Writers* (Lewisburg: Bucknell University Press, and London: Associated University Press, 1976), pp. 172–182.

"MacGowran on Beckett," interview by Richard Toscan, *Theatre Quarterly*, vol. 3, no. 2, July–Sept. 1973, pp. 15–22.

McMillan, Dougald and Martha Fehsenfeld, *Beckett in the Theatre: The Author as Practical Playwright and Director* (London: John Calder, 1988).

Marowitz, Charles, *Prospero's Staff: Acting and Directing in the Contemporary Theatre* (Bloomington and Indianapolis: Indiana University Press, 1986).

Materialien zu Becketts Endspiel, reports and essays, list of performances (Frankfurt-on-Main: Suhrkamp, 1968).

Materialen zu Becketts Warten auf Godot, ed. Ursula Dreysse, vol. 1 (Frankfurt-on-Main: Suhrkamp, 1973).

Materialen zu Becketts Warten auf Godot, ed. Hartmut Engelhardt and Dieter Mettler, vol. 2 (Frankfurt-on-Main: Suhrkamp, 1979).

Matousek, Mark, "Schneider on Beckett, Understanding, Differently," *Village Voice*, July 3, 1984, p. 97.

Mayer, Hans and Uwe Johnson, eds., *Das Werk von Samuel Beckett: Berliner Colloquium*, (Frankfurt-on-Main: Suhrkamp, 1975).

Melchinger, Siegfried, "Regie Samuel Beckett: Der Autor im Umgang mit der Technik," *Theater heute*, May 1966, pp. 12–15.

Mercier, Vivian, *Beckett/Beckett* (NY: Oxford University Press, 1977).

Müller, Heiner, "Brief an Robert Wilson," program insert for *Death Destruction & Detroit II*, Schaubühne am Lehniner Platz, 1987.

Murch, Anne C., "Quoting from Godot," *Journal of Beckett Studies* 9, 1984, pp. 114–115.

Murphy, Vincent, J., "Being and Perception: Beckett's *Film*," *Modern Drama*, vol. 18, no. 1, March 1975, pp. 43–48.

O'Brien, Eoin, *The Beckett Country: Samuel Beckett's Ireland* (Dublin: Black Cat Press, and London: Faber & Faber, 1986).

Pavis, Patrice, *Languages of the Stage* (NY: PAJ Publications, 1982).
Piette, Alain, "Beckett After the Deluge," *Theater*, vol. 15, no. 3, Summer/Fall 1984, pp. 54–57.
Poggioli, Renato, *The Theory of the Avant-Garde*, trans. Gerald Fitzgerald (NY: Harper & Row, 1968).
Pountney, Rosemary, "Practical Aspects of Theatre, Radio and Television 1: On Acting Mouth in 'Not I,'" *Journal of Beckett Studies* 1, Winter 1976, pp. 81–85.
Rabkin, Gerald, "Is There a Text on this Stage?," *Performing Arts Journal* 26/27, vol. 9, nos. 2/3, pp. 142–159.
Reid, Alec, *All I Can Manage, More Than I Could: An Approach to the Plays of Samuel Beckett* (Dublin: Dolmen, 1968).
    "Beckett, The Camera, and Jack MacGowran," in *Myth and Reality in Irish Literature*, ed. Joseph Ronsley (Waterloo, Ontario: Wilfrid Laurier University Press, 1977), pp. 219–225.
Revue d'Esthétique: Samuel Beckett, ed. Pierre Chabert, special number, 1986.
Roach, Joseph R., *The Player's Passion: Studies in the Science of Acting* (Newark: University of Delaware Press, 1985).
Robbe-Grillet, Alain, *For a New Novel: Essays on Fiction*, trans. Richard Howard (NY: Grove Press, 1965).
Robinson, Michael, *The Long Sonata of the Dead: A Study of Samuel Beckett* (NY: Grove Press, 1969).
Rülicke-Weiler, Käthe, *Die Dramaturgie Brechts* (Berlin: Deb, 1966).
Samuel Beckett inszeniert das Endspiel, photographs: Rosemarie Clausen and rehearsal diary: Michael Haerdter (Frankfurt-on-Main: Suhrkamp, 1969).
Samuel Beckett inszeniert Glückliche Tage, rehearsal diary: Alfred Hübner, photographs: Horst Güldemeister (Frankfurt-on-Main: Suhrkamp, 1976).
Schechner, Richard, *The End of Humanism* (NY: PAJ Publication, 1982).
Schneider, Alan, "'Any Way You Like, Alan': Working with Beckett," *Theatre Quarterly*, vol. 5, no. 19, Sept.–Nov. 1975, pp. 27–38.
    "Director as Dogsbody," *Theatre Quarterly*, vol. 3, no. 10, April–June 1973, pp. 25–30.
    Entrances: An American Director's Journey (NY: Viking, 1986).
    "On Directing *Film*," in Samuel Beckett, *Film* (NY: Grove Press, 1969), pp. 63–94.
    "What Does A Director Do?," *New York Theatre Review*, Spring/Summer 1977, pp. 16–17.
Shenker, Israel, interview with Beckett, *New York Times*, May 5, 1956, section 2, pp. 1, 3.
Sherzer, Dina, "Beckett's *Endgame*, or What Talk Can Do," *Modern Drama*, vol. 22, no. 3, Sept. 1979, pp. 291–303.
Simon, Richard Keller, "Dialectical Laughter: A Study of *Endgame*," *Modern Drama*, vol. 25, no. 4, Dec. 1982, pp. 505–513.
Simpson, Alan, *Beckett and Behan and a Theatre in Dublin* (London: Routledge & Kegan Paul, 1962).
States, Bert O., *The Shape of Paradox: An Essay on 'Waiting for Godot'* (Berkeley, Los Angeles, London: University of California Press, 1978).

Suvin, Darko, "Beckett's Purgatory of the Individual," *TDR* vol. 11, no. 4, Summer 1967, pp. 23–36.

Völker, Klaus, ed., *Beckett in Berlin* (Berlin: Frölich & Kaufmann, 1986).

Worth, Katharine, ed., *Beckett the Shape Changer* (London and Boston: Routledge & Kegan Paul, 1975).

Worthen, William, B., "Beckett's Actor," *Modern Drama*, vol. 26, no. 4, Dec. 1983, pp. 415–424.

  The Idea of the Actor: Drama and the Ethics of Performance (Princeton: Princeton University Press, 1984).

Young, Jordan R., *The Beckett Actor* (Beverly Hills, CA: Moonstone Press, 1987).

Zilliacus, Clas, *Beckett and Broadcasting* (Abo [Finland]: Abo Akademi, 1976).

  "Beckett Versus Brecht in Helsinki," *Journal of Beckett Studies* 6, Autumn 1980, pp. 129–133.

  "Three Times *Godot*: Beckett, Brecht, Bulatovic," *Comparative Drama* 4, Spring 1970, pp. 3–17.

Zipes, Jack, "Beckett in Germany/Germany in Beckett," *New German Critique* 26, Spring/Summer 1982, pp. 151–158.

Zurbrugg, Nicholas, ed., *The Review of Contemporary Fiction* (Samuel Beckett number), vol. 7, no. 2, Summer 1987.

Index

8 95
216 299

Printed in the United States
18660LVS00004B/73-75